D1089866

Also by Wendell H. Oswalt

Mission of Change in Alaska
Napaskiak: An Alaskan Eskimo Community
This Land Was Theirs
Alaskan Eskimos
Understanding Our Culture
Other Peoples, Other Customs
Habitat and Technology
An Anthropological Analysis of Food-Getting Technology
Kolmakovskiy Redoubt
Life Cycles and Lifeways: An Introduction to Cultural Anthropology
Bashful No Longer: An Alaskan Eskimo Ethnohistory, 1788–1988

Eskimos and Explorers

Wendell H. Oswalt

University of California, Los Angeles

SECOND EDITION

UNIVERSITY OF NEBRASKA PRESS
LINCOLN AND LONDON

⊗

First Bison Books printing: 1999
Most recent printing indicated by the last digit below:
10   9   8   7   6   5   4   3   2   1

Library of Congress Cataloging-in-Publication Data
Oswalt, Wendell H.
Eskimos and explorers / Wendell H. Oswalt.—2nd ed.
p.   cm.
Includes bibliographical references and index.
ISBN 0-8032-8613-9 (pbk.: alk. paper)
1. Eskimos—History.   2. Eskimos—Social life and customs.
3. Explorers—Arctic regions.   4. Arctic regions—Discovery and
exploration.   I. Title.
E99.E7079   1999
970'.004971—dc21
99-13969   CIP

Reprinted from the original 1979 edition by Chandler & Sharp Publishers, Inc., Novato CA.

CONTENTS

Illustrations

MAPS

Preface to the Second Edition

To prepare a new edition of this book twenty years after initial publication is personally gratifying. It suggests an enduring interest in Eskimos among both the general public and anthropologists. Judging from the many books, monographs, and articles about Eskimos that have appeared in recent years, Westerners remain fascinated by life in the "frozen north." My dominant purpose is to trace the emergence of Eskimos from the era when Europeans thought of them as more legendary than real to the time when the last of Eskimo country was explored. The narrative begins in Greenland about A.D. 1000, eventually moves to Canada, and reaches northern Alaska in the 1800s. When Eskimos of southwestern Alaska are described, a shift is made back in time to the early 1700s to accommodate Russian penetration into Alaska. Since this was the earliest effective contact from the west, the historical regression is reasonable in terms of organization.

With the passage of time, and as one chapter leads to the next, increasing numbers of persons wrote about Eskimos until their lifeway gradually took form and was stripped of its more fanciful embellishments. By 1745 the Eskimos of southwestern Greenland were well described by Hans P. Egede, and his account became an acceptable standard against which all later reports could be judged. While sketchy or quaint observations about Eskimos in the 1600s are worthy of attention, reports of similar quality but dating after 1745 are not germane because we know so much by that time. In a like manner many good reports by nineteenth-century explorers are not considered because by then we already have innumberable accounts about the Eskimo boats, clothing, housing, and so on that they were most likely to describe. By beginning in Greenland and working westward, sources that present new data were dramatically reduced in number by the time Alaska was reached, and much needless or largely uninformative repetition is avoided.

As Eskimo culture came to be appreciated by Europeans and Euro-Americans, one aspect of Eskimo life has been praised but seldom given adequate stress in general accounts—the aptness of the technology, which enabled Eskimos to live for so long and so successfully in the far north. One of my most conscious goals has been to represent these Eskimo manufactures adequately on a regional basis. If indeed Eskimo culture is best typified by its artifacts, they must not be slighted in a presentation devoted to these people.

The reader must excuse the early explorers, and me, for not dealing with the racial affinities of Eskimos in modern terms, and the same is true for the nature of their language. To do so would detract from the goal of presenting Eskimos as they were viewed by the men who first encountered them. Much the same is true of Eskimo art. Though it is widely acclaimed and purchased in recent times, Eskimo art rarely was singled out for attention by explorers. Furthermore many, even most, works from the recent past were produced for sale to outsiders and were not a part of early historic Eskimo culture.

The first nine chapters and the appendixes remain the same as in the previous edition. In this revision, however, the concluding chapter, "Before and After Explorers," has been revised extensively. Developments in the recent past have resulted in substantial changes in our knowledge of Eskimo prehistory and their language classification. In addition, the revised chapter focuses on changes that took place during the last twenty years, especially regarding the political status of Eskimos.

At the end of each chapter, a notes section documents the sources and provides a guide to further reading. After rewriting the final chapter, the prehistory text was reviewed and revised by Don E. Dumond. James W. VanStone reviewed the entire chapter, and I included his recommended changes. My debt to each of them is great.

Since the original edition of this book appeared, the word "Eskimo" has been attacked with some vigor and requires comment.

The word "Esquimawes," from which Eskimo is derived, was introduced into English in 1584 and is thus long established. Yet it is offensive to some, possibly most, Eskimos because it is not their self-identification. Eskimos in Canada much prefer the word Inuit or a variant, meaning "people," and the same is true in northern Alaska. Greenlandic Eskimos call themselves Kalaallit, meaning "Greenlanders," not Inuit, although this term would be fitting. Most Eskimos in southwestern Alaska and others in Siberia call themselves Yuit or a variant, meaning "people" in their Eskimoan languages; some Eskimos in Alaska regard themselves as Koniag and others consider themselves Aleuts. In sum, the only generic designation that embraces *all* of these people is "Eskimo."

W.H.O.

An Introduction

Why Eskimos?

Eskimos are for many reasons the most exotic people in the world. After all, what is more demanding than living in a land where it is nearly always cold? What is more unprecedented than a diet of meat or a house built from snow? What could be kinder than never punishing children or more pacific than being ignorant of war? What is more bizarre than killing one's children or aged parents without showing emotion? What is more daring than hunting great whales from frail skin-covered boats or facing a polar bear when protected by nothing more than a spear backed by bravery? These sometimes overstated qualities of the Eskimo life-style stand in inviting contrast with those of all other peoples.

More truth than fiction has produced the Eskimo stereotype, but these people also are remarkable in less familiar ways. Some Eskimos customarily went barefoot and wore sleeveless garments throughout the year. Others ate fish as a steady diet and never killed a great whale or saw a polar bear. Although Eskimos are visualized as occupying barren, icebound coasts, some lived at the edges of great coastal forests or so far inland that they never saw the sea. Surprisingly, some Eskimos never sledded behind a dog

1

team or hunted seals at their breathing holes. Sad perhaps, but indisputable, most never lived in snowhouses.

When European explorers met peoples in the New World, they called them Indians except for those people that we still know as Eskimos. Justly or unjustly Eskimos were judged as distinct from other Native Americans, probably because they lived so far north and seemed so different from Indians in appearance and the manner in which they lived. The technology of Eskimos is now recognized as without parallel and their varied means for taking game unmatched among other aboriginal hunters; these qualities of Eskimos were not stressed by many early observers. Eskimos also stood apart from other aboriginal peoples because they controlled more land than did any other group. As the imperialists of the north they developed notable and often unique means for survival. Finally some Eskimos were among the first and others were among the last New World peoples discovered by Europeans.

Admiration for Eskimos approaches awe when Euro-Americans consider the ability of these people to thrive in the far north. The cold and danger of arctic living conjure visions of great adventures. Arctic conditions certainly gave Eskimo culture a unique cast. In addition the remoteness of these people contributed to their survival into modern times. The inaccessibility of their homeland and its lack of economic importance until recently meant that intrusions by Westerners seldom were intensive. European explorers ventured to the American arctic with trepidation; whether the travels were in the tenth or nineteenth century, danger and the possibility of disaster were ever present. Sooner or later most arctic explorers discovered Eskimos. Some reports of these meetings are short, even cryptic, but others describe Eskimos in expansive detail. As remarkable as it may seem, the accounts span nearly eight centuries. The last aboriginal Eskimos were discovered early in the twentieth century, and since then none have been unaffected by outside influences.

Eskimos have attracted widespread and lasting attention because of their highly adaptive means for arctic living. Perhaps this is best reflected in the things that they made; their elaborate harpoons, kayaks, and skin clothing were produced from severely limited resources. As important as these forms were to support life in the far north, artifacts alone do not fully account for our fascination with Eskimos. We appreciate sophisticated technology, but certain aspects of Eskimo social life may have even greater appeal. The premium that they placed on personal freedom unfettered by rigid social constraints is important, as is the laxity of their sexual code. Among Eskimos we find that a strong positive value placed on hard work was vital to the survival of small family units. Theirs was a simpler reality than ours, it required fewer social encumbrances, and it serves as a positive model for individual achievement, especially since theirs was such a demanding environment.

Sadly but certainly, traditional Eskimo culture has perished; but history and anthropology provide a means to view it once again. From the reports of explorers and others, Eskimos slowly emerge in all their uniqueness. The first vague reports represent them as far more mystical than real. Some early explorers described them as savages or even as cannibals who worshiped the sun and ate only raw meat. Eskimos apparently were considered by some to be pygmies who warred with birds and died at the age of eight. Many years passed before the Eskimo way of life came to be appreciated as a highly resourceful adaptation to arctic conditions. By tracing the discovery of Eskimos and increasing awareness of their lifestyle, we may not only plot the increments of their early history, but come to better understand the changes in attitudes toward them. In this way we can come to appreciate, Why Eskimos?

CHAPTER

1

The Norse Experience

Eskimos call themselves *Inuit* or *Yuit*, both words meaning "real people" and reflecting their supremely confident attitude toward the remainder of humanity. Eskimos exploited the greatest expanse of polar land, and they justly deserve their reputation as the most successful conquerors of the arctic. The names first applied to Eskimos by foreigners do not reflect that view, however. Indians in northwestern Canada called them "Enemy-feet" and "Enemies of the Open Country," to indicate their strained relationship. Scandinavians first called them *Skrellings*, which translates "barbarians" or possibly pygmies and may have implied the supernatural qualities of gnomes and trolls. The earliest English use of the word *Eskimos*, or more correctly *Esquimawes*, is in an essay about colonizing eastern North America, titled *Discourse on Western Planting*. It was written in 1584 by Richard Hakluyt, who is justly famous for compiling and editing the works of English explorers. However, this study was not published until 1877. Hakluyt referred to the Esquimawes of Grande Bay, identified with the northern sector of the Gulf of St. Lawrence, yet his source for the term is a mystery. We do know that the word means "eaters of raw flesh" and was originated by Algonkian-speaking Indians in eastern Canada,

5

probably as a derogatory label rather than a neutral term of reference.

Eskimo origins are obscure but not entirely unknown after nearly 100 years of intermittently intensive study. As a racial group they probably emerged in eastern Asia during comparatively recent times. Their unique culture coalesced as they became intensive sea-mammal hunters, possibly along the coasts of the Bering Sea. Although regional differences existed at the beginnings of Eskimo history, their overall culture formed a highly distinct configuration. In general the Eskimo lifeway focused on the exploitation of sea mammals, especially seals, along treeless coasts in the American arctic and subarctic. Alternatively Eskimos were inland hunters of caribou or were fishermen along coasts and rivers. Among their most characteristic manufactures were harpoons, tailor-made skin clothing, oil-burning lamps, and skin-covered boats known as kayaks and umiaks. Social ties were closest among small groups of related persons, and organized political action seldom prevailed. Spirits controlled by shamans dominated religious life, but formal ceremonies were limited primarily to Eskimos in Alaska. The Eskimo languages are distinct from all others but have distant ties with those spoken by other peoples in eastern Siberia, a further indication of their origins. At the beginning of their history Eskimos controlled the vast region from Greenland and Labrador across northern Canada to Alaska and beyond to the eastern fringe of Siberia.

Formal history began when the distant past was recorded in reliable written accounts. Oral narratives, however, may include truth as great as that of words on parchment or paper, and legendary tales sometimes may be authenticated in unexpected ways. For example, in the recent past Eskimo children at Point Hope, Alaska, were cautioned against wandering about at night with the warning that they might meet "a man with ivory eyes." Tradition led generations of parents to admonish children in this manner. When archaeologists discovered and excavated burials near the village in 1940, they found that the skulls of some males had been fitted with ivory eyes, including jet inlays as pupils. As surprising as it may seem, the men with the ivory eyes had been buried nearly 2000 years ago, and the burial practice was abandoned shortly thereafter. This particular tradition does not bear on critical events, but its verification does illustrate that details about the remote past may find a firm place in the oral heritage of a nonliterate people. An even more dramatic example of the accuracy of Eskimo lore was recorded by Charles F. Hall. When he visited Canadian Eskimos living on Baffin Island in 1861, an old woman related that long ago two ships arrived with white men aboard, the next year three ships came, and the following year many ships appeared. She added that the Eskimos captured five crew members, who wintered among them for one or more years. During that time the strangers built a large boat with a mast and sails. After considerable difficulty they launched the boat in open water and sailed away, never to be heard of again. We know that on his first voyage Martin Frobisher sailed two ships to the area and that local Eskimos captured five sailors. Frobisher returned the following year with three vessels, and the next year he arrived with 14 ships. Remarkably, the Frobisher expeditions were in 1576-8, nearly 300 years before the interview by Hall.

Icelanders, the Europeans living nearest to Eskimos, had a compelling interest in history. The Scandinavians who began to settle Iceland in A.D. 874 were not fierce Vikings in long ships seeking plunder and glory. Instead they were venturesome Norse traders and settlers who pioneered routes and founded colonies along northern seas. Oral narratives told of their achievements, and after being written around 1200, these tales came to be known as *sagas*. Among these Norse adventure stories and family histories *The Greenlanders' Saga*, written in the early 1300s, is the most important. *The Saga of Eric the Red* possibly was recorded somewhat later. Norse tales describing voyages in the New World are well known. No one denies that certain episodes ar distorted, some quite clearly exaggerated, and still others fabricated, yet the corpus is far more historical than legendary. Voyages that began in southwestern Norway eventually led to the discovery of North America, and the sagas describing them are among the greatest adventure stories of all times. Fortunately they include reports about American peoples.

The saga *The King's Mirror*, dating about 1250, gives three reasons for sailing to Greenland: curiosity, the quest for wealth, and the spirit of competition. So it may have been, but disputes between Norsemen were the more immediate cause for a number of crucial westward sailings. First there was Thorvald Asvaldsson, a combative man who lived with his wife and family in southwestern

Norway until he killed a man in about 970. According to the local legal system the punishment for homicide was loss of property and either banishment or payment of *wergild*. Since payment was difficult after one's property had been seized, it was expedient to flee. Thorvald sailed for a remote sector of northwestern Iceland since homestead sites in more favorable and accessible localities of the island were occupied. With him was his family, including a child named Eric but called Eric the Red because of his red hair. After Thorvald's death Eric married and moved to a less remote locality. Here he killed a number of persons and consequently was forced to move to another district. Again he became embroiled in murderous conflicts, and banishment from all Icelandic territory for three years compelled him to venture elsewhere. He decided to investigate earlier reports by Icelanders of land to the west.

Icelanders were among the earliest maritime adventurers of the Middle Ages. Their typical vessel, called a *knarr*, was clinker built; that is, the hull was made of overlapped planks nailed in place, and the seams were caulked with tar-soaked animal hair. These Icelandic ships probably were well over 50 feet long, at least 15 feet wide, and partially decked fore and aft. They were rigged with a large square sail of coarse cloth and guided by a steerboard. When the *hillingar* effect, an optical phenomenon, prevailed, Greenland could be seen from the mountains of northwestern Iceland or from a knarr near the shore of northwestern Iceland. Hillingar is an Icelandic word for the optical displacement of an observed image in an upward direction from its real location. Thus a person could see beyond the normal horizon. This form of arctic mirage prevails when the ground or water surface is much colder than the air above. Eric the Red had lived in northwestern Iceland and must have been aware of this unknown land beyond the horizon; he sailed toward it in 982. He possibly saw the towering outline of the East Greenland coast but was unable to land there because of great masses of ice tightly packed along the shore. Eric rounded Cape Farewell and sailed north along the west coast. For three years he explored the fjords along southwestern Greenland. After returning to Iceland and finding that he could not resolve his old disputes, Eric decided to settle in the land found during his exile. Eric the Red not only has the distinction of being the first European explorer of this island, but he was the first real-estate promoter in the New World. He called his discovery "Greenland" with the clear hope of persuading others to settle there with him.

As a propagandist Eric the Red was highly successful, for in the summer of 986 colonists on 25 ships left Iceland for Greenland. The greatest famine in early Icelandic history had occurred in 976, and in the aftermath many people had little or nothing to lose by following Eric. The 14 vessels that arrived in Greenland carried a total of about 350 people in addition to cattle, horses, sheep, and other personal property. These and later immigrants established themselves in the southwestern sector near modern Julianehaab and Godthaab. The Norse settlers found the remains of dwellings, parts of boats, and stone tools, all belonging to Eskimos of an earlier era. Many years passed before Eskimos and whites met in Greenland, although those Norsemen who ventured on to Labrador and Newfoundland soon encountered Native Americans.

At this point the misadventure of Bjarni Herjolfsson, a shipowner who traded between Norway and Iceland, deserves comment. Bjarni planned to winter in Iceland with his father, but when he found that the old man had sailed for Greenland with Eric, Bjarni decided to join his father there. He sailed west, but the first land he sighted was flat and wooded. He knew this was not Greenland and sailed northward, once again sighting forests along the coast. Finally, by coursing before a wind from the southwest, Bjarni arrived at the settlement where his father was staying. Although Bjarni did not land in North America, his was the first Westerner's view of the continent in historic times.

The Greenland colonists raised stock, hunted, and attempted to farm but without success. As the settlements expanded, construction efforts were hampered by a scarcity of timber. There were stone and turf aplenty for walls but no timber for beams. The few stands of trees that grew in Greenland were birch, adequate for firewood but not suitable for construction. The only local source of large timber was driftwood. Piled high on some beaches when the Norse arrived, the supply soon was depleted. Thus timber for roof beams and, of greater importance, for building oceangoing ships was unavailable.

The urge for new adventures and the knowledge that large trees grew on the lands seen by Bjarni led to voyages south and west. The second son of Eric, Leif Ericsson, was a youth when the Greenland colony was established. In the summer of 1001 he sailed with a crew of 35 to explore and obtain wood. Their first landfall was Baffin Island, designated as Flatstone Land (Helluland), and since it seemed without merit, they sailed farther south. The next land they sighted was along the southern coast of Labrador, forested inland from an expansive and gently sloping beach. Leif named it Wood Land (Markland). Not content with Markland, he sailed to an island, probably Belle Isle, and then to northern Newfoundland. The Norse wintered there and called this country "Vinland." What the "vin" of Vinland meant to these Norse has been subject to more controversy than any three-letter word deserves. Traditionally "vin" has been taken to mean wine, and it has been assumed that wild grapes were found by the Norse. The problem is that wild grapes do not now grow in northern Newfoundland although they may have in Leif's time. Alternatively "vin" may have referred to wild berries, not wild grapes, used to make wine. Once the word had meant grassy plain, meadow, or pasture, but these meanings were passing out of use at the time of Norse travels to Vinland.

Leif and his party built temporary dwellings and wintered at a place they named Leifsbudir. Little was recorded about their stay, and no mention was made of any contacts with other people. Soon after the party returned to Greenland, Eric the Red died, and his eldest son, Leif's brother Thorvald, was the next to sail for Vinland. In 1004-5 he wintered in the structures built by Leif. During the second summer, an exploring party led by Thorvald sailed north to a river flowing from east to west, which presumably was the English River in Hamilton Inlet of Labrador. Here they made the first recorded contacts with Native Americans. They discovered three skin boats drawn up on shore, with three men sleeping beneath each. Eight of these men were captured and killed, but the ninth escaped in one of the vessels. In the distance the Norse saw mounds that they thought were houses, and from that direction a large number of men soon came in skin boats to attack the Norse vessel. Thorvald died from an arrow wound and was buried on a cape with crosses raised at his head and feet.

The ethnographic evidence about this encounter with New World people is not detailed enough to verify their ethnic identity. If indeed three men were sleeping beneath three different skin boats, it seems likely that they were Indians. (Or are the threes magical numbers?) Three men could not be expected to fit under a kayak, which is a relatively small vessel usually designed to carry one person, but three men could sleep under a large Indian canoe. It is unlikely that the boats were Eskimo umiaks because one man could not have launched and escaped in such a large vessel. It long has been debated on the basis of information in the sagas whether the attackers were Eskimos or Indians. A separate line of evidence seems to resolve the question. Archaeological excavations by William W. Fitzhugh clearly indicate that Algonkian Indians lived in the Hamilton Inlet region of Labrador at the time, and they probably occupied coastal Labrador to the south.

The third exploratory voyage to Vinland was led by Thorfinn Karlsefni and is recorded in *The Greenlanders' Saga*; encounters with aboriginal people are mentioned although only in brief. *The Saga of Eric the Red* is far more expansive, obviously embellished, and combines the three voyages into one; furthermore, it partially contradicts the other major source. The text to follow is a reasonable summary of the combined accounts.

Thorfinn Karlsefni was a trader who plied between Norway and Greenland, and in 1006, or perhaps a few years later, he wintered in Greenland with Leif. Here he married Gudrid, the widow of one of Leif's brothers. He apparently decided to settle in Vinland, possibly because the desirable sites for homesteads in Greenland had been taken. His party of 65 persons, including 5 women, took along their personal property as well as livestock. Following the colonists' first winter at Leifsbudir, a number of Skrellings appeared from the nearby forest carrying packets of pelts. At first they were frightened by the bellowing of a bull, but after being reassured, they began trading their furs. The Skrellings were anxious to obtain weapons, but since the Norse would not give them up, the trade reportedly was confined to cow's milk. The next year most of the Norse party sailed south to a place called Hop, which means "landlocked bay"; here the abundant fish were relished after the difficult winter. One morning a number of skin boats appeared at Hop, and the people in them put ashore. They were "small [dark] ill favoured men, and had ugly hair on their heads. They had big eyes and were broad in the cheeks." They looked around in astonishment and then launched their boats to head southward. Karlsefni and his party wintered at Hop, and in the spring the Skrellings arrived in a large number of skin boats. They hoped to trade for weapons, but the Norse would exchange only red cloth. (This episode is reported in *The Greenlanders' Saga* as taking place at Leifsbudir.) Three weeks later many boats arrived from the south, and the Skrellings attacked. Their major weapons were large ball-shaped objects, resembling the stomachs of sheep, which were flung from poles. When one of these missiles was hurled, it "made a hideous noise where it came down," and the frightened Norse began to flee. They did not rally even when goaded by Freydis, a nonlegitimate daughter of Eric, nor would they give her a weapon. Finally Freydis seized the sword of a dead Norseman, and as the Skrellings rushed toward her, she exposed her breasts and slapped them with the sword. This bizarre behavior so terrified the Skrellings that they fled in their boats. The intriguing Skrelling weapon is the only clue to the identity of the attackers. Possibly this form of missile was made by sewing a large stone inside a fresh skin that tightened about the stone as it dried. Such a pouch was attached to a pole and hurled as a weapon by Algonkian Indians. Alternatively the weapon may have been an Eskimo harpoon with an inflated bladder attached to the shaft. In truth no one can say with certainty whether the Norse encountered Eskimos or Indians, or both. Nonetheless the Skrellings clearly caused the Norse to abandon the thought of settling permanently in Vinland.

Controversy and speculation have surrounded the Norse sagas and their fit with verified historic events. At the heart of the issue are the locations of Vinland and, more specifically, of the settlement of Leifsbudir. Americanists are indebted to Helge Ingstad for discovering and excavating a site of the Norse in Vinland. The settlement appears to have been Leifsbudir, and it was found in 1960 near L'Anse aux Meadows along Épaves Bay at the northern tip of Newfoundland. The remains of large and small rectangular dwellings with dirt floors were uncovered. Most included stone-lined fireplaces with ember pits nearby. These turf-walled structures are similar to Norse dwellings in Greenland, and they are unlike houses built in the area by Eskimos or Indians. One structure had at least five rooms and was about 70 feet long and 55 feet wide. Outdoor pits containing stones that had been exposed to fire presumably were the remains of cooking pits such as those found at Norse sites in Greenland. Conclusive evidence that this was not a prehistoric Eskimo or Indian site was the presence of a smithy anvil near a hearth as well as iron slag, indicating that iron was processed from bog iron common at the site. Near the smithy was a concentration of charcoal, and nearby slag indicated the location of a kiln. The few artifacts found in association with the structures included a strip of smelted copper, part of a bone needle "of the type used by the Norsemen," a whetstone, some stone tools, rivets, and rusty nails. Also recovered in the 1960s were a stone lamp similar to those used in Iceland during the Middle Ages and, most importantly, a soapstone spindle whorl of a form common to the Norse. In 1974 during further excavation of one of the larger houses there was found a spherical clear glass bead of a form common during the late Viking period. This bead was recovered from beneath one wall and is clearly associated with the construction period of the dwelling. Eskimo and Indian artifacts were found at the site but not in intimate association with Norse remains. They appear instead to have been left by parties camping in the locality in later times.

The scarcity of artifacts at the site results from a number of factors. Soil conditions were unfavorable for the preservation of organic materials. The settlement was occupied for a brief span, and when the residents left, they probably took most of their artifacts with them. Then too it is likely that in later years Eskimos and Indians removed most other artifacts. Further evidence to support Norse occupancy is that radiocarbon dates for charcoal associated with the structural remains cluster around A.D. 1000.

Following the voyage of Karlsefni, repeated trips apparently were made from Greenland to Markland for timber. A reference to such a voyage in the Icelandic annals for 1347 noted that a small vessel with a crew of 17 left Greenland for Markland but lost its anchor and was driven to Iceland. This is the final Norse reference to the region where Leif Ericsson settled temporarily and made such a fleeting imprint on the history of discovery.

*　　　*　　　*

In Vinland contacts between the Norse and Native Americans were few, brief, and usually hostile. Eskimos were not encountered by the Norse when they settled Greenland; instead they found the ruins of a people who had vanished. Before we turn to the reappearance of Eskimos, the Greenlandic Norse colonization must be described in brief.

The Norse colony in Greenland apparently reached its greatest development in the 1100s; at this time the population may have peaked at about 5000. The Greenlandic Norse established nearly 300 homesteads, about 20 churches, a Benedictine convent, and an Augustinian monastery. The communities were grouped in two clusters, the Eastern Settlement and the Western Settlement, both along fjords on the southwestern coast. The colonists dressed in garments of skin and homespun, and most artifacts—including some iron tools—appear to have been made locally. Their economy was based on fishing, hunting, and pastoralism. Sheep were raised in larger numbers than cattle on pasturages often described as excellent. The butter, cheese, and milk produced were important supplements to the flesh of animals, birds, and fish.

Trade was active between Norwegians and the Greenlandic Norse, and sailings were common in the 1000s and 1100s. The most important exports were walrus tusks, walrus hides, and the skins of caribou, foxes, polar bears, seals, and sheep. More un- usual exports included living polar bears and falcons, and most especially "unicorn horns." The Norse in Greenland knew long before most other Europeans that the "unicorn" was a sea mam- mal. The horn was greatly valued by Europeans, who pulverized it into medicinal powder. A container made from the horn was thought to neutralize poison, and for many years the food of French kings was placed in "unicorn horn" vessels before being served. The horn was considered a gift fit for an emperor, a king, or a queen; Elizabeth I of England kept one in her wardrobe to exhibit. In actual fact the "horn" is the tusk of a narwhal. These whales are found only in the open water of the far north, and a pod may include hundreds or even thousands of animals. They are relatively small whales, seldom over 20 feet in length, and males have a left canine that twists in a spiral and grows as long as 10 feet. Many theories have been advanced to explain the presence of this hollow-tipped and brittle tusk. Modern Baffin Island Eskimos point out that the ends of narwhal tusks are polished, generally on the underside. They say this wear results from the narwhal's scraping the bottom of the sea to obtain cod and sculpin. Early sources about Greenland mention the same use, to stir up the bottom for food, and another—less likely—to make breathing holes in the ice.

Eric the Red may have died believing in the Norse gods, but his son Leif introduced Christianity to Greenland. In 999 Leif sailed to

Norway and met King Olaf Tryggvasson at Trondheim. The king had made Christianity the official religion, and he persuaded Leif to become a Christian and to attempt converting the Greenland colonists. Although his father rebuffed his proselytizing, Leif's mother not only accepted Christianity but had a small church built at Brattalid, Eric's homestead and the principal community. This was the first Christian church in the New World. By about 1020 most Norse in Greenland were Roman Catholics, and because homesteads were so scattered numerous churches were built to accommodate them. It was difficult to obtain clergy for these distant parishes, and Greenland did not have its own bishop until 1125. Between 1376 and 1378 the last bishop died at his post.

An episcopal see was established in the Eastern Settlement at Gardar in 1126, and its church buildings were the most elaborate in Greenland. Archaeological excavators uncovered the remains of two rectangular churches; each had three walls built of stones and a fourth of turf and wood, with the older and smaller church foundation beneath the later one. The more recent cathedral, dedicated to St. Nicholas, was about 89 feet long and up to 43 feet wide. The residence was quite large, and the bishop's hall, which measured about 55 by 26 feet, was larger than any other hall in Greenland. The home field encompassed 37 acres, and the byres could accommodate over 100 cows. One storehouse, reputed to have held tithes, measured about 33 by 17 feet, and the stone lintel over one doorway weighed an estimated three tons. The site also included a smithy and additional storehouses.

Political life appears to have been largely of the Icelandic form, with a parliament and courts to settle disputes between residents or with visitors from Norway. By 1261 the Greenland colony voluntarily, if reluctantly, accepted the rule of the Norwegian king, but the remoteness of the island kept this political tie loose. Sailing from Norway to Greenland was dangerous at best, and a round trip typically required not less than a year. Seven successful sailings are known to have occurred during the 1100s and 13 in the 1200s, which suggests that completed voyages were relatively infrequent.

In the 1300s the Greenland trade appears to have diminished as pelts became available in reliable quantities from Russia and as ivory was obtained from Africa. Another factor affecting trade was that the population of the Western Settlement perished about

1350, and because men from that locality had sailed north most often to hunt walrus and narwhal for their tusks, these major exports were no longer available in significant numbers. The Black Death, a form of plague, struck Bergen, the chief port involved in the Greenland trade, especially hard in 1349 and recurred throughout the century in less virulent form. At this time too traders from Hanseatic ports in northern Germany came to dominate northern shipping at the expense of merchants from southern Norway. By about 1400 the Norse colonists in Greenland were badly neglected although they were not forgotten.

*   *   *

Before Norse colonization, Greenland was populated by aboriginal people, but the time of initial settlement has not been positively determined. Not so long ago it was thought that Eskimos first arrived in Greenland within the Christian era, but sites found in 1947 in Peary Land, north Greenland, had been occupied around 2000 B.C. by people from the northern islands of Canada (Independence I culture). The stone tools recovered are strikingly similar to some from Alaska (Denbigh flint culture) that have been dated about 3000 B.C. and are associated with emerging Eskimo culture in the western American arctic (Arctic small tool tradition). In Peary Land this stoneworking tradition endured until about 700 B.C., and a later one (Independence II culture) spread over a broad area in northeastern Greenland. From about 1400 to 700 B.C. other migrants from Canada pushed into western Greenland, occupied the southwestern coast, and then ranged along the southeastern shore (Sarqaq culture). About 100 B.C. yet another thrust from northwest to southeast began (Dorset culture), and the remains of these Eskimos were found by the Norse.

A fascinating but unanswered question is why Eskimos were not living in southwestern Greenland when the Norse settled there. Eskimos may have exhausted the local supply of driftwood and then either died out or pushed on to live elsewhere. Another group of Eskimos (Thule culture) entered northwestern Greenland from Canada about A.D. 1200, and their descendants established the site found near Upernivik on Inugsuk Island to the north of the Norse settlements. These Eskimos hunted on sea ice, and they also were learning to hunt more efficiently from kayaks. As their technology for hunting from kayaks in the winter developed, they were able to range farther south.

The earliest mention of Greenlandic Eskimos in the literature dates from about 1200 and is as follows: "On the other side of Greenland, toward the North, hunters have found some little people whom they call Skrellings; their situation is that when they are hurt by weapons their sores become white without bleeding, but when they are mortally wounded their blood will hardly stop running. They have no iron at all; they use missiles made of walrus tusks and sharp stones for knives." This brief account has a ring of truth amidst the fantasy. We know that the only Eskimos encountered by the Norse came from the northwest. The absence of iron and use of stone knives are reasonable, and missiles made from walrus tusks are no doubt harpoons.

As Eskimos filtered south along the western coast, they first encountered Norse at the Western Settlement, which more accurately should be called the "Northwestern" Settlement. About 300 miles farther south was the Eastern Settlement, again more precisely the "Southwestern" Settlement. The homesteads of the Eastern Settlement were far more numerous, larger, and more productive than were those farther north. The Norse of the Western Settlement apparently depended heavily on hunting, fishing, and fowling for food. It was these Norse who most often boated northward in the summer to the uninhabited area known as *Nordsetr.* Here they hunted, collected wood, and obtained skins and ivory for export. According to the account cited in the previous paragraph, they met Eskimos on their travels in about 1200. Tangible evidence of Norse ventures to the far north is a runic stone recovered in the Upernivik District, about 600 miles north of the Western Settlement. The characteristics of the inscription, which consists mainly of the names of three men, date it in the late 1200s. An excavated Eskimo site on Inugsuk Island dates about 1300 or somewhat later. Artifacts of Norse origin recovered at this site include a piece of metal from a church bell, a fragment of woven woolen cloth very similar to that found in Norse graves to the south, staved wooden containers or coopers, saws made from baleen, and wrought-iron blades. Small wooden dolls carved in an Eskimo style have clothing of the type common to the Greenlandic Norse, which suggests that these Eskimos had seen Norsemen (Figure 1-1). The Norse objects at Inugsuk may have been obtained

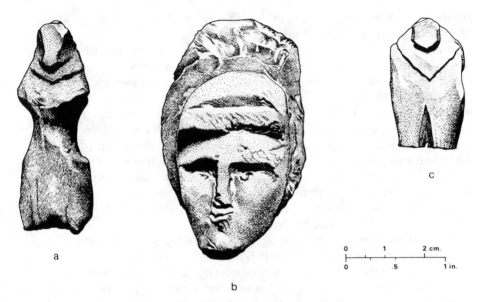

a

b

c

0   1   2 cm.

0   .5   1 in.

Figure 1-1 Artifacts from the Eskimo site at Inugsuk, Upernivik District of West Greenland, showing evidence of Norse-Eskimo contacts. The wooden dolls (a, c) are carved in a different style from Eskimo dolls and the clothing resembles that worn by the medieval Norse. The wooden carving of a face (b) has un-Eskimo facial features and style of headdress. (From Mathiassen, 1931; redrawn by Patrick Finnerty)

by the Eskimos as the result of direct contact with people at the Western Settlement, but it also is possible that they were traded to the northern groups by other Eskimos who already had pushed to the south.

We know very little about what happened when Eskimos and Norse first met at the Western Settlement; presumably relations were both friendly and hostile. As the years passed, the Eskimos apparently became aggressive, and about 1350 a party of Norse from the Eastern Settlement was sent to the Western Settlement to drive out the troublesome Eskimos. When they arrived, they found neither Eskimos nor Norsemen. The 90 homesteads of the Western Settlement seem to have been abandoned abruptly at about this time; the cattle and sheep of the Norse were still grazing in the vicinity. After the Eskimos gained control of this area, they moved southward and attacked the people of the Eastern Settlement. In 1379 Eskimos reportedly "killed eighteen men, and captured two swains and one bondswoman." This was not a final encounter, however, since the Eastern Settlement continued to exist through most of the 1400s. Eskimo legends mention the Norse and occasionally discuss them at some length, but they do not provide adequate information about abandonment of the Western Settlement.

The last written record linking the Greenland colony with Scandinavia is a marriage certificate issued at Gardar on April 16, 1409. Two priests certified that on three consecutive Sundays they had read the banns for a couple, and no one having raised any objections they were pronounced man and wife. Nothing in the document suggests that the Eastern Settlement was disintegrating— quite the contrary. However, it appears that no ship was sent to Greenland during the late 1300s or through much of the next century. The priests at the marriage ceremony had been bound from Norway to Iceland, but after landing in Greenland by accident had spent four years there. Communities in the Eastern Settlement apparently were occupied until after 1480. In excavated graves were caps of a distinctive type fashionable after 1450 in Burgundy! Although it is possible that ships from England accidentally reached Greenland in the 1400s, the Burgundian cap was most reasonably introduced by Basque whalers who sailed to the far north at that time.

A final historical footnote is offered by Jon Greenlander, an Icelander who was given his last name because of his many accidental sailings to Greenland. He reportedly left Hamburg on a vessel bound for Iceland about 1540, but the ship was driven to Greenland in a storm. According to a later copy of his story, he sailed into a fjord and saw a boathouse and dwellings similar to those built in Iceland. On the beach was the body of a man dressed in a coat made of homespun and sealskins. The blade of the knife at his side appeared to have been nearly worn away by sharpening. Mute and poignant evidence such as this probably existed at diverse homesteads as the Eastern Settlement passed into extinction.

An Eskimophile might attribute the demise of the Norse colony to the adaptive superiority of Eskimo culture, but it is more likely that Eskimos dealt only one among several blows that ended the

Norse era. No one really knows which factors contributed most to the death of the colony. Climatic conditions apparently grew more severe in the 1300s and 1400s and made it increasingly difficult for the Norse to keep their sheep and cattle alive through the winter. A trend toward colder weather would favor the southward movement of Eskimos, and this first would affect the people of the Western Settlement. Eskimo methods of hunting seals on the ice became more successful in the long fjords as the colder climate produced thick ice in many of these localities. Thus, fur-clad Eskimos with sophisticated weapons designed to take sea mammals on the ice or at its edges began hunting in the region exploited by the Norse dressed in medieval European clothing and apparently using less adequate weapons and boats. Eskimo equipment was as innovative as the Norse presumably was conservative. As the Eskimos pushed southward, they came into direct competition with the Norse. This made it increasingly difficult for the Norse to obtain ivory and skins for the European trade; however, the market for such products had declined as trade networks opened with Russia for similar products. As the trading decreased, social ties with Iceland waned, and religious bonds with Norway finally shattered. The altered trade pattern, coupled with the aftermath of the Black Death and the decline of the merchant fleets from Bergen, led to the abandonment of Greenland by Scandinavians.

The artifacts found by the Norse in western Greenland and the absence of their makers during the early settlement years lent mystery and perhaps a supernatural air to the Skrellings. Even after Eskimo and Norse hunters had met, very little is recorded about the contacts, although it seems that they were not intimate and friendly. Few Eskimo artifacts have been recovered from Norse homesteads, and most Norse objects found in Eskimo sites could have been obtained from abandoned settlements. There is no indication from the human remains recovered that Eskimos and Norse intermarried. The earliest known illustration of a Skrelling depicts him as a dwarf, and as the Middle Ages ended Eskimos remained a mystical people.

NOTES

STUDIES OF ESKIMOS.   An immense amount has been written about Eskimos, probably more than about any other aboriginal people. The book-

Figure 1-2 These are the earliest known illustrations of Eskimos. They appear on *Carta marina*, a map of Scandinavia and the islands of the north Atlantic Ocean. The map with Greenland in two parts was prepared by Olaus Magnus and issued first as a woodcut in 1539. In the upper figure the Eskimo is depicted as a dwarf fighting a Norseman. In the lower figure the bowman is shooting at a European ship. Near it is a strange vessel sometimes described as an Eskimo kayak or umiak, although it looks like neither. These representations of Eskimos and the boat appear to be products of the artist's imagination. (From Lynam, 1949)

Figure 1-3 *Carta marina* issued as a copper engraving in 1572. (From Lynam, 1949)

length works of two authors are outstanding. *The Eskimos* by Edward M. Weyer (1932) is the most comprehensive and widely respected study of Eskimo aboriginal lifeways on a regional and comparative basis. A less technical account ranging from Eskimo prehistory to ethnographic descriptions and historic changes is *The Eskimos* by the Danish ethnographer Kaj Birket-Smith; this book has appeared in three English editions (1936, 1959b, 1971). *Alaskan Eskimos* (1967) by Wendell H. Oswalt is a regional ethnography. A more lengthy bibliography is included in the Notes to Chapter 10.

The most comprehensive bibliographic source is the *Arctic Bibliography*, which is annotated. Volumes one through three appeared in 1953; in 1975 the sixteenth and final volume in the series was published. The journal with the most articles devoted to Eskimo studies is *Arctic Anthropology* (1962-   ), published by the University of Wisconsin. The American series with the most intensive coverage is *Anthropological Papers of the University of Alaska* (1952-   ). Laval University in Quebec recently launched a new journal devoted to Eskimos, *Études Inuit Studies* (1977-   ). In Europe the most important series is the publication of the Danish Kommissionen for videnskabelige undersøgelser i Grønland *Meddelelser om Grønland* (1879-   ).

WORDS FOR ESKIMOS.   Most authors agree that the term *Eskimo* is from an Algonkian language spoken by Indians in the vicinity of the St. Lawrence River; whenever a particular tribe is identified as originator of the term, it is the Abnaki (*see* Birket-Smith, 1959b, 7-8; Hodge, 1907, pt. 1, 436). The Danish linguist and ethnographer William Thalbitzer (1914, 542-3; 1950, 564) felt that the word originally was "Excomminquois," coined by Jesuits in eastern Canada to refer to pagan peoples to the north. "Esquimawes" was used first by Richard Hakluyt in 1584, although this work was not published until much later (Hakluyt, 1877, 88). Since the Jesuits did not begin their missionizing effort until 1605, it would appear that "Eskimo" clearly is of Algonkian origin and not derived from *excommunicated*. My efforts to locate the source from which Richard Hakluyt obtained the word have failed.

The words cited as used by Athapaskan Indians in northwestern Canada to refer to Eskimos were recorded by Émile Petitot (1970, v. 2, 94).

ESKIMO FOLKTALES VALIDATED.   The skulls with ivory eyes were found near Point Hope, Alaska, and belong to persons of the Ipiutak culture. The finds are described and the myth about men with ivory eyes is mentioned in the site report by Helge Larsen and Froelich G. Rainey (1948, 120). It should be added, however, that a sacred mask used at Point Hope in historic times had ivory eyes (Rainey, 1947, 248). Charles F. Hall (1865, 277-80) recorded the old Eskimo woman's story about the voyages of Martin Frobisher.

ESKIMO PREHISTORY. The most comprehensive book about Eskimo archaeology is by Hans-Georg Bandi (1969). The discussion of finds from Greenland by the historian Finn Gad (1971) is excellent. The archaeological record of Norse contacts with Eskimos is best for the Inugsuk Island site excavated and reported on by Therkel Mathiassen (1931).

ARCTIC MIRAGE. The navigational implications of the hillingar effect are discussed by H. L. Sawatzky and W. H. Lehn (1976). The ability of an observer to sight Greenland from northwestern Iceland is presented by Vilhjalmur Stefansson (1943, 43) among others.

NORSE SAGAS. The translated texts by Gwyn Jones (1964) have been followed, and included in these are valuable data about Norse settlements in Greenland. Much of the same information is covered in a work by Helge Ingstad (1966). A critical review of information conveyed in the sagas is provided by Henrik M. Jansen (1972).

HISTORY OF GREENLAND. The accounts by Finnur Jonsson (1928), Samuel E. Morison (1971), and Carl O. Sauer (1968) overlap and provide different perspectives. The most thorough analysis of Eskimo and Norse data alike is in the work of Finn Gad (1971, 1973).

ABANDONMENT OF NORSE SETTLEMENTS IN GREENLAND. Since the Norse are of interest primarily in terms of their contacts with Eskimos, no effort is made to review all of the conflicting explanations about Norse abandonment. Gad (1971, 131-2) and Jones (1964, 54-61) consider changing climatic conditions to have had some effect, but Sauer (1968, 155-7), among others, discounts this possibility. Fridtjof Nansen (1911, v. 2, 104-13) and Vilhjalmur Stefansson (1938, xxvi-xxxiii) felt that the Norse were assimilated by Eskimos. This theme is developed most fully by Tryggvi J. Oleson (1963, 70-86). Based on an analysis of blood groups found in modern Greenland; Ib Persson (1969) suggests that the historic population of the Julianehaab district may have been derived from an Eskimo-Norse mixture.

VINLAND. For the Norse travels to Labrador and Newfoundland I have depended heavily on Ingstad (1969), and this work is again the primary source about the Norse settlement in Newfoundland near L'Anse aux Meadows. The 1974 finds at the site are reported by Donald A. Harris (1974). G. M. Gathorne-Hardy (1921, 172-87) offers a thoughtful evaluation of the ethnographic evidence and favors the identification of Skrellings in Vinland as Indians. Sauer (1968, 126-32) likewise surveys the data and concludes that the people contacted were Algonkian Indians. Archaeological studies in Labrador by William W. Fitzhugh (1972) provide the best evidence by far for Indian occupancy at that time.

NARWHAL. Very little is known about this small, toothed whale. Perhaps the best summary of its appearance and habits is by Fred Bruemmer (1966). Appended as a note to this article is the suggestion that a narwhal used its tusk to stir up bottom-feeding fish as food. It does not appear that the tusk was used to pierce ice to form breathing holes as sometimes was reported in early accounts (e.g., Egede, 1745, 79).

THE EARLIEST ILLUSTRATIONS OF ESKIMOS.   Edward Lynam (1949) reproduced the 1539 and 1572 maps by Olaus Magnus. As Birket-Smith (1959a, 5) and William C. Sturtevant (1976, 449, fn. 25) have pointed out, the Eskimos illustrated on *Carta marina* appear to be products of the artist's imagination since they have no distinguishable Eskimo characteristics.

CHAPTER

2

Early Northern Encounters

Eskimos were introduced to history largely as a footnote to the English search for a northwest waterway to Asia and the Danish desire to reestablish ties with the old Norse colony in Greenland. In the early 1500s ships from northern Europe and England sailed by accident or design to Greenland and beyond, but we know little about these travels and any contacts with Native Americans. The first notable accounts about Eskimos are an indirect product of the passage quest by Martin Frobisher, an English explorer whose credentials as a seaman were excellent. Born in Yorkshire, he was raised by an uncle, Sir John York of London, a merchant in the African trade. Frobisher went to sea at the age of 14 and later became the captain of a privateer. He was an impatient person, irascible and stern, yet at the same time compassionate. He appears to have been an inspiring leader whom subordinates admired when they did not fear him. For years Frobisher sought sponsors of a search for a northwest passage, and through the efforts of Michael Lok, a financier of considerable means, he finally succeeded. In 1576 Frobisher was given command of the bark *Gabriel*, and with its crew of 18 he sailed in the company of the *Michael*, a vessel of similar design and complement. When the ships encountered pack ice off Greenland, the captain of the *Michael* turned back to England, where he falsely reported that the *Gabriel* had been lost. This was nearly true since Frobisher's ship almost sank in a terrible storm off south Greenland. After the storm Frobisher sailed briskly to the south and then westward to discover a broad waterway between what appeared to be two landmasses, America and Asia. The captain named the passage "Frobisher's Strait" and felt that it was the northern counterpart of the Strait of Magellan. After sailing along his strait for about 150 miles, Frobisher was convinced that this was the northern border of Cathay. Actually he had discovered a great bay, which now bears his name, along southeastern Baffin Island.

On August 19, 1576, Frobisher, his sailing master Christopher Hall, and others landed on an island at the mouth of the bay and climbed a hill for a better view. They thought they sighted porpoises or seals at sea, but as the forms drew near, they proved to be men in small skin-covered boats. Before the English could descend the hill, the people landed on the island and attempted to cut the sailors off from their boat. Only by rushing to the landing were Frobisher and his men able to avoid an obvious trap. These strangers did not stand in awe of whites and their great ships. Instead they clearly and cleverly attempted to take advantage of the newcomers. In written history this is the first clear account of an English-Eskimo encounter, but apparently these Eskimos were already familiar with Europeans, judging from their initial response to Frobisher, the iron that they possessed, and the acrobatics they later performed in the ship's rigging in the manner of sailors.

Following the safe return of the Englishmen to the *Gabriel* the still trusting Christopher Hall went ashore to visit the people and "gaue euery of them a threadden point." He saw men and women similarly dressed in sealskin garments. The women's faces were marked with blue tattoos around their eyes and down their cheeks. In later times pubescent Baffin Island girls were tattooed either by pricking the skin and rubbing a mixture of plant juice and soot into the wounds or by sewing thread coated with the same mixture through the skin. Women also had tattooed limbs and breasts, no doubt in each instance to enhance their beauty. According to Hall the people looked like Tartars with their broad faces, flat noses, long black hair, and brownish complexions. Hall is the first West-erner known to have taken field notes about Eskimos, and al-though unable to understand their language, he recorded 17 words with English translations, no doubt by pointing to forms and writing the word spoken. After this friendly visit Hall returned to the ship with an Eskimo, and later in the day numerous Eskimos visited the English.

The day following these amicable contacts an English boat with five men aboard went ashore. Their reception was unexpected—they were captured by the people. During the next few days Frobisher attempted different strategies to recover his men and the boat, but to no avail. When Eskimos in kayaks and large open skin boats (umiaks) paddled toward the ship, Frobisher planned to sink an umiak and take the passengers hostage. However, as the ship's crew prepared to fire, the Eskimos grew wary and withdrew beyond ordnance range. The Eskimo response again suggests their familiarity with Europeans. Frobisher next held out a bell to lure a nearby kayaker. When the Eskimo was within arm's length, Fro-bisher seized the man and lifted him, kayak and all, out of the water onto the ship's deck. The distraught Eskimo reportedly bit his tongue in two but did not die from the wound. The English hoped to exchange their captive for the missing sailors, but this proved impossible. Reluctantly the *Gabriel* set sail for England without its full crew but with an Eskimo and his kayak aboard.

Frobisher's captive made a great impression on the stay-at-home English, as Michael Lok conveys in a brief contemporary account:

> they aryved at Harwich on the ij day of October in safety where they taryed to refresh their sick and weake men, and so came to London with their ship Gabriel the ixth day of October and there were joyfully received with the great admiration of the people, bringing with them their strange man and his bote, which was such a wonder onto the whole city and to the rest of the realm that heard of it as seemed never to have happened the like great matter to any man's knowledge.

Lok described the man as being of dark complexion and having a fat body, short legs, long black hair tied in a knot above his forehead, and a little beard. The captive had become ill on the return voyage and did not live long to impress the curious. The Flemish artist Lucas de Heere, who was in England at the time, made a wash drawing of this man (Figure 2-1). The Eskimo is not portrayed as described by Lok; instead of being fat and having short legs, he resembles a European dressed in stylized Eskimo clothing.

When Frobisher was at southeastern Baffin Island, he sent men ashore to obtain objects to substantiate the claim of discovery. Among the souvenirs from Hall's Islet was a piece of heavy black stone that seemed to have a high metallic content. In England, the stone was judged worthless by several assayers, but another one reportedly derived flakes of gold from it. His conclusion that it contained gold was supported by a mineralogist. On the basis of this evidence the Company of Cathay was chartered, and a polar gold rush was in the making. Lok was governor of the company, and Frobisher became the High Admiral. Queen Elizabeth made a significant contribution to the enterprise, and three ships were outfitted for the voyage. They sailed in 1577, and when they arrived at the islands near the northern entrance to Frobisher Bay, the miners aboard began digging "gold ore."

On this voyage Frobisher hoped to capture Eskimos and exchange them for the five sailors seized the previous year. In an initial attempt to take two Eskimo men, Frobisher and his sailing master nearly were overpowered, and they fled to the safety of a waiting boat. While escaping, Frobisher was shot in the buttocks with an arrow, earning him the dubious distinction of being the first Englishman known to have been wounded by an Eskimo. Another man from the English boat was able to capture one of the Eskimos involved in the scuffle. During the weeks to follow the Eskimos were wary and kept their distance. The English found garments belonging to the captured sailors at a camp from which everyone had fled. In the hope that the people would return and that their countrymen might be among them, gifts were left at the camp, and the English planned to return and take the Eskimos by surprise. The following day one party approached overland, and a second set out in two boats. After discovering that the Eskimos were gone from the campsite, the land party moved on and found an occupied camp near the coast. The Eskimos saw the attackers approaching and fled in a kayak and an umiak. The English fired at them to delay their escape and to attract the attention of their boat crews. In their haste the Eskimos had taken too few paddles and rather than be overtaken by the English, they landed and appar-

Figure 2-1 This wash drawing of the Baffin Island Eskimo captured and taken to England by Martin Frobisher in 1576 is one of
the earliest illustrations of a living Eskimo. (Courtesy of the University Library, Gent)

ently climbed to the top of rocks along the shore. From there they launched arrows at their assailants, who responded with arrows and shots from muskets. The Eskimos shot all of their arrows and returned fire with arrows shot at them by the English "until both weapons & life utterly failed them." In desperation a number of the wounded jumped into the sea, preferring death by drowning to capture. The others escaped on foot except for an old woman and another woman with a small child on her back. Hiding amidst some rocks, the younger woman was mistaken for a man, and a shot wounded the child before the three were seized. The sailors considered the old woman a witch and removed her boots to see whether she had cloven feet. When this proved not to be the case, she was released, but the mother and child were taken away. A pen and watercolor drawing was made of this skirmish by John White, who may have been a member of the expedition. A copy of this drawing, possibly made about 1610, is reproduced as Figure 2-2. Following this episode the Eskimos were so cautious and such "craftie villains" that no others were captured, and nothing was learned about the lost sailors.

Although friendly face-to-face contacts did not occur on this voyage, the English did encounter some people with whom they communicated by gestures from a distance, and they inspected a number of settlements from which people had fled. The descriptions of Eskimos by Dionyse Settle are the best ones recorded from the Frobisher voyages. Settle was a "gentleman" in search of adventure. Men such as Settle were the intellectual ancestors of naturalists who later sailed on ships probing the arctic and other distant parts of the earth. Even though Settle had an opportunity to observe the captives at his leisure, his account is more typical of reports by observers involved in brief and unfriendly contacts, irrespective of whether the record was made in the sixteenth or nineteenth century. He noted that the Eskimo men, who wore their hair rather long, were "of a large corporature, and good proportion." A woman's long hair was arranged in loops on each side of her face, with the remainder rolled into a knot. A description of blue coloring on the faces and wrists of some women is a reference to their tattoos. The garment covering a woman's upper body had a hood and a tail. Men and women wore undertrousers or "hose" that fitted snugly from their waists to their knees, and other hose were drawn over these. Women were known to wear

Figure 2-2 The first historical illustration of a skirmish between explorers and Eskimos. The drawing is of the major conflict between Frobisher's men and Baffin Island Eskimos in 1577. (© British Museum)

two or three pairs of hose at a time, and the openings at the tops served as pockets for small objects.

Descriptions of Eskimo housing and weapons were compiled by Settle following visits at abandoned settlements and observations during brief encounters. Their summer dwellings were sealskin tents; their winter houses had walls of stone and whales' bones roofed with skins. Their wooden bows were backed with strips of sinew and were strung with sinew, while wooden arrows had four feather vanes and arrowpoints made from stone or iron. Another weapon was described as having many bone forks at one end and others along the middle of the shaft. This was "cast out of an instrument of wood, very readily." This is an abbreviated description of a bird spear hurled with a throwing-board (spear-thrower). A second "dart," probably a lance, had a long bone point sharpened on two sides; Settle wrote that this "I take to be their most hurtfull weapon."

Settle reported a diet of raw flesh, including dogs, fish, and fowl, but also noted that these people sometimes prepared soup from boiled meat, blood, and water. He thought they were cannibals and wrote "what knowledge they haue of God, or what Idol they adore, wee haue no perfect intelligence." His most curious statement was that the Eskimos made signs which led him to believe they had a very large man, a king, who was carried about on the shoulders of others.

The description of Eskimos by Settle is brief compared with his account of the problems the English had with them, the hardships of the voyage, and English efforts to mine gold. An Eskimo's appearance was strange and clearly worthy of more than passing note, but it was not especially intriguing. Their customs were curious, yet they were "countrie people," not uncouth barbarians. "They neither use table, stoole, or table cloth," a delightful observation that they were quite un-English and by implication uncivilized.

When the ship bearing the three captive Eskimos arrived at Bristol, they quickly became the center of widespread interest. These were indeed exotic people since they dressed in skin clothing and "fed only upon raw flesh." In addition the woman nursed her child while it was on her back by "casting her breasts over her shoulders." The man launched his kayak in the harbor and demonstrated hunting ducks on the wing, hurling his bird dart with a throwing-board as illustrated in the French edition of Settle's account (Figure 2-3). Contrary to English expectations the captives behaved in a civil manner and were not at all savage. When presented to Queen Elizabeth, they were duly respectful, and she was so impressed by them that she granted the man permission to hunt swans on the Thames, an act for which poachers were punished by hanging.

The captive trio did not live in England for very long. The man died of pneumonia after about two months, while the mother and child survived only a little longer. Their appearance was recorded

Figure 2-3 Woodcut, probably based on an original painting by John White, of a Baffin Island Eskimo hunting with a bird spear hurled from a throwing-board while in a kayak. The woodcut appears in the 1578 French edition of Settle's account of the voyage in 1577. (Reproduced by permission of The British Library)

in numerous paintings, but the only two surviving originals are watercolors by John White, the Elizabethan artist famous for the watercolors he made of Indians in the Virginia Colony. White's illustrations of Indians are well-known because they were reproduced as engravings by Theodore de Bry for the book *America*, published first in 1590. However, the watercolors of Eskimos were not prepared as engravings by de Bry and seldom have appeared in print. The White originals are reproduced as Figures 2-4 and 2-5.

Frobisher sailed on his final voyage to Baffin Island in 1578. He

Figure 2-4 John White's water-color of the Baffin Island Eskimo man captured and taken to England by the Frobisher expedition in 1577. (© British Museum)

Figure 2-5 John White's water-color of the Baffin Island Eskimo woman and child captured and taken to England by the Frobisher expedition in 1577. (© British Museum)

commanded a large fleet of ships that were to bring back ore of supposedly great value. The vessels had many difficulties reaching their destination because of stormy weather and ice-clogged seas, and when they arrived at Frobisher Bay, the severe weather handicapped their mining efforts. Nonetheless they recovered hundreds of tons of ore before returning to England in early September. For five years efforts were made to smelt the ore and retrieve its riches but to no avail. On this final venture Baffin Island Eskimos were sighted, but they were very cautious and could not be approached. The fleet chaplain on this third voyage, Master Wolfall, was the first missionary to the Eskimos, but he was unable to "reform those Infidels" since he met none.

The only other ethnographic information of substance from the expeditions of Frobisher is in the report by George Best. He was in an excellent position to provide a summary since he participated in all voyages. Best described the Eskimos as warlike, subtle, and sharp-witted with strangers but friendly and kindhearted with one another. Best noted that their umiaks were fitted with masts and sails made by sewing skins or bladders together and that they ate grass, an observation also offered by Settle. Most of his other descriptions parallel those of Settle. Best's account of what he assumed to be a curing technique is particularly informative.

> For when their heads do ake, they tye a great stone with a string unto a sticke, and with certaine prayers & wordes done to the sticke, they lift up the stone from ground, which sometimes with all a mans force they cannot stir, & sometime againe they lifte as easily as a feather, and hope thereby with certaine ceremonious words to have ease and helpe.

This is an instance of comparatively complex behavior being transmitted from Eskimos to an Englishman without the benefit of language. From the reports of later observers we know that the "stone-lifting" ritual was performed to determine whether the patient would survive an illness.

Men who participated in the voyages of Frobisher referred to Eskimos by a number of different words, and these provide insight into the manner in which sixteenth-century Englishmen viewed aborigines. Eskimos usually were called "people," or less often "countrie people." When they caused the English minor problems, they were "craftie people" or "villains." "Savage" was used occasionally in neutral contexts but was more often found in descriptions of difficulties between Eskimos and English. At times Eskimos might disparagingly be called "cannibals." In sum, Eskimos were often "people" and by inference were accepted by the English as similar to themselves. In retrospect it is curious that the English did not coin a national label for the inhabitants of the newfound land.

*   *   *

When Frobisher first anchored at the entrance of the bay that bears his name, he planned to carry off three or four people. He had been requested to do so by Queen Elizabeth but was cautioned not to give offense in the process. His captive Eskimos were among the first aboriginal Americans introduced to Elizabethan England. The English were to become increasingly exposed to indigenous peoples from diverse areas of the New World, but none represented highly developed cultures such as the Aztec and Inca. One rationale for taking captives from afar was to train interpreters, and the other was to provide the heathen with an opportunity to see the workings of Christianity and civilization close at hand. A more pragmatic reason, and probably the one most on the minds of explorers, was that Americans were compelling public attractions.

In terms of Christian doctrine, the English found it difficult to explain the existence of "countrie people" such as those discovered by Frobisher. The sons of Noah giving rise to the human races numbered only three. Scriptures derived Asiatics from Shem, Africans from Ham, and Europeans from Japhet, leaving no ancestor for an undiscovered region. Had New World peoples, living at what was perceived as the earth's end, been giants, pygmies, or human-like monsters, they would have fitted into a nonhuman category. However, the Eskimos and Indians taken to England were eminently human both in appearance and behavior. Could it be that New World peoples were descendants of the lost tribes of Israel or of other lost peoples? Or were they simply humanlike but not human? To confuse the issue further, Eskimos differed from Indians, and striking distinctions among Indians soon became apparent. None of these peoples could be easily fitted into the belief system of the explorers and their countrymen.

*   *   *

At the time of Frobisher's voyages and even before, the Danes and Norwegians had planned to return to Greenland. They hoped to contact the earlier settlers and convert them from Catholicism to the Lutheran faith established in the homeland during the Reformation. However, wars and other pressing domestic problems interfered with their plans.

In 1579, partly in response to the success of Frobisher, the Danish-Norwegian government of King Frederik II had two ships outfitted for a voyage to Greenland led by the English navigator, James Alday. The goals of the expedition were to reclaim the country for the Norwegian crown and to convert the people to the Lutheran faith. The sailing was delayed until one of the vessels could be replaced, and once begun, the voyage was hampered by very stormy seas. Greenland was sighted, but the amount of ice near the shore made landing there impossible.

Many knowledgeable persons still reasoned that a navigable northwest passage existed, and another Englishman, John Davis, soon embarked on three searching expeditions. When Davis first sailed from Dartmouth harbor, he was 36 years old, had about 20 years of experience at sea, and was highly regarded as a sea captain and navigator. Accounts about him and his voyages to the American arctic reveal a kind and competent leadership. His first venture was backed by merchants, and letters of patent were granted by Queen Elizabeth for "the search and discoverie of the North-west Passage to China." In 1585, 23 persons sailed on the *Sunneshine*, including four musicians to entertain and obtain the goodwill of any savages encountered. The *Mooneshine* had a complement of 19. Sighting the east coast of Greenland, Davis called it "The land of Desolation," and unable to penetrate the sea ice to land, he sailed on. After rounding Cape Farewell without seeing it, they anchored at a fjord in the old Western Settlement near modern Godthaab. The chronicler of the voyage was John Janes, described as a "Marchant." He reported landing on one island where artifacts were found and then on another where he and others climbed to the top of a high rock. They were sighted by "the people of the country" who "made a lamentable noyse." The noise was returned in kind by the English as both a sign of friendship and warning to their companions on the ships. Soon about a dozen Eskimo "canoes" floated offshore, but the paddlers were reluctant to land. More of the English went ashore, including the four musicians who played as others danced. The English imitated Eskimo signs of friendship, and a kayaker was emboldened to approach nearer than the others. Some sailors removed their caps and stockings, tossing them to the man as gifts. Since it now was late in the day, the sailors returned to the ships, and the Eskimos went to their homes.

The next morning nearly 40 kayaks approached the ships, and the paddlers gestured that the English were welcome ashore. When the sailors did not respond promptly, an Eskimo climbed on a rock to dance, display sealskins, and beat a drum. The English took to their boats, and before landing they pointed to the sun and struck their chests, imitating an Eskimo sign that they had seen the previous day. Janes shook hands with an Eskimo who in turn kissed his hand, a very un-Eskimo greeting, clearly indicating familiarity with Europeans. The English soon were trading for clothing, kayaks, and skins, and did so a second time before favorable winds led Davis to sail on. These were the only direct contacts between Davis's men and Eskimos, and Janes wrote of their amiability, "They are a very tractable people, voyde of craft or double dealing, and easie to be brought to any civilitie or good order: but wee judge them to bee Idolaters and to worship the Sunne."

The ships crossed Davis Strait to Baffin Island and entered Cumberland Sound, which is wide, deep, and seemed almost endless. Davis thought that it had a western outlet because there were powerful tides, whales swam from the west, and the water was the same color as that seen in the main ocean. He felt that this was indeed a route to Cathay, but since the season was growing late, he turned back to England without knowing that this "passage" was in fact a sound. Surely another voyage would show the way to the Orient, and Davis was prepared to make a second attempt.

The following year (1586) Davis commanded the barks *Mooneshine* and *Mermayde* and sailed west again, seeking a through waterway. The *Sunneshine* and *North Starre* under Richard Pope attempted to reach Cathay by sailing along the eastern coast of Greenland and over the North Pole, which seemed a reasonable enterprise to some geographers. In describing the second voyage Davis reported that his vessels were "mightily pestered with yce and snow" off south Greenland, but that they finally arrived in the vicinity of Godthaab, where they had met friendly Eskimos the previous year. Davis went ashore, distributed knives to the men, and asked for nothing in return. The English soon were amicably trading for fish and skins, but the Eskimos' desire for iron proved insatiable. They soon were taking anything that could be carried off, even a boat. Davis found them "marvellous theevish" but so disarmingly open in their thefts that their behavior was at first considered more humorous than malicious. Soon, however, the constant thefts became a problem, and a small cannon and an arquebus were fired. This led to the abrupt departure of the Eskimos, but they returned shortly to make peace. When Davis came back to his barks after exploring in a pinnace, he found the crews angry at the Eskimos. They had stolen an anchor, had cut the cable on one of the ships, and were hurling heavy stones from slings at the English. The sailors blamed the lenient policies of Davis for these difficulties, and even his patience ended when a heavy stone struck a sailor. An armed party was sent by boat to punish the Eskimos, but they escaped in their speedy kayaks. When the Eskimos returned again to make peace, the worst thief was held hostage until the anchor could be retrieved. Before an exchange could be negotiated, a favorable wind came up, and Davis sailed off. The Eskimo captive soon adjusted to the ship's routine and was pleased with a gift of English clothing from Davis, but it is reported that before long he died.

Sailing north, the English landed in the vicinity of the Arctic Circle, establishing brief but friendly trading contacts with local Eskimos. After the less manageable *Mermayde* left for England, the *Mooneshine* crossed Davis Strait and sailed south along the coast of Labrador. The crew fished near Hamilton Inlet and caught a huge number of cod. Some men were sent ashore at a nearby bay to process the fish. Afterwards they returned to the ship, and when five sailors later went to retrieve the fish, they were set upon by "brutish people." The attackers fled as the *Mooneshine* drew near enough to fire in their direction. Two of the men on shore were killed with arrows, and the others were wounded. To make matters worse a storm came up, and the bark nearly was driven ashore among the "Canibals." Following this tragedy and near-disaster, the *Mooneshine* turned back to the safety of England.

After the futile effort of the *Sunneshine* and *North Starre* to sail over the North Pole, they headed for southwest Greenland to meet

Davis as previously arranged. The ships arrived in the vicinity of Godthaab after Davis had left, and at first the Eskimos were hostile, no doubt because Davis had taken one of their men. Friendly contacts soon were established, however, and a short while later they sailed south to another harbor, again encountering Eskimos. Sealskins were obtained, as was a kayak, but the kayak was not satisfactory to the captain. In the dispute that followed, Eskimos launched darts at the sailors and hit one man. The English returned fire with arrows, killing three Eskimos and wounding others. A few days later the vessels sailed for England, but after a storm the *North Starre* was never seen again.

Davis considered the second voyage successful and willingly committed himself to another attempt. After obtaining the necessary backing, he sailed west again in 1587 with the barks *Sunneshine* and *Elizabeth* and the pinnace *Ellin*. The *Sunneshine* began to leak badly, and the pinnace often was extremely slow. To complicate matters further, some sailors were on the verge of mutiny when they learned that the vessels were not sailing directly to the cod-fishing grounds discovered the previous year. The vessels finally arrived again in the Godthaab area, and trade with the Eskimos began. Again John Janes, the chronicler of the first Davis voyage, was a member of the crew. He wrote that on June 16 "the people came presently to us, after the old manner" to trade sealskins. The English went ashore and began building a second pinnace from materials that they had brought with them on the *Elizabeth*. Soon after their arrival they seized "a very strong lustie young fellow" as a hostage to insure the good behavior of the Eskimos, yet this was not to be. Before the pinnace could be launched, the Eskimos pulled boards off to obtain the nails. The English shot arrows at the Eskimos, who turned the pinnace on its side for protection. When a blank shot was fired from a cannon, the Eskimos fled in their kayaks, but they had the presence of mind to take along the nail-filled boards. The English decided to complete the dismantling of the pinnace and to use it later for cod fishing.

Since the prospect of a great harvest of fish was far more attractive to the sailors than exploring, it was decided that the crews of the two barks would sail for the Labrador fishing grounds and meet Davis there later. In the meantime he was to explore northward in the *Ellin*. When he passed beyond the Arctic Circle in the pinnace and was about 30 miles at sea, kayaks approached the vessel. Their occupants were willing to trade anything, including their kayaks and clothing, for "pinnes, needles, bracelets, nailes, knives, bels, looking glasses, and other small trifles." The pinnace reached Upernivik, and there seemed to be open sea ahead. Sailing west they encountered pack ice and adverse winds that prevented them from venturing northward, and so they turned south along the pack ice to once again trade with Eskimos at sea. After sailing about 150 miles they reached Cumberland Sound, a locality discovered on the first voyage along Baffin Island. As they continued their journey south, not many days had passed before they encountered "a very great gulfe, the water whirling and roring, as it were the meeting of tides." This was a great strait, later named Hudson Strait, but it went unrecognized as such. On a map prepared with places discovered by Davis it was labeled "The furious overfall," which indeed it was. Davis eventually arrived at the rendezvous but found that the two barks already had left for England. He had no choice except to sail the pinnace back to England, which was in itself an achievement of note.

About 1600 Christian IV, the Danish and Norwegian king, embarked on a program of maritime expansion. His goals were to reassert the old tradition of Norsemen as traders who controlled the northern seas, to reestablish ties with Greenland, and to locate the old settlers. Before undertaking commercial ventures, he decided to determine the best route to Greenland and turned to his brother-in-law, James I of England, for aid. The English had more recent familiarity with northern waters, and Christian IV enlisted a Scot, John Cunningham, to lead the Danish expedition, which involved three naval vessels. Cunningham was in command of the *Trost*, and it was accompanied by the *Katten* and the *Røde Løve* or *Løven*. The *Løven*, older and slower than the others, was under the command of Godske Lindenov, a Danish nobleman. Cunningham apparently did not trust his own abilities as a navigator since he engaged James Hall as his pilot aboard the *Trost*. Very little is known about Hall except that he was English and later emerged as a key figure in a series of investigations. The *Katten* was commanded by John Knight, another Englishman numbered among the seekers of the Northwest Passage.

In 1605 after an uneventful crossing of the Atlantic the vessels became separated in a fog off south Greenland. When they reunited, Lindenov obtained a chart of the sailing directions from Hall, lest they become separated again. Differences between Lindenov and the English, however, led him to sail off on the *Løven* to explore. Although difficulties were encountered with ice floes, the *Løven* reached southwestern Greenland, and the crew landed to trade with Eskimos for skins and narwhal tusks. After two Eskimo men and their kayaks were seized, the *Løven* sailed for Denmark. The Eskimos initially proved difficult passengers and were said to have bitten like dogs. They became more tractable as the voyage progressed, and when the ship arrived in Copenhagen, the crew received a royal welcome. The Eskimos performed before the king and queen to the apparent pleasure of all. In one display they raced their kayaks against a boat propelled with 16 oars and were able to keep abreast.

The *Trost* and *Katten* sailed on to just south of the Arctic Circle. After anchoring the vessels at the head of a bay and formally claiming the country, Cunningham and Hall walked along the bank of a nearby river and then climbed to higher ground, from which they spied four Eskimos and skin tents farther along the riverbank. As the English approached, three of the Eskimos fled on foot and the fourth took to his kayak. Hall and Cunningham boarded a boat that had been following along the shore and were rowed toward the kayaker. "Hee, holding up his hands towards the Sunne, cryed *Yota*, wee doing the like and shewing to him a knife, hee presently came unto us and tooke the same of the Captaine." Although these and other early explorers did not know it, this word or a similar one meant "we are friends." As the Eskimo paddled away, Hall and Cunningham went ashore to inspect the abandoned camp. In a pot with a stone bottom and baleen sides, seal meat was cooking in seal oil over the flame of a stone lamp. Another utensil contained a freshly cooked dog's head, and scattered about to dry were seal meat and small fish. The most impressive artifacts were two boats covered with sealskins. They were some 20 feet in length and were rigged with sails made from sewn intestines. During the next few days Eskimos arrived to exchange clothing, sealskins, and weapons for old nails, pins, needles, and "other trifles."

Hall traveled north on the *Katten* as Cunningham waited on the *Trost* for his return. Contrary winds soon forced the *Katten* to seek shelter in a cove that Hall named "Sling Road." Soon after the small vessel had anchored near the shore, some 30 Eskimos arrived in kayaks. The visitors apparently reasoned that the pinnace with its small crew was vulnerable to attack. The Eskimos paddled ashore to find stones that they hurled at the vessel with slings. After a falcon was fired, the Eskimos took to their kayaks, only to return a few hours later with twice their original number. The Eskimos readied their attack, but the pinnace crew was prepared and fired on them as more stones were hurled. When they heard a shot fired, the "Barbarus people" ducked behind the rocks out of harm's way, a clear indication of familiarity with European firearms. The situation grew tense, and the pinnace crew welcomed the favorable winds that released them. Hall ventured just short of Disko Island, and as the *Katten* was returning to the rendezvous with the *Trost* the crew located a deposit of "silver ore." In accounts of the voyage this discovery is not mentioned—for obvious reasons—but it appears to have provided the primary impetus for the next sailing and probably was the purpose behind yet another voyage. James Hall prepared the first detailed maps of Greenland, one of which is reproduced as Figure 2-6. This map depicts not only kayaks and a tent but also men holding different types of weapons.

After Hall returned on the pinnace, preparations were made to leave as soon as possible. Before they sailed away, the English captured three Eskimo men, and another was killed during the encounter. As they departed, a large number of Eskimos attempted to attack the kidnappers, but a cannon was fired and frightened them off. When the *Katten* and *Trost* arrived in Copenhagen, the three Eskimos proved a fascinating attraction. They exhibited their boating skills by performing dance-like patterns in their kayaks before a captivated audience. The Spanish ambassador to Denmark witnessed the performance and was so impressed that he gave the men a large sum of money. The Eskimos bought the most fashionable clothing, including hats with ostrich feathers, swords, and spurs. After they appeared in this garb, they were termed the "Greenland Grandees." Although the three men were well treated, in the spring they attempted unsuccessfully to escape in their kayaks. The Danes planned to return them to Greenland so that they might tell their countrymen of the good treatment they had received. On their return voyage, however, two of the Eskimos died, and the fate of the third is not known.

Figure 2-6 In 1605 James Hall made the first detailed surveys of localities in Greenland. This is the map of Itivdleq Fjord located about 180 miles north of Godthaab. (From Gosch, 1897) The man on the left in the upper section is holding a spear or harpoon, while those at the top and bottom center have bird darts in hand. The person at the lower left is preparing to hurl a rock from a sling, while a bow and arrow are held by the man at the lower right.

In characterizing Greenlandic Eskimos, Hall described them as "a kinde of *Samoites*," referring to the Samoyed who lived in western Siberia. They were "a reasonable stature, being browne of colour" and a warlike nation of wanderers who ate their meat raw or slightly boiled and apparently worshipped the sun. Once again as a result of limited contacts with Eskimos the descriptions are thin and elaborated with speculations.

An expedition was organized on a grand scale in 1606, with Lindenov in command of five vessels, but only two ships, the *Trost* and *Örnen*, appear to have reached Greenland. The primary purpose of the voyage was to mine the ore found the previous year, and with Hall as pilot, the ships visited only the fjords explored earlier. The ore was judged high in silver content, and the crews were to mine as much as possible. When they reached the deposit, the crews worked feverishly and traded very little with Eskimos. One sailor was put ashore as punishment for some misdeed and soon was killed by Eskimos. Before the ore-laden ships sailed homeward, four Eskimos and their kayaks were seized to take back to Denmark, but one man jumped overboard.

The next year Hall sailed with a Danish expedition organized primarily to locate the old Norse settlers, but when masses of ice prevented any landings, they returned to Denmark. In 1612 Hall set out on a fourth and final voyage that apparently was a joint mining and trading venture sponsored by London merchants. The *Patience* and *Heart's Ease* set sail, with Hall in command of the former vessel. Two accounts of the 1612 voyage exist, one by John Gatonbe, quartermaster of the *Patience*, and the second by William Baffin. The "savages" who approached the ships in the Godthaab area gave the usual greeting of friendship and soon were trading, especially for iron. On a nearby island the ships' carpenters set about reassembling a large and a small boat. A watch was kept to prevent Eskimo thefts, but one night when these sailors were huddled in a shelter before a fire, a musket was stolen. On the day the larger boat was launched, a sailor seized an Eskimo, presumably in the hope of recovering the gun, but another Eskimo threw a harpoon and mortally wounded the captor. The captive Eskimo was taken aboard ship, where he was given a coat, a knife, and a mirror. Before long two "aged men and rulers of the rest, came, with great reverence" to return the musket and seek the release of the captive. By signs the English indicated that they were willing to give up the man, his kayak, and weapons. When freed he jumped overboard, and as he reached the shore the Eskimos cut the coat from his back.

Shortly before departing the Godthaab area, Hall assembled the ships' crews to hear orders about future barter with the people. Trading was to be the exclusive right of Mr. Wilkinson, a "doer" or merchant representing the organizers of the venture. Rain and contrary winds delayed the ships' departure, but on arriving at an anchorage about 50 miles to the north Hall left the *Patience* and sailed off on the smaller *Heart's Ease* to the "silver" mine. He and three others were in a small boat when an Eskimo, presumably in a kayak, offered to exchange a harpoon for a piece of iron. As Hall picked up the iron, the kayaker hurled a harpoon at him, and he died from the wound. At this time some 150 kayakers were nearby, and the sailors were unprepared to defend themselves. The Eskimos did not launch a general attack at this most opportune moment, however. Presumably Hall was killed as revenge for the murder and seizure of local Eskimos by the Danish expedition in 1605. The crew sailed on to the mine, but a goldsmith who accompanied them judged the ore worthless. After the death of Hall, disputes arose over the hierarchy of command, and it was nearly a month before the ships sailed around south Greenland headed for England.

Figure 2-7   A West Greenland Eskimo in his kayak as observed by the Hall expedition to West Greenland in 1612. The original caption follows: "The fashion of the savages rowing in their boats, the boats being made of seal skins, and clos'd in, all but the place where he rows in her, and that is clos'd about him when he sits in her, from his waste downward. His oar hath two webs, and he useth both hands to row with." (From Gosch, 1897)

Baffin's interest in watercraft led him to describe Eskimo boats in considerable detail. He reported that one umiak was 32 feet long, while kayaks were about 20 feet in length and about 2 feet wide (Figure 2-7). He commented on the swiftness of kayaks: "they will row so swiftly that it is almost incredible; for no ship in the world is able to keepe way with them, although shee haue neuer so good a gale of wind." He remarked further that much of their sustenance was obtained from their boats and that the larger ones transported household goods from one camp to another. Baffin also reported that food apparently was eaten raw, and he too thought that the Eskimos worshipped the sun. He did not consider them to be man-eaters, as did some of the others on the voyage, because they did not take advantage of an opportunity to kill and eat three sailors.

The life and doings of William Baffin before he sailed to Greenland with James Hall in 1612 are unknown. After his return Baffin entered the service of the Muscovy Company, sailing with whaling vessels to Spitzbergen (1613, 1614). He then joined the Company of Merchants of London, Discoverers of the North-West Passage, who had sponsored Henry Hudson (1610) and Thomas Button (1612) before the formal organization of the company. Robert Bylot was in command of the next attempt, and Baffin served as his pilot. In 1615, Baffin sailed the *Discovery* into Hudson Strait to Southampton Island before turning back after encountering great masses of ice. The following year he sailed again on the same vessel and explored the great bay that now bears his name. However, on these two voyages Eskimos were seen only at a distance or traded with briefly.

John Davis, James Hall, and William Baffin were the men most responsible for exploring and mapping the western coast of Greenland. With geographical discovery and cartography as primary goals, gathering information about Eskimos was of little concern. In fact their purposes would have been served better if no people had been encountered. The trade goods obtained from Eskimos apparently had no great value, and food provided by Eskimos did not contribute significantly to the welfare of these explorers. Neither was it possible to learn very much about the region from Eskimos, given the problems of communication.

Possibly the first comparative or ethnological statement about Eskimo life was made by Davis in 1586. After seeing people in the Godthaab area, he sailed farther north and landed in Greenland again. He stated that they "differ not from the other, neither in theyr canoas nor apparell, yet in theyr pronuntiation more plaine than the others, and nothing hollow in their throat." While near Godthaab, Davis compiled a list of 40 southwest Greenland words and phrases with English translations. Later studies show that the Eskimo terms were accurately recorded and translated, a remarkable feat considering the difficulties Europeans have with certain Eskimo sounds and the fact that neither the informants nor the ethnographer knew the language of the other.

Of the concepts attributed to Eskimos during the first 200 years of their history, none was more often mentioned than sun worship. What could be more logical than for these arctic people to revere their major source of light and heat? The sun, as the dispeller of cold and darkness, was a reasonable object for veneration, even for deification, but as the particulars of Eskimo religious life later came to be understood, the sun rarely was reported as important. Occasionally the sun was accorded ritual attention as among the Iglulik Eskimos living along northwestern Hudson Bay. When the sun first appeared after the winter solstice, Iglulik children put out the flames of lamps, and the lamps were relighted to greet the new sun. A small number of similar rituals are reported elsewhere, but in nearly every instance they were unimportant. Only in West Greenland, where sun worship is most often reported, did the sun's return command clear recognition, but even there the "Sunfeast" is thought by some to have been a minor ritual. Over 200 years ago the historian David Crantz attempted to dispel the notion that West Greenland Eskimos stressed the sun in their religious life. He pointed out that early in the morning when people left their houses and faced the rising sun "in deep meditation" it was to observe weather conditions. Other examples of Eskimo sun worship likewise may be discounted.

Eskimo tales about the origin of the sun and moon were a part of their mythological background to reality. The essence of a widespread but locally varying myth is that a man seduced a woman in the dark, and since she could not determine her lover's identity before he left her side, she marked him with soot from a lamp. She later found that her lover had been her brother. In her shame the girl cut off her breasts and offered them to her brother to eat since he was so taken with her. The sister then fled into the sky to become the sun. The brother followed her to become the moon, and he still pursues his sister across the heavens. This myth is reported from Alaska to Greenland and is unquestionably of a common origin.

The moon, as opposed to the sun, was a potent supernatural force, and it was most malevolent in East Greenland. Here people believed that during a lunar eclipse the moon came to earth to steal the souls of nonconformists. Among Eskimos of the Bering Sea region the moon was associated with disease, and an eclipse fore-shadowed an epidemic unless the sickness could be averted by shamans. These people also believed, however, that a great deal of good was derived from the moon. The manlike moon controlled the abundance of game on earth, and in times of food stress shamans reportedly visited the moon with the aid of spirits that they controlled. The shaman's purpose was to induce the moon to release animals as food. In the Canadian arctic the moon some-times was associated with hunting success, and rituals involving water or snow were performed for vague or specific purposes. The moon's influence on tides was widely recognized, but tides were relatively unimportant in the activities of Eskimos. The moon was thought to affect the fertility of females; the timing of the menstrual cycle in relation to the phases of the moon no doubt was the source of this concept. In general the moon was masculine, and some-times it was powerful, in clear opposition to the sun, which was female and weak.

We reason that the sun is a source of more direct earthly good than the moon and are prepared to support this position with a wealth of evidence. Yet Eskimos attributed few benefits to the sun. The assumption by explorers that the Greenlandic Eskimo greeting of pointing to the sun had a supernatural significance was ill-founded. Later studies show that for most Eskimos the sun simply existed: it was just there. Misinterpretations of the sun's impor-tance give us pause when judging any behavior of the Eskimos on our terms. If there was a failing of explorers that was greater than all others in the interpretation of Eskimos, it was their Westerniza-tion of Eskimo concepts.

NOTES

THE THREE VOYAGES OF MARTIN FROBISHER.   Vilhjalmur Stefansson (1938) assembled all the known accounts of these voyages in a two-volume work that includes a long introduction with a wealth of background and inter-pretive information. The tattooing practices of Baffin Island Eskimos are reported in an ethnography by Franz Boas (1888a, 561) based on his field-work among them in 1883-4. Details about the personality of Frobisher are from the biography about him by William McFee (1928).

THE EARLIEST ILLUSTRATIONS OF ESKIMOS.   Articles devoted to the subject by Birket-Smith (1959a) and Paul H. Hulton (1961) deal with most of the early representations of Eskimos from life. Illustrations of Eskimos by John White are catalogued by Hulton and David B. Quinn (1964, 141-5).

ABORIGINES IN EUROPE.   The reception of aborigines in Elizabethan England is best presented by Sidney Lee (1929, 263-301). Books by Roy H. Pearce (1953), Margaret T. Hodgen (1964), and a third edited by Fredi Chiappelli (1976) are key sources about the intrusion of "primitive peoples" on European thinking.

THE THREE VOYAGES OF JOHN DAVIS.   The Hakluyt Society edition of these voyages edited by Albert H. Markham (1880) is the primary source. The identification of landfalls and distances by Morison (1971, 583-605) is followed, and particulars about the life of Davis are from the biography by Clements R. Markham (n.d.).

THE FOUR VOYAGES OF JAMES HALL.   C. C. A. Gosch (1897) published the firsthand accounts of Hall's explorations for the Hakluyt Society. Supplementary information was drawn from the introduction by Gosch and from Gad (1971, 217-9). The meaning of the Eskimo greeting, "yota," is supplied by William Thalbitzer (1914, 677).

THE 1615 AND 1616 VOYAGES OF WILLIAM BAFFIN.   Eskimos were not encountered on the sailing to Southampton Island in 1615 although people were seen at a distance in "one great cannoo" and an abandoned Eskimo summer camp was visited. The 1616 voyage that led to the discovery of Baffin Bay was exceedingly important in terms of geographical discovery, but of marginal importance in terms of Eskimos. They were met near Disko Island in Greenland and in the Upernivik region, with comments offered about tattooing, eating raw meat, and sun worship. Accounts of the five voyages of Baffin and pertinent elaborations were published by Clements R. Markham (1881).

THE SUN AND MOON.   Weyer (1932, 381-9) summarizes the attitudes, beliefs, ceremonies, and rituals involving the sun and moon; he likewise references many primary sources. David Crantz (1767, v. 1, 196-7) partially explains why voyagers were mistaken about Eskimo beliefs involving the sun. However, no one has adequately accounted for the particular salute to the sun used as a greeting by West Greenland and Eastern Canadian Eskimos. The Iglulik "new fire" ritual is reported in brief by Knud Rasmussen (1929, 183).

CHAPTER

3

The "Perfect Craze"

In the course of the most magnificent failure in navigational history Westerners met Eskimos time and again. Miller Christy called the search for a northern sea route to the Far East a "perfect craze," and the Northwest Passage best symbolized this elusive waterway. The "furious overfall" that the pinnace of Davis had crossed in 1587 seemed a promising threshold to the passage, and backers of the newly formed Company of the East India Fellowship felt that this discovery deserved further investigation. In 1602 George Waymouth was given command of the *Discovery* and *God-speede* with instructions to "passe on forwarde in those seas by the Norwest, or as he shall finde the passadge best to lye towards the parts or kingdom of Cataya or China." The vessels were outfitted for a 16-month voyage, but soon after they arrived in Hudson Strait the cold and ice seemed almost overwhelming to the crew. A mutiny organized by John Cartwright, "our preacher," resulted in a return to England without any accomplishment, and no Eskimos were encountered.

The sponsors of Waymouth did not abandon hope, and in 1606 they commissioned John Knight to sail the *Hopewell* on a similar search. After a slow and uneventful crossing of the North Atlantic their trials began in earnest. Off the Labrador coast they were battered by masses of ice, and the aftermath of several storms found them in the midst of crushing ice. Fortunately the north-central coast was sighted, and they managed to reach a cove. The surf badly damaged the vessel, however, and it was beached. At this point Knight's account ends, and the narrative was continued by Oliver Browne, "one of the Company." Knight and five others set off by boat in search of an adequate harbor. Landing on a large island, Knight and three others reconnoitered, leaving two sailors at the boat. The well-armed men walked over the crest of a high hill and never were seen again. The waiting sailors repeatedly trumpeted and fired a musket before returning to the ship. Subsequent searches proved fruitless. The eight survivors camped on shore as they labored to lighten the bark, which was pounding on rocks in the cove. During a heavy rain a few nights later about 50 Eskimos attacked and nearly seized a small boat before being driven off by musket fire. As they fled in umiaks, ice partially blocked their escape, and the English fired on them a dozen times. The "shot caused them to cry out very sore one to another." This was the first and last encounter with the "Savages of the Countrie" or "Countrey people" whom Browne described as "very little people, tawnie coloured, thin or no beards, and flat nosed, and Man-eaters." After extraordinary efforts the sorely taxed crew freed the bark and finally made it seaworthy enough to carry them to Newfoundland. After European fishermen helped the crew make additional repairs, the *Hopewell* returned to England.

No man was more enchanted by the Perfect Craze than Henry Hudson, nor was any contemporary explorer quite so perplexing a person. Yet in terms of Eskimology he is a peripheral shadow. Hudson's effort to discover a route across the North Pole (1607) failed, and the same was true of his search for a northeast passage (1608). On his third voyage (1609) he sailed northeast from Holland, but after encountering ice off the coast of Norway he turned west and eventually discovered the Hudson River. His final voyage (1610) was from England and was again a search for a northwest passage. He reached the "furious overfall" in late June and encountered great masses of churning ice and fog. Despite the weather and dissension among his crew, the *Discovery* managed to sail through Hudson Strait into a seemingly endless expanse of water, Hudson Bay. Instead of setting a course to the west,

Hudson curiously sailed south along the eastern shore until he reached James Bay. He lingered there so long that the company was forced to spend a wretched winter along the southern shore. The ship was freed from the ice in the late spring and reached open water, but in late June some of the sailors mutinied from fear of starvation, Hudson's vacillations, and his favoritism. Hudson and

Figure 3-1 In 1619, Jens Munk sailed from Denmark to Hudson Bay in search of a Northwest Passage. His only contact with Eskimos was in Hudson Strait, where he traded with the people briefly. This illustration of the encounter forms part of a woodcut depicting episodes on the voyage. The artist apparently thought that all aborigines went about naked. (From Gosch, 1897, v. 2)

eight others were cast adrift in a small boat, and the *Discovery* sailed north. At the eastern entrance to the bay the mutineers and their accomplices landed on a small island in search of food and soon encountered "savages." A sailor was exchanged for an Eskimo as a hostage, and they bartered with the people briefly but spent most of the day killing birds for food on the return voyage. Because the Eskimos had seemed friendly, most of the sailors were lightly armed when they went ashore to trade for food. Suddenly they were attacked, and two men "had their bowels cut." One died somewhat later "swearing and cursing in a most fearfull manner." The leader of the mutiny was killed with an arrow, and the other sailors hastily reboarded the ship and sailed on. During their return trip the worst troublemaker died "for meere want," but the others were rescued off Ireland. Most of Hudson's journals were destroyed by Abacuk Prickett, who was in tacit, if not open, league with the mutineers. His self-serving account is the only record about most of the voyage. Luke Foxe later wrote an often-quoted sentence that deserves to be cited once again: "Well, *Pricket*, I am in great doubt of thy fidelity to Master *Hudson*."

Contrary to expectations the mutineers were not tried and hanged for their compounded crimes. The reason was simple. Their knowledge was of great value to the merchants of London because they apparently had discovered the Northwest Passage. The survivors, especially Prickett and Robert Bylot, the navigator of the bark on the return voyage, knew the route beyond the overfall. Therefore when Thomas Button sailed with the *Resolution* and *Discovery* Bylot and Prickett were members of the party. Little is known of this voyage, sponsored by "The Company of Merchants of London, Discoverers of the North-West Passage." Apparently its directors were convinced that the results would be valuable to their competitors, and firsthand accounts were suppressed originally and later lost. The ships departed in April 1612, and after entering Hudson Bay, they sailed west and landed south of present-day Eskimo Point at a locality named "Hope's checked," which requires no further comment. From there they turned to the south and wintered at Port Nelson, where many men died. The *Resolution* apparently was abandoned before the following spring, and further probes to the west for a waterway were unsuccessful. Failure was their only reward, and yet another expedition returned to England without achieving this most elusive goal.

The description of the 1631 voyage to Hudson Bay by the forthright if not boastful Luke Foxe contributes very little to our understanding of Eskimos. On an island off the northwestern coast the sailors took the wood covering Eskimo graves for firewood. Foxe reported that the skeletons were "not above 4 foot long," and given their small stature he remarked, "God send me better for my adventures than these." The bodies probably were flexed before burial, and therefore the graves were short, giving the impression that the people were dwarfs. Foxe also noted that the weapons in some graves were tipped with copper or iron.

Old ideas and old, determined men die hard. The old idea is of course the Perfect Craze, and James Knight was the old man. He had a long and distinguished career with the Hudson's Bay Company before he became a lost explorer. In 1718 he sailed to England to convince the "Committee" that since little was known about the northwestern sector of Hudson Bay, a passage to the Orient might be found there. Furthermore he felt certain that a river flowing to the sea in this region exposed accessible deposits of copper and gold. In the spring of 1719 the frigate *Albany* and the sloop *Discovery* were placed under the jurisdiction of Knight, and the vessels left England. Nothing was heard of them after their departure, and in 1721 the *Whale-Bone* was sent to Churchill to prepare for a search the next summer. Under the command of John Scroggs, the vessel sailed about 90 miles north of Eskimo Point, and Scroggs "doth affirm that Every Man was killed by the Eskemoes."

Samuel Hearne, another longtime Hudson's Bay Company employee and a great explorer in his own right, commented on the disappearance of the Knight party. He felt that the evidence reported by Scroggs was not proof of the men's fate. Optimists in England still hoped that the vessels might have sailed through the Northwest Passage to California and on to the South Seas. In the summer of 1767, new evidence was found by whalers. For a number of years whaling sloops had sailed along the western shore of Hudson Bay. They met at Marble Island because it had a good harbor and whales were plentiful in the vicinity. This particular summer they found a new harbor on the island, and near it were seen guns, an anvil, and many other manufactures as well as the ruins of a house. In the water near the head of the harbor were the sunken hulls of a ship and a sloop. Among the artifacts recovered was the figurehead of the *Albany*, conclusive proof that these were remains from the Knight expedition. In 1769 several Eskimos, including two old persons, visited the Hudson's Bay Company whalers at Marble Island. An English-speaking Eskimo employed by the company learned from the elderly Eskimos that the vessels arrived late one fall and the larger vessel was damaged at the harbor entrance. The English, who numbered about 50 at the time, began building a house. When the Eskimos saw them again the next spring, 1720, there were fewer whites. Although they seemed unhealthy, they were working hard, probably building a boat. By the beginning of the second winter they numbered only 20. Some Eskimos wintered nearby and provided the English with meat and oil until they left for the mainland in the spring. When the Eskimos returned in the summer, they found five starving men. They bartered for seal meat and blubber but ate it so ravenously that three of them died. The two survivors often walked to the top of a nearby rock and watched for rescuers. After one died, his companion expired while attempting to dig a grave.

The northwestern sector of Hudson Bay remained unexplored following the failure of James Knight. The idea that a passage might exist there intrigued some men and made crusaders of others. Heading the list of avid devotees was Arthur Dobbs, an Irishman who had served in the Irish House of Commons and later held high administrative posts in Ireland. He attempted to convince the Hudson's Bay Company Committee to launch a systematic exploration, but after its trading sloops had probed the northwestern coast in the late 1730s, the company concluded that a passage probably was nonexistent. Dobbs was convinced that company officials would continue to be obstructionistic, and so he turned to the Admiralty. He enlisted the cooperation of Christopher Middleton, an experienced commander of Hudson's Bay Company vessels and a man with scientific interests. Middleton entered the King's service and was placed in command of two vessels that were to seek a passage once again. Middleton commanded the *Furnace*, while William Moor was captain of the *Discovery*. They wintered at the mouth of the Churchill River and sailed north in the summer of 1742. After entering Wager Bay, Middleton became convinced that no passage existed there or to the south and that if one existed to the north it would be too ice-filled for navigation. On this seemingly final note he returned to England.

The interest of Arthur Dobbs was undiminished, and he next formed the "North West Committee" by public subscription. The *Dobbs*, commanded by William Moor, and the *California*, with Francis Smith as captain, sailed from England in 1746. One of the two chroniclers for the voyage was Henry Ellis, about whom comparatively little is known. He appears to have been wealthy and was a subscriber of the expedition. On the basis of family connections, or possibly because of his scientific writings about the voyage, Ellis later became governor of Georgia (1758-61) and then of Nova Scotia (1761-3). The second chronicler presumably was Charles Swaine, but his work was signed only as "the Clerk of the *California*." After cruising in the northwest, they put in at Marble

Island and then sailed south to winter near York Factory. In the summer, Moor, Ellis, and eight sailors explored the coast north of the Churchill River. They set out in a modified longboat christened the *Resolution* and journeyed north, planning to meet the larger vessels near Marble Island. In shallow, rock-strewn waters along the way the *Resolution* was buffeted by tides and was in a very dangerous situation when an old Eskimo man saw its plight. He paddled ahead in his kayak and guided the ship to safety. Additional probes between headlands proved futile. Moor and his men did not reach the head of Chesterfield Inlet but did explore Wager Bay further without finding a passage to the west.

The backers of Moor's search were very specific about dealings with "Eskimaux Indians" along Hudson Strait. Barter was carried out to ensure their friendship, but the crews were not to linger long in the process nor be particularly concerned with reaping a profit. Neither were they to seize any people against their will, but if individuals volunteered to sail to England, they were to be taken aboard.

After the first encounter with Eskimos along the islands in Hudson Strait, Henry Ellis devoted nine pages of text to these people. In the author's words the sketch was included because it "may possibly prove entertaining to the Reader." Ellis wrote more about Canadian Eskimos than had anyone since the voyages of Martin Frobisher nearly 175 years earlier. The descriptions of Eskimos by Swaine are somewhat less comprehensive, possibly because his contacts with them were not intensive. Swaine's interpretations, however, are sometimes superior to those of Ellis and are considered whenever appropriate.

The Eskimos seen first by Ellis at islands in Hudson Strait were great flatterers who were "much addicted to pilfer from Strangers." Their overwhelming desire for iron and their willingness to steal iron artifacts were noted many times before and after the 1740s. When Europeans began trading with aboriginal peoples, iron tools always were popular, but Canadian Eskimos had fewer opportunities than most peoples to obtain iron. Ellis remarked that these people were "stripping themselves almost naked" to exchange clothing for knives and other metal products. These Eskimos probably reasoned, as did others, that the quantity of metal aboard a ship was staggering and that iron objects therefore legitimately could be taken. However, they willingly offered essential possessions, such as clothing, in exchange. Why was their demand for iron so great? The answer seems clear. Although most aboriginal hunters made comparatively few artifacts to use in their food quest, Eskimos required many such forms. Persons in any hunting society found iron tools valuable because they kept an edge far better than stone-bladed tools. To Eskimos this cutting quality of iron tools was even more important because the raw materials they used to make essential parts of their often complicated weapons were hard organic substances such as antler, bone, and ivory. These materials were difficult to work with stone tools, especially since some parts were quite small. With an iron-bladed knife an able craftsman could work more quickly and easily. As iron became available in quantity, weapon points were made from it, and these were obviously superior to earlier forms fashioned from stone. Obtaining iron from the south was difficult since the trade routes were overextended by the time they reached the arctic, especially the isolated islands. Northern Eskimos coveted iron because they realized that the metal increased their chances for survival.

We have come to expect writings about Eskimos or other exotic peoples to include curious or amusing incidents. Anecdotes add color and often are intended to point up the naivete of aboriginal peoples. Ellis, for example, reported about Eskimo boys captured by Indians and taken to English trading stations, where they were raised. Here they learned something of the language and customs of their hosts. When one of them saw an Englishman butchering a seal, the Eskimo collected as much oil as he could with his hands and licked it off, saying, *"Ah! commend me to my own dear Country, where I could get my Belly full of this."* Ellis then wrote "it would be no difficult matter to civilize them, if their Trade was worth the Labour." The incident and the addendum are far from meaningless words. The Eskimo preferred to give up civilized life to live among his own people; to an Englishman this was incomprehensible except as an anecdote. The remark that it would be comparatively easy to civilize Eskimos reflects the pervasive European view that Eskimo culture was simplistic. An Eskimo's commitment to his culture, however, was no less than that of the Englishman to his. The learnings involved differ, yet to be an Eskimo hunter of note may have required as much knowledge—or even more—than to be an English gentleman. A comparison such as this escaped Ellis as it has escaped many commentators on Eskimo culture.

Among the observers thus far encountered Ellis was the first to describe in detail the most remarkable weapon ever conceived by hunters, the Eskimo harpoon. This weapon was used mainly against seals, walrus, and whales. Many different harpoon styles were made, with their use dependent on the species sought and on hunting conditions. Since harpoons were essential weapons among maritime Eskimos, they will be mentioned repeatedly, and it may be helpful to describe them in detail at this point.

Of all the animals hunted by people none are more inherently difficult to harvest than the sea mammals living in arctic and subarctic waters. One obvious but critical reason is that a hunter could not hope to survive for more than a few minutes if he fell into that very cold water. When seals, or other species, are hunted in open water, the human predator must first have sound watercraft, such as the Eskimo kayak or umiak; thus good boats were an essential preadaptation to sea-mammal hunting. Moreover, while a hunter could travel only on the water's surface, a seal could escape by swimming beneath it. For hunting sea mammals it would be ideal to have a weapon that would kill the quarry immediately and somehow keep it from sinking, but no such weapon was developed, possibly because a lethal wound would be difficult to inflict on an animal that exposes such a small amount of its body and for such a short period of time. The best alternative is to wound and thereby impede the free movement of an animal. The most effective means ever developed for both wounding and holding sea mammals is the toggle-headed harpoon, whether it is hand hurled or shot from a gun. A toggling harpoon head is designed to cut beneath the skin and to turn sideways in the flesh as the animal pulls away. Aboriginal harpoon heads were designed not to kill but to provide a technological hold on an animal.

The design of a harpoon was adapted to the size and habits of the sea mammal hunted. A harpoon used against a 150-pound harbor seal was much smaller and lighter than one for taking a 600-pound bearded seal, or a 1700-pound walrus, or a whale weighing many tons. Just as the size of the prey was critical, so were its habitats. Seals, for example, live in open water, but they also maintain small breathing holes in thick winter ice, sleep near large breathing holes in the spring, and swim along leads in masses of ice. The harpoons used under these varied conditions had certain modifications in design.

The account by Ellis effectively introduces the principal forms of harpoons used along northern Hudson Bay. The one for taking large seals, walrus, and small whales will illustrate the toggle-headed type (Figure 3-2, A). It consisted of a stout wooden shaft (1) with an ivory ice pick (2) lashed onto the base with a thong. The weapon was readied for launching by holding it with one's finger against an ivory finger rest (3) lashed to the shaft at the weapon's balance point. At the forward end of the shaft was fitted and

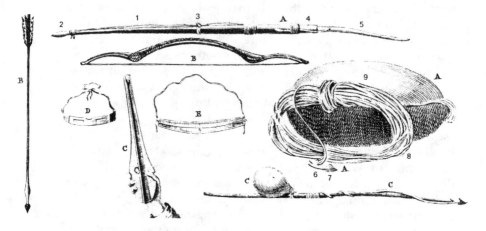

Figure 3-2 Illustrations of Hudson Strait area Eskimo manufactures by Henry Ellis in 1746. His caption reads as follows: "A The Great Harpoon for Whales wth its Barb Coil & Buoy. B The Bow & Arrow. C The Small Harpoon, its Bladder & Barb, with the Instrument to dart it at the Seals. D The Snow Eyes. E The Breast Ornament made of a Seahorse Tooth." The numbers have been added to the original engraving. (From Ellis, 1748)

bound an ivory socketpiece (4) that had a hole at one end to receive an ivory foreshaft (5). The ivory harpoon head (6) had a hole in the base that fitted over the end of the foreshaft. The iron harpoon blade (7) was pegged to the harpoon head, as a stone blade would have been before contact. A long line (8) was tied through a hole in the harpoon head, and the head was kept in place by holding the line taut by means of a small ivory attachment placed on it and fitted over a second peg of ivory on the shaft; the line led on to an inflated sealskin (9).

In open water during the summer and fall men hunted sea

mammals from kayaks with harpoons. A harpoon was placed lengthwise along the foredeck, and its coiled line rested in a wooden line holder lashed on the kayak in front of the manhole. This line led along the right side of the vessel, past the manhole, to an inflated sealskin float tied on the aft decking. The float was made by skinning out a seal through its mouth, which was enlarged somewhat, so that the number of holes in the skin would be minimal. All openings except at the mouth were closed with thongs; here an ivory nozzle was lashed in place. The skin was inflated by blowing into the nozzle, and the nozzle opening was closed with a stopper. After a hunter launched his harpoon, he quickly untied the thong that held the float in place, and as the animal sounded the float was dragged along behind, slowing the quarry until it could be killed.

Other forms of harpoons were used under specific conditions or for particular species. The second harpoon illustrated by Ellis (Figure 3-2, C, lower right) was for taking small seals from a kayak. This weapon had the same basic parts as the harpoon just described, but the shaft was lighter and the harpoon point attached with a short thong. An inflated bladder was connected to the shaft, and the weapon was launched with a throwing-board, also illustrated by Ellis (Figure 3-2, C, left front). A throwing-board artifactually lengthened a hunter's arm, presumably enabling him to hurl his weapon with greater thrust. The basal end of a harpoon shaft was set into a groove in the throwing-board. When the harpoon was thrown, the point penetrated the seal's flesh and became detached from the foreshaft but remained tied to the shaft. The sounding seal pulled the shaft and its attached bladder through the water. As the animal tired, the hunter killed it with a knife or lance. A much larger harpoon, again of the same basic design, was launched from an umiak at a whale. In this instance the end of the harpoon line was tied to three sealskin floats, which greatly increased the drag.

Ellis illustrated a bow made from three mortised pieces of wood as the most ingenious weapon of Eskimos (Figure 3-2, B). Woven cords of sinew were attached to the back of the bow shaft for strengthening and providing greater thrust for the arrow. From later sources we know that bow shafts were made from one long piece of wood if available, and alternatively from spliced sections of wood or caribou antler. Bone-pointed arrows were carried in a

Figure 3-3 Hudson Strait area Eskimos as illustrated by Henry Ellis. On the ground at the left are a harpoon and float. The central figures are making fire with a strap drill, and the person facing away is a woman with a child in one of her large-topped boots. The man in the kayak to the right is preparing to launch a small sealing harpoon. (From Ellis, 1748)

skin quiver and were used mainly against caribou. Men stalked individual animals or hid behind rocks and waited to intercept a herd; an able hunter could kill three animals in a herd before the others fled. Most Eskimos preferred to drive caribou into lakes because large numbers then could be speared from kayaks.

Skin clothing, which made arctic living possible, understandably attracted the attention of Ellis. He described garments made from the skins of birds, seal, and "deer." The latter also were called "reindeer" by some observers, but in the United States reindeer has come to mean the domestic species first introduced to Alaska from Siberia in 1891. The wild North American cousin of the reindeer, to which Ellis referred, is the caribou. In the Old World, domestic animals of this genus are called reindeer, and the un-tamed ones are termed wild reindeer or simply reindeer.

Men wore thigh-length, hooded parkas made from the skins of birds, caribou, or seals and trimmed with strips of different colored skin; a woman's parka was of similar design but included a long tail. "Parka" is an anglicized Russian word meaning a loose-fitting upper garment of skin made by peoples in eastern Siberia. Both sexes appear to have worn close-fitting breeches with a drawstring at the waist. Over skin socks the men wore short boots, but the boots of women were long, with wide tops that might be held open with strips of baleen. The top of a woman's boot was large enough to accommodate a small child, as indicated in an illustration by Ellis of a standing woman (Figure 3-3). The custom of placing a baby in the top of the mother's boot was confined largely to the northern sector of Hudson Bay.

Ellis and many later observers reported that Eskimo mothers carried babies in their parka hoods. This commonly is accepted as a widespread Eskimo custom, but babies seldom were carried in the hood of a parka. An Eskimo mother usually had a pouch-like recess at the upper back of her parka for her child. The infant's weight might be supported by a strap that passed beneath the baby and over the mother's breasts on the outside of the garment. Carrying a baby in a hood would negate the purpose of the hood and probably would choke the mother as well.

The *Resolution* sailed north along the western shore of Hudson Bay in the summer of 1747, and Eskimos occasionally were met. Ellis devoted a few pages to what probably were coastal bands of Caribou Eskimos. He considered them essentially the same as people along Hudson Strait but went on to note "that these are a more affable, friendly and better disposed Sort of Folks, as well as more accomplished Artists in those several Branches of Mechanicks, which they have been taught by one common Mistress, Necessity, which is the sole Mother of Invention amongst them." The ability of Eskimos to make fire with a strap drill serves as an example, and the process was illustrated (Figure 3-3). The lower end of a wooden shaft rested on a fireboard, and the upper end was fitted into a bearing. A length of thong looped around the shaft was pulled back and forth rapidly to rotate the shaft; this friction produced sparks that smoldered on the fireboard and then ignited wood or dry moss. Ellis no doubt also considered Eskimo "Snow-Eyes" to have been originated by necessity. These wooden goggles with small eye slits (Figure 3-2, D) were worn in the spring to protect the eyes from the sun's glare on the snow, thereby preventing snow blindness.

As one of the first writers to describe Canadian Eskimos in a thoughtful manner, Ellis understandably stressed such concrete qualities as manufactures, but he commented also on nonmaterial aspects of their lives. They "are the only Nation that eat Animal

Food absolutely raw," and some people thought they were closely related to the Greenlanders. Hudson Bay Eskimos and Greenlanders had beards and a "whiteness of their Skin" that contrasted with Indians. Thus Ellis distinguished Eskimos from Indians on the basis of dietary habits and physical characteristics. According to Swaine many persons believed that Eskimos always ate flesh raw, but he noted that Eskimos cooked meat when they had the opportunity.

Efforts by the crews of the *Dobbs* and *California* to find a passage along one quadrant of Hudson Bay failed, and they returned to England in October 1747. Ellis still felt that such a waterway might exist. He had concluded that in the north trees do not grow on narrow peninsulas or islands as they do on the continental masses. Since the land fronting northwestern Hudson Bay was bare of trees, he felt that it must be a peninsula, even though it might not include a passage.

To dispel the feeble but lingering hope of a passage along Chesterfield Inlet, William Christopher examined the inlet from the sloop *Churchill* in 1760. He turned back when he found a river, but the Hudson's Bay Company officials sponsoring the venture remained interested since this waterway might offer access deep into the interior. In 1762 the company sent two vessels up the inlet, and one traveled the 230 miles to Baker Lake at the end.

By now it was clear that no strait led from western Hudson Bay, but along with this realization a new and different hope emerged. Beyond the divide of rivers flowing into northwestern Hudson Bay might be a major river draining into the Pacific Ocean. This was a reasonable assumption since Cook Inlet, the deep bay discovered by James Cook in 1778 along the Gulf of Alaska, seemed to be the drainage of a great river. Alexander Mackenzie was quite certain that "Cook's River" originated in northwestern Canada. To verify his supposition he left Fort Chipewyan with a small party in June 1789. After traveling in birch-bark canoes to the Slave River and then along the western shore of Great Slave Lake, they began to descend a great river, to be called the Mackenzie. At first their hopes were high since the river flowed fast and to the west, but as mountains appeared in the west, the river coursed northwest and then north to parallel but not pass between them. By mid-July they had reached the river mouth and the "Hyperborean sea." Approaching the coast they passed from Indian to Eskimo country but did not encounter Eskimos, although their camp and home sites were found. Mackenzie commented on the artifacts he saw around the camps of the "Esquimaux" or "Esquimaux Indians," but he could write little about the people.

Renewed interest in the Northwest Passage came about in an unexpected manner, and for those intimately involved the prospects were exciting. In the summer of 1815 and the two that followed, ships sailing the north Atlantic encountered unprecedented ice conditions. Northern waters were open as never before, with ice drifting farther south than had been reported previously. Even the east coast of Greenland was relatively free of ice. An Englishman, John Barrow, was captivated by the implications and formulated a plan to expand the geographical knowledge of the arctic. Barrow, a largely self-educated person, devoted his career to the civil administration of the navy. In his nearly 40 years as Second Secretary of the Admiralty, he was England's most influential nonexplorer interested in the arctic. Barrow's proposal was approved by the Royal Society, the First Lord of the Admiralty, and the Prime Minister. Two ships were to sail west of Spitzbergen toward the North Pole, and two others were to seek the Northwest Passage among the islands west of Greenland. Earlier explorers had not been able to penetrate the Polar Sea, although William Baffin might have done so if he had entered Lancaster Sound from Baffin Bay. The fact that water flowed north through Bering Strait, south in Davis Strait, and south from Spitzbergen convinced Barrow that these currents swept unimpeded from the Pacific to the Atlantic. Those who doubted that any positive gain could result from efforts to find the route could not be ignored. These "Utilitarians," as Barrow labeled them, felt that the search was not worth the effort. He was quick to stress that the practical results, even though they need not include a passage to China, could not be measured before the passage was negotiated. Who could have known that the whale-fishery would expand following the discoveries of Davis, or that Frobisher would lead the way to the eventual development of the great northern fur trade? Barrow was certain that knowledge gained from a renewed effort was a valid goal and in keeping with the great English tradition of maritime explorations.

In 1818 two ships ventured forth once again on the Northwest Passage quest. The commander of the *Alexander* was William E. Parry; John Ross commanded the *Isabella* and the expedition.

Among the supernumeraries aboard the *Isabella* was John Sackhouse (Jack Saccheous, Hans Zakaeus), a Greenlandic Eskimo raised at Disko Island. He had stowed away on a whaler bound for Scotland and later was enlisted as an interpreter by Ross. The results of the expedition were disappointing to Barrow, and he placed the blame directly on the leadership of Ross. Although Eskimologists do not share this view, perhaps they should be more cautious in the interpretation of descriptions by Ross.

In mid-June the ships reached Disko Island off West Greenland, a place where whalers usually waited for improved ice conditions before sailing farther north. The expedition paused at the island, and Sackhouse served as "master of ceremonies to a ball on the deck of His Majesty's ships in the icy seas of Greenland." The guests were local people of Danish and Eskimo ancestry. After the ball was over, the ships proceeded north, and Melville Bay was named by Ross, although he did not actually discover it since whalers operated in the vicinity. Barrow was certain that whalers previously had ranged even farther north, an observation that bears on subsequent events.

When the *Alexander* and *Isabella* anchored off Greenland a short distance north of Melville Bay, Eskimos driving eight sleds were seen across the ice. The sleds stopped comparatively near the ships, and Sackhouse went forth carrying a white flag and presents. The dialect of Eskimo spoken by Sackhouse was different from theirs, and initially he was unable to communicate with them. At first the strangers would not approach but were pleased to receive a knife that he threw to them. As a gesture of appreciation they pulled their noses, and friendly contacts were established (Figure 3-4). Ross called them "Arctic Highlanders," and his remarks about them may be unique in the annals of ethnography. "They exist in a corner of the world by far the most secluded which has yet been discovered, and have no knowledge of any thing but what originates, or is found, in their own country; nor have they any tradition how they came to this spot, or from whence they came; having, until the moment of our arrival, believed themselves to be the only inhabitants of the universe, and that all the rest of the world was a mass of ice."

Even though these Eskimos first thought the English to be spirits, they soon were enticed aboard one of the ships. The size of the wood used in the ship's construction impressed them greatly since

Figure 3-4 A portion of a painting by John Sackhouse depicting the meeting of the Arctic Highlanders, or Polar Eskimos, with William E. Parry and John Ross in 1818. Sackhouse is shown in a beaver hat trading with two Eskimos. (From Ross, 1819)

the only wood they knew was from plants "with stems no thicker than the finger." Ross cited the absence of wood as one reason that they had no boats; the other reason was the short season during which boats could be used. The scarcity of wood also accounted for the fact that their sleds were made from bones and skins and their harpoon shafts fashioned from narwhal tusks. After introductions aboard ship the visitors were loaded with presents, and they promised to return. Ross learned from Sackhouse that when the ships were sighted the women and children were sent to the mountains. The men who approached the ships came to ask the English to go away and do them no harm. The people were described as dirty copper in color, about five feet in height, and of corpulent build. Their summer clothing included hooded sealskin parkas with birdskin liners, trousers of dog or bear skin, and sealskin boots. Ross was told that they wore cloaks of bearskin in the winter, and he learned that they lived in semisubterranean stone houses. Seals and narwhal were preferred foods, but the Eskimos ate their dogs when food supplies were low.

   Ross was distressed by their lack of cleanliness and wrote, "The habits of this people appear to be filthy in the extreme; their faces, hands, and bodies, are covered with oil and dirt, and they look as if they never had washed themselves since they were born." Similar observations about Eskimos occur time and again in accounts by explorers. As Kaj Birket-Smith, the great Danish ethnographer of Eskimos, wrote, "The fact is that even the Eskimos' best friends cannot hide the fact that cleanliness is not one of their great qualities."

Comparatively little information was obtained about Eskimo social life, but even so Ross is more expansive on the topic than any other voyagers cited thus far. Sackhouse no doubt was the one who reported that a man or woman initially took a single spouse and that if the woman bore an offspring neither man nor wife could take an additional mate. If a woman was barren, either of the pair could take another spouse and yet another, until a child was born. When men asked for gifts from the English, the presents were said to be for their wives, and one man spoke well of his wife because she had six sons. The Eskimos also reported that "their king" lived to the north with many persons who gave him a portion of all that they caught or found. The king was described as a strong and good man who lived in a stone house nearly as large as a ship. Ross also wrote, "They could not be made to understand what was meant by war, nor had they any warlike weapons."

Through Sackhouse a man was questioned about Eskimo religion, and Ross learned that they had conjurers or sorcerers. Such a person had the "power to raise a storm, or make a calm, and to drive off seals, or bring them." These abilities were passed from old to young, and there usually was one such person in each family. He also wrote, "Although there is certainly no proof whatever that this people have any idea of a Supreme Being, or of a spirit, good or bad, the circumstances of their having conjurers, and of their going to the moon after death, are of a nature to prevent any conclusion from being drawn to that effect." Ross regretted that linguistic barriers prevented learning more about the subject.

After the expedition returned, John Barrow was extremely harsh in his criticism of John Ross. He maintained that Ross never went ashore nor could have seen what he reported. Yet the ethnographic sketch by Ross is reasonable and generally acceptable when compared with later descriptions of the same Eskimos. Barrow was provoked because Ross sailed home without entering

Lancaster Sound. The other two ships, the ones that attempted to reach the North Pole in 1818, failed to achieve their goal.

In 1819 the *Hecla* and *Griper* set out for what John Barrow called "that magnificent piece of water called Sir James Lancaster's Sound." The expedition was commanded by William E. Parry, and Frederick W. Beechey was an officer aboard the *Hecla*. They entered Lancaster Sound on the first of August and sailed west briskly in a broad channel of open water. Surely this was the greatest moment in the Passage quest since that August day in 1610 when Henry Hudson labored beyond the "furious overfall" on the *Discovery*. Parry was lured south by the inviting entrance to an inlet but turned back after finding it blocked by ice and continued west. In early September the ships dropped anchor for the first time off southeastern Melville Island, where they remained for 10 months. During the winter they faced neither serious danger nor privation, and on August 1, 1820, they were able to sail west. Ice floes frequently threatened to crush the ships, and only by sailing dangerously near the beach were they able to approach the western end of the island. Finally so much ice was encountered that further progress proved impossible, and they regretfully turned east. From Lancaster Sound they sailed south along the east coast of Baffin Island and met whalers who reported seeing Eskimos along a particular inlet. Parry decided to contact these people and examine the area, which was across from Disko Island.

After the ships anchored in the inlet, four Eskimos came aboard, and friendly contacts were established. The following day the English visited the Eskimos on the mainland, and about seven pages are devoted to their observations. The camp included two tents accommodating 17 persons, and the word *pilletay*, translated by Parry as "give me," resounded throughout the visit. Axes, knives, needles, and brass kettles were bartered, as were luxury items such as uniform buttons. In spite of the fact that Parry went out of his way to meet these people, his account about them is unexceptional. The *Hecla* and *Griper* returned to England with Parry convinced that a passage could be navigated even during a sailing season of seven weeks or less. What of the future? Cumberland "strait" in Baffin Island as well as the northwestern coast of Hudson Bay deserved closer inspection. Parry's ships had sailed east from Melville Island to the entrance of Lancaster Sound in six days, yet five weeks were required to cover the same distance on the trip west; this suggested that a passage might be negotiated more easily by sailing east from northern Alaska.

With the exception of Parry the explorers cited met Eskimos who were near when they sailed by or anchored. Eskimo contacts were unplanned in the course of geographical discoveries. John Ross is a partial exception since he attempted to find the "king" of the Arctic Highlanders. With exploration as their primary goal, the English numbered Eskimos among the curiosities of distant lands rather than as subjects for study. If these people were described in more detail than walrus or whales, it was because more could be written about them on the basis of short-term observations. Before the period ending in 1819, if it may be considered a period, trade and curiosity were the only purpose for close contacts. It will be recalled too that except for the English-speaking Eskimo who accompanied John Ross to Greenland in 1818, no one could communicate with Eskimos except by signs. Thus even if the English had been fascinated by Eskimos in their native land—which they were not—observations could not have been very sophisticated given the barriers to communication.

The fleeting glimpses of Eskimos by these explorers include appreciative remarks about their manufactures and observations about their appearance. The virtues of Eskimo boats, clothing, and weapons escaped few observers. Likewise English travelers usually commented about the physical attributes of Eskimos. They all agreed that Eskimos usually were of short stature, perhaps averaging slightly above five feet, and more observant persons remarked that they had relatively short limbs. The words corpulent, fat, and plump are common in the descriptions but were modified by some reporters, such as Henry Ellis, who wrote that they were only "inclinable to be fat." The earliest autopsy of an Eskimo was made in 1577 by Edward Doddinge. After examining the body of a man who died after Frobisher brought him to England, Doddinge did not comment on his general morphology but did mention his "incurable gluttony," suggesting that he was fat. The Eskimo stereotype is of fat, fur-clad individuals.

Around the world people in hot countries usually weigh less, with allowance made for comparative stature, than those living in cold regions. Precisely why people tend to be heavier in colder climates is not entirely clear. The temptation is to apply the Bergmann "effect" about the bodily form of other animals to people.

Bergmann suggested that the body size of an animal species will be greater among a population in a cold environment than for one in warm surroundings. The Allen "effect" also seems to apply; it states that appendages decrease in size in colder regions. For arctic animals a massive body, short limbs, and diminutive tail seem to be the best cold adaptations. In these terms Eskimos should have very short arms and legs and massive bodies. It might seem logical too that Eskimos would acquire an insulating layer of fat in the winter as do caribou and seals.

The Allen and Bergmann effects may apply to the morphology of many arctic-dwelling mammals, but they cannot be extended to Eskimos directly because Eskimos modified their habitat by cultural means. Their winter housing was well adapted to the cold, and dwellings often were described as very hot. Of greater importance, Eskimos had developed the finest aboriginal cold-weather clothing known and were thus encased in an artificial environment during severe weather. Their warm-to-hot houses and excellent garments led Vilhjalmur Stefansson to describe their physical environment somewhat dramatically as subtropical or tropical. Since Eskimos have lived in the arctic only about 5000 years, there probably has not been sufficient time for them to make any major morphological adaptations to the cold even remotely comparable to those of other arctic-dwelling mammals.

Evaluations of aboriginal Eskimo morphology based on more than casual observation are few. Even thin Eskimos, if they had substantial trunks, short legs, and bulky skin clothing, would seem fat; moreover, heavy persons would appear plump if not gross. Although most detailed reports about Eskimo appearance were made after their clothing, diet, and housing had changed as a result of Western influences, expansive observations of the East Greenland Eskimos in the vicinity of Angmagsalik were made within a few years of their initial contact. Gustav Holm wrote in an introductory statement, "The people of Angmagsalik are of middle height, slenderly built, and well-proportioned." In a detailed account of their appearance Søren Hansen noted that "the body is comparatively long, but at the same time it is broad and strongly built. The chest especially is powerfully developed in a quite unusual degree," and there is no mention that they were fat. When George F. Lyon described the aboriginal Iglulik Eskimos in north-central Canada in 1821-3, he wrote "few amongst them are in the slightest degree inclined to corpulency." In northern Alaska in 1881-3, when essentially aboriginal conditions still prevailed among these Eskimos, a random series of Eskimo heights and weights was recorded. For 42 adult males height averaged 5 feet 4 inches and weight 154 pounds. For 30 women the height averaged 5 feet and the weight 136 pounds. An earlier observer of the same people noted, "These people are by no means the dwarfish race they were formerly supposed to be. In stature they are not inferior to many other races, and are robust, muscular, and active, inclining rather to spareness than corpulence." These references give the impression that Eskimos probably were muscular and compactly built more often than stout.

A perspective on cold adaptation is derived from more recent studies of Eskimo physiology. The synopsis of data by Jacques LeBlanc is especially relevant. Under test conditions Eskimos and non-Eskimos alike begin to perspire or shiver at the same skin temperatures; thus these responses of contemporary Eskimos are much the same as those of persons who do not live in cold settings. Yet when the hands of Eskimos and non-Eskimos are exposed to either cold water or cold air, the blood in Eskimo hands circulates at significantly higher temperatures than it does in the controls, and Eskimos have a reduced cold sensation. In the cold-air test at $-5°$ ($-21°C$) for 30 minutes the Eskimos were able to use their hands effectively. Of the white subjects, 25 percent completed the experiment, but the others suffered frostbite or could not tolerate the pain. Thus it appears that the hands of Eskimos had adjusted physiologically to the cold. This adaptation seems reasonable in terms of their subsistence activities. Aboriginal Eskimos had mittens rather than gloves to protect their hands from the cold. Since numerous tasks, from harnessing dogs to freeing fish from gill nets and shooting arrows, are cumbersome with mittens on, their hands were bared, which may account for this cold tolerance. Eskimos also have a psychological attitude about cold that is different from our own, and while they feel the cold they have learned to live with it and even expect to be frostbitten.

NOTES

THE VOYAGES OF GEORGE WAYMOUTH AND JOHN KNIGHT.   The background for these sailings is described by Thomas Rundall (1849), who reprinted the accounts of the Waymouth and Knight voyages as summarized by Samuel Purchas. Knight's report in its original form appears in the 1906 Glasgow edition of *Hakluytus Posthumus: or, Purchas His Pilgrimes* (v. 14, 353-65).

THE 1610 VOYAGE OF HENRY HUDSON.   Original and secondary sources about the voyages of Hudson were compiled by G. M. Asher (1860). The quotation from Luke Foxe about Abacuk Prickett appears in *The Voyages of Captain Luke Foxe and Captain Thomas James* edited by Miller Christy (1894, v. 1, 162). In the same volume Christy called the search for a northern passage to Asia a "perfect craze" (Introduction, i).

THE VOYAGES OF THOMAS BUTTON AND LUKE FOXE.   Miller Christy (1894) in his edition of Foxe includes all accounts about the travels of Button. Christy's long and thoughtful introduction provides a wealth of background information about searchers for the Northwest Passage.

THE VOYAGE OF JENS MUNK.   His 1619-20 travels from Denmark to Hudson Bay were a heroic adventure, but he is not mentioned in the text because his contact with Eskimos was minimal. The woodcut depicting the meeting, reproduced as Figure 3-1, is from the edition of Munk's travels edited by C. C. A. Gosch (1897, v. 2).

JAMES KNIGHT, HIS VOYAGE AND FATE.   The two vessels under Knight's command sailed from England in 1719 but disappeared. The fate of the Knight party is reported by Samuel Hearne in the introduction to *A Journey from Prince of Wales's Fort in Hudson's Bay to the Northern Ocean*, which was published first in 1795. In recent years this work often has been reprinted; the best edition is the one edited by Richard Glover in 1958. Extensive background material about Knight as an employee of the Hudson's Bay Company and his ill-fated voyage is included in the three-volume work *Hudson's Bay Company* by E. E. Rich (1960, v. 1).

THE VOYAGE ORGANIZED BY ARTHUR DOBBS.   This 1746-7 passage search was described by two participants, Henry Ellis (1748) and the "Clerk of the *California*" (1748-9), who presumably was Charles Swaine. Background information about this voyage is provided by Rich (1960, v. 1, 556-86). Swaine later enlisted the support of Benjamin Franklin and Philadelphia merchants to outfit a vessel to search for the Northwest Passage as well as to promote commercial and political interests. Captain Swaine sailed the *Argo* from Philadelphia in 1753 but could not penetrate the ice in Hudson Bay. The next year he set off again but met with even less success (Labaree, 1961, v. 4, 381-2).

Biographical information about Ellis is from *The Dictionary of National Biography* (1959-60, v. 6, 696-7). The Hudson Strait Eskimo descriptions by Ellis and Swaine are supplemented by the 1883-4 observations of Baffin Island Eskimos by Franz Boas (1888a).

CHESTERFIELD INLET AS A "STRAIT."   Trips up the inlet from 1760 to 1782 demonstrated that this was not a Northwest Passage and are summarized by Rich (1960, v. 1, 627-8).

ALEXANDER MACKENZIE. His travels down the Mackenzie River are reported in his book *Voyages from Montreal*. The third American edition of 1803 was consulted.

THE VOYAGES OF JOHN ROSS (1818) AND WILLIAM E. PARRY (1819-20). The background to these sailings and others is detailed by John Barrow (n.d.), who was the most persistent promoter of arctic explorations in England from 1817 to 1845. Christopher Lloyd (1970) wrote a biography of Barrow, and we have Barrow's autobiography (1847). The account of the "Arctic Highlanders" appears in the volume by Ross (1819). Parry (1821) described his attempt to penetrate Lancaster Sound, and a separate report of this voyage was authored by Alexander Fisher (1821), the surgeon on the *Hecla* with Parry. Fisher's summary statement (1821, 278-9) about Eskimos merits inclusion. "I think we may take it for granted, that all the Esquimaux tribes scattered along the shores of Greenland, North America, and its adjacent islands, are the same race of people, and, as far as our observations go, their appearance, dress, manners, mode of living, as well as their language, tend to confirm this point."

FAT ESKIMOS? Among the many persons who judged Eskimos as fat was Henry Ellis (1748, 132), who observed them in the Hudson Strait area. However, William E. Parry (1821, 282), while commenting on the appearance of people on eastern Baffin Island, did not mention that they were fat. The autopsy of an Eskimo in 1577 by Edward Doddinge, written in Latin, was published by Stefansson (1938, v. 2, 135-7) in a compilation of Frobisher's arctic travels. Stefansson (1922, 76-7) reasoned that Eskimos had created a hot environment in their clothing and dwellings. The volume edited by William Thalbitzer (1914, 27, 159) is the source of Angmagsalik Eskimo appearance. George F. Lyon (1824, 308) noted how few Iglulik Eskimos were fat. The Point Barrow area observations are from Patrick H. Ray (1885, 50); the source of the quotation about the same people is John Simpson (1875, 238).

The Allen and Bergmann effects are discussed, with special reference to Eskimos, by Charles G. Wilber (1957) and Stanley M. Garn (1958). The appropriateness of Eskimo clothing can be expressed in terms of the "clo," a unit for measuring insulation. A clo is the insulation required to maintain a sitting man comfortably at 70° F. with a relative humidity of less than 50 percent. A man's business suit would provide the necessary insulation. An Eskimo's double layer of caribou-skin garments, according to Jacques Le Blanc (1975, 8-9), provides 8 to 10 clos and offers relative comfort in temperatures as low as −50° F.

CHAPTER

4

West Greenlanders

The Danes were long convinced that the Greenlanders captured were survivors of the medieval Norse colony. On six occasions between 1607 and 1654 ships sailed for Greenland to trade and to search for descendants of the early settlers. Although no Norse were found and the trade with Eskimos proved unprofitable, about 30 Eskimos were captured and brought back on Danish-Norwegian and Dutch vessels, enabling the curious and stay-at-home ethnographers to make firsthand observations. An early Eskimologist was Claus C. Lyschander, the Danish-Norwegian royal historiographer. He apparently saw the three Eskimos taken to Copenhagen in 1605 and had access to the writings of Frobisher and Davis. In 1608 Lyschander published a long narrative poem in which Eskimos were portrayed as untrustworthy "wild beasts," who sometimes ate animals before they were even dead.

The most famous captives were a man, two women, and a girl seized by David U. Dannel in 1654 near modern Godthaab. When they reached Bergen, the four became the subjects of the earliest known painting of Greenlandic Eskimos (Figure 4-1). Although they were under the care of the ship's surgeon, Reinhold Horn, the man died on the trip to Copenhagen. Later Horn, who learned

75

Figure 4-1 This, the earliest known painting of Greenlandic Eskimos, is of persons from the Godthaab area and was painted at Bergen. The names of these people appear in German above their heads. The inscription behind the man reads, "In their small leather ships, the Greenlanders sail hither and thither on the ocean; from animals and birds they get their clothes. The cold land of Midnight. Bergen, September 28th, 1654." (Courtesy of the Danish National Museum)

enough Eskimo to converse with the three survivors, took them to Gottorp to live with Adam Olearius. A scholar with ethnological interests, Olearius had written a book about his experiences in the Orient. In the 1656 edition of this work he included a chapter about Greenland based on historical sources, his observations of the captives, and information provided by Horn.

The appearance of the women reminded Olearius of Samoyeds who lived in western Siberia or, in more general terms, Tartars. The younger woman, about 25 years old, looked different from the others and was considered more perceptive. He felt that she might be a descendant of the Norse settlers and based his conclusion on her more discriminating taste for foods; she did not eat intestines and liver or "unclean" animals as did the others. However, on the basis of Biblical evidence Greenlanders were judged descendants of Ham; their color was lighter than that of Negroes because of mixture with other peoples. Although Olearius described their appearance, he was more interested in their language. After compiling a list of over 100 words, he concluded that their language was unrelated to any spoken in Europe but seemed to resemble that of the Tartars. Eskimo clothing, kayaks, and hunting methods were described in brief. He presumed that these people worshipped the sun and reported that the women had no pubic hair and did not menstruate. His conclusion was that they were savages who lived like animals "for they do not possess high intelligence, breeding, politeness, chastity." The contribution by Olearius is notable because it is the first extended account of Greenlandic Eskimo culture.

The voyage of a Dutch trading vessel in 1656 under the direction of Nicholas Tunes deserves mention. He visited West Greenland, and his descriptions include comments about the Eskimos' ability to construct small boats and the skill with which these vessels were handled. Tunes remarked that their boats "have neither sails, nor masts, nor rudder, nor compass, nor anchor, nor the slightest piece of all this large amount of gear that is required in order to make our ships seaworthy." He continued that "moreover, they can have no disputes in these vessels, since one man is master, the sailor, the purveyor, and pilot." Tunes reported seeing people of two distinct physical types living in harmony but with different occupations. The group who "enjoy hunting" were "very tall, well-built, rather white and skilled in running." The other people were fishermen, "much smaller, of an olive-hued complexion, and rather well proportioned limbs except they have short stocky legs." This is the clearest written indication that some Norse survived in West Greenland and lived with Eskimos.

Tunes conveyed an idyllic view of social life. The people "seem of a happy, hardy, and courageous nature." Furthermore, "even though they are one of the poorest and most barbaric nations that the sun shines on, they believe they are very happy and the most favored people in the world. And they have such a good opinion of their way of life that they consider the civility of all other peoples as unseemly, savage, and as ridiculous as imaginable." Finally, "the comfort of beautiful, sumptuous buildings, worldly reputation, the delights of banquets, the knowledge of beautiful things and all that we value the pleasantness and the happiness of in life not yet having penetrated to them, they are not as tormented by the thought of possessing them which could interrupt the gentle peace which they enjoy." These indeed were savages most noble. Yet they ate their foods raw and worshipped the sun, or so Tunes wrote.

Nearly 100 years later the fables, fabrications, and fancies about West Greenland Eskimos would be dispelled, and the modern history of Greenland would begin. The individual most responsible for the recolonization of the old Norse colony was Hans P. Egede. Born in northern Norway, Egede was educated as a Lutheran minister at a time of revived interest in the old colony. He developed a plan to settle there and protestantize the descendants of the early Norse settlers, but his proposal was ignored. In 1718 he moved to Bergen and encouraged the local merchants to send ships to Greenland. His plan, put before King Frederik IV of Denmark, had the support of the Missionary Society and Bergen merchants and led to the creation of the Bergen Greenland Company. Three ships finally were outfitted for the voyage, and on July 3, 1721, they landed on an island in the old Western Settlement area, near modern Godthaab, that Egede named Island of Hope. For 15 years Egede worked as a missionary among the Eskimos of West Greenland. On returning to Denmark he wrote about his experiences, and his best-known work, appearing in 1741, was translated into English as A Description of Greenland (1745). This book put Greenland back on the map and is the first major work about Eskimos.

When Egede arrived in Greenland, and for tens of thousands of years before, the island was nearly covered by a huge ice cap and was inhabitable only along its littoral amongst islands and fjords. The western sector that he came to know so well was a labyrinth of bays and peninsulas, sounds, and skerres in which barren and lichen-covered rock formations dominated. In sheltered areas, as along fjords and short rivers, were meadows of grasses dotted with berry bushes and other low-growing plant cover. Storms, rain, and fog characterized the summer, ice and snow the winter. The land offered little, but its configuration provided the resources essential for human occupancy. Streams and rivers afforded fresh water, and there were sheltered spots where houses could be built and boats launched. The plant kingdom was poorly represented, and nearly all useful wood was obtained as drift along the shore. The land provided stone for knife and weapon blades, and some areas had soapstone that could be made into containers. The economic welfare of the people was based primarily on marine resources, fish, seals, and whales. In many localities caribou herds were a dependable source of food, but hares and ptarmigan were not significant in the diet.

Egede searched in vain for descendants of the old Norse colonists, but he found people near Godthaab whom he called by the forthright term "Greenlanders." He introduces them as follows:

> As every Nation has its peculiar Way of living and of getting their Livelihood, suiting their Genius and Temper to the Nature and Produce of the Country they inhabit; so the *Greenlanders* likewise have theirs, peculiar to themselves and their Country. And though their Way and Customs may seem to others mean and silly, yet they are such, as very well serve their Turn, and which we can find no Fault with.

In these opening sentences Egede conveys far greater tolerance and understanding than one might expect from an eighteenth-century Protestant missionary among the heathen.

Egede devoted about 100 pages of his book to the people of southwest Greenland. His knowledge of Eskimos was far more profound than that of any previous writer. He not only lived among them for many years but learned their language and usually maintained a sympathetic attitude toward their life-style.

Egede's account deserves special attention because most of the customs he described prevailed among Eskimos all across the north. His report about southwest Greenland is supplemented by the observations of David Crantz in 1767 and the later work of Kaj Birket-Smith. In 1918 Birket-Smith spent three months in the area to the north talking with Eskimos about their old way of living. He then attempted to reconstruct aboriginal conditions before European influences had come to dominate. These combined accounts characterize Eskimo life from Cape Farewell to the Upernivik area.

When the reports of Egede and later observers are compared, allowance must be made for the devastating effects of exotic diseases. Egede was able to observe a viable and largely undisturbed cultural system. However, in terms of aboriginal demographic and cultural conditions, Birket-Smith was dealing with a remnant population. A terrible smallpox epidemic struck in 1734 and another about 1800. In 1785-6 a disease similar to the plague devastated the population; even though mortality rates are unknown, it is clear that in some localities everyone died. When a virgin population is exposed to a new disease, the results often are disastrous. Unless they were recorded shortly after historic contact, accounts about aboriginal conditions probably are not accurate.

The ethos of a people is possibly the most difficult quality to capture in an ethnographic report. Even astute observers may be ill-equipped to convey the subtleties of values and attitudes that characterize the behavior of another people. Egede described Greenlanders as good-natured, peaceful, and loving, lacking in envy or hate. He claimed that they deplored a thief and kept the seventh commandment except under particular circumstances. They were phlegmatic, and their "stupidity," which should be read "ignorance," resulted from a lack of education. Egede depicted a rude and physically unclean but strangely flawless and nearly noble people. Birket-Smith was more cautious in his comments on their attitudes. He acknowledged their gaiety, generosity, and simplicity of faith but confessed his inability to probe beyond these superficial impressions. Instead he contrasted these congenial aspects of their personalities with a darker side reflected in their folktales filled with accounts of meanness, murder, and torture.

Egede writes that in the winter men wore hooded, knee-length parkas made from skins of birds, caribou, or seals. They also wore short trousers with the hair side inward, stockings of caribou or sealskin, and sealskin boots. Women's clothing was much the same as that of men with the addition of waistcoats made from the skins of young caribou and underpants worn beneath their trousers. A specialized garment was a suit of dehaired sealskins worn by a man when hunting great whales from an umiak. The suit had a head opening that could be tightened around the face with a drawstring, and mittens and boots were sewn directly onto the garment. It was entered through a large hole at the chest, and this was closed with a drawstring after air had been trapped inside. If a man fell overboard during the confusion of a hunt, the air inside the suit kept him afloat for several hours. Men in these suits also were able to jump into the water to butcher a whale after it was killed. A daring hunter might even climb on the back of a wounded whale to make the kill.

These clothing descriptions, plus the illustrations in this and other chapters, convey the basic information, but the niceties of Greenlandic garment design are many and should not go unmentioned. For example, skin mittens made for winter use and for hunting from kayaks had two thumbs so that they could be worn on either hand. In severe weather men wore an extra and oversized pair of trousers, made of dog skin with the hair side inward, and an extra pair of boots. In terms of hunting effectiveness in extreme cold, details such as these loom large. We know too that in the southern sector during early historic times poor people wore parkas made from dog skins, a distinction indicating that the society was not fully egalitarian.

Egede, as the first writer to detail Eskimo activities in winter, provided essential information about their major adaptive modes. The winter houses of stone and turf had low flat roofs, and along one side were windows framed with wood and covered with sewn strips of seal intestines or halibut stomachs (Figure 4-2, 3). A dwelling was entered through a low tunnel designed to keep out much of the cold, and the house interior was insulated with skins from old umiaks. Along the wall opposite the windows was a plank platform covered with skins; here people lounged or worked during the day and slept at night. As many as eight families lived together, and roof support posts separated their compartments. In front of each section of bench belonging to a family was a semilunar lamp mounted on a stand. The lamp burned seal blubber on

Figure 4-2 Cutaway showing a section of a West Greenland house. (From Crantz, 1767)

a moss wick, and a cooking pot was hung above it. The lamps not only cooked food but provided light and heat. Other important furnishings included racks suspended above lamps for drying garments and tubs filled with urine. Urine was used as soap and to process skins; in these hot houses the odor of urine was very strong, or as Egede wrote, "their Urine-Tubs smell most insufferably, and strikes one, that is not accustomed to it, to the very Heart." Egede's straightforward account provides valuable insight into the cultural adjustments of these people. The low ceilings, entrance passages, window materials, and the lamp-pot-drying rack combination, were refined adjustments to life in a cold and treeless subarctic littoral. Only after details such as these were available *in the context of daily living* could the subtleties and integration of Eskimo culture begin to be appreciated.

As spring approached at the end of March, families began moving into tents for the summer. These were semicircular, pole-framed, and covered with two layers of skins; the outermost skins were soaked with fat as a water repellent. The tent entrance, which also served as a window, was fitted with a flap of sewn intestines (Figure 4-4). Each family head owned a tent as well as an umiak to transport the tent and other belongings from one camp to another.

Birket-Smith and other later observers wrote that winter settlements usually were built on islands or near headlands where boats could be beached and hunting grounds were accessible. Families frequently moved from one locality to another, but no one could settle in a village without permission from local residents. A sense of common political purpose was absent since communities included neither chiefs nor councils of elders. The advice of charismatic leaders or wise men was sought and heeded because experience had proved that they were thoughtful persons. Personal behavior was guided by custom, and the exploitation of local resources was open to all on an equal basis. One of the most important obligations to fellow villagers was that every able-bodied man hunt and divide his harvest in a carefully prescribed manner.

As winter hunting methods were described, we begin to appreciate the appropriateness of Eskimo weapons, especially those for taking seals. The most common species was the ringed seal, so named because of the white rings on its fur. These seals weigh up to 200 pounds and often live beneath unbroken expanses of ice in bays or fjords during the winter. They use their claws to scratch breathing holes in the ice and to keep the holes open throughout the winter. A hunter located one of these small openings and then settled himself to wait for a seal to appear. He sat on a one-legged stool and rested his feet on another stool with three legs (Figure 4-5, left foreground). When—and if—a seal visited the hole, the hunter struck it with his harpoon; the harpoon head detached from the shaft but remained fastened to a hand-held line. After the wounded seal had thrashed about and exhausted himself at the end of the harpoon line, the hunter enlarged the hole with an ice pick, pulled the seal to the surface, and killed it with a blow from his fist. This, the *maupok* or waiting technique of hunting seals, was one of the few means for obtaining fresh meat in the middle of winter and thus was a crucial adaptation for survival.

Another sealing technique was to chop a large hole in winter ice or to find a large hole made by seals in the spring. Near this

Figure 4-3   A West Greenland man, his kayak, and a winter house in the background. (From Crantz, 1767)

Figure 4-4   A West Greenland woman in front of a summer tent. (From Crantz, 1767)

opening a small hole was chopped, and a long-shafted harpoon was inserted in it. One man stood poised to thrust the harpoon as another man stretched out on a bench and peered into the small hole (Figure 4-5, right foreground). The man looking into the hole covered his head so that he could see deep into the water; thus this technique was named "peep sealing." As a seal swimming toward the larger opening passed beneath the poised harpoon, the man peering into the water cried out. The second man immediately thrust the harpoon downward, and if the harpoon head struck the seal, he played it to exhaustion with the handline.

In the spring a seal enlarged a breathing hole so that it could climb onto the ice to sun itself. However, a basking seal was cautious and slept less than a minute before looking about for any sign of danger. Each time the seal slept a hunter crawled closer. If the seal noticed the strange form nearby, the man pretended to be another seal by imitating its sounds and movements. When the hunter was close enough he launched a long-shafted harpoon, and the wounded animal was played at the end of the line until it could be killed (Figure 4-5, lower center). In ethnographic accounts this sealing technique is called *utok*, from the word for a basking seal. Another approach was taken in the spring when currents produced large holes in the ice. Many seals might gather at these openings, and they could be harpooned at the edge of the ice (Figure 4-5, right background). From later reports we know that a similar technique of harpooning was used during the winter at openings in ice floes or along open water adjacent to firm ice. Seals sometimes were lured to the surface by placing an ice pick in the water and whistling along the shaft. A man might also run back and forth, dragging an ice pick on the ice as a lure, and then quietly return to the open water and harpoon any curious seal that appeared. A hunter sometimes hauled his kayak to these spots to retrieve the kill.

In the open waters of summer, seals were taken from kayaks with harpoons to which floats were attached by lines (Figure 4-6). A harpooned animal pulled the shaft and the bladder or sealskin float beneath the water as it sounded. The drag of the float and blood loss from the wound soon exhausted the seal, and it surfaced for air. The hunter attempted to be near the spot to repeatedly stab the seal with a stone-bladed lance. It finally was killed with a small lance that had a dagger-like ivory blade. The wounds

Figure 4-5 West Greenland sealing techniques. (From Egede, 1818)

Figure 4-6 Greenlanders hunting from kayaks. (From Crantz, 1767)

of the dead seal were closed with wooden plugs to prevent loss of blood, and the hunter blew air through the seal's nostrils into its lungs, making it more buoyant and easier to tow ashore. A kayak used in this type of hunting was about 17 feet long, two feet wide, and slightly rounded on the bottom. It was propelled with a double-bladed paddle, and as long as he was paddling, an experienced kayaker was not likely to capsize. Dead in the water, however, he could easily turn over if he did not balance the vessel by placing the paddle beneath a strap in front of the manhole with one blade resting in the water.

Of all the hunting methods none quite compares in organization and daring with that required to kill great whales, yet the description by Egede is prosaic. Whales were hunted from umiaks, and in an effort not to offend the prey the female paddlers wore their best clothing and men put on clean flotation suits. A whale was struck with one harpoon after another. Since each harpoon head was attached to a sealskin float with a line, the wounded animal soon tired from dragging multiple floats through the water. When the

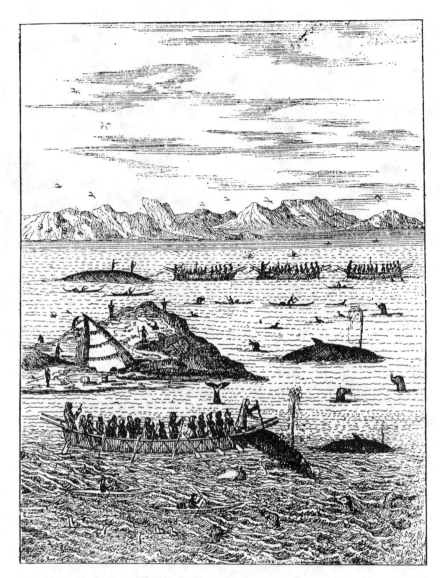

Figure 4-7 A West Greenland whale-hunting scene around an island where a tent is standing. (From Egede, 1818)

floats surfaced, the paddlers positioned themselves for another harpoon strike or for dealing death wounds with lances (Figure 4-7). We know little more than Egede conveys except that amulets were carried to avert disaster. A more practical measure was attaching sealskin floats to the umiak gunwales to prevent it from sinking if it capsized. Hunting southern right whales declined abruptly in early historic times following their intensive exploitation by European whalers.

Even these brief accounts of sea-mammal hunting adaptations to subarctic coasts convey the specialized qualities of the harpoons used at different times of the year and under specific conditions. Whether a harpoon shaft was long or short and whether the head was attached to a handline or to a separate flotation arrangement are refinements of artifact design. Complicated harpoons skillfully used were only part of the food-getting complex. Lore and knowledge about sea mammals also were vital to their capture. Predicting the movement of an animal in water, imitating its behavior on ice, and understanding its curiosity or cautiousness were necessary accompaniments to the use of well-adapted weapons.

Compared with hunting sea mammals, taking game on land and catching fish were prosaic pursuits, and they contributed far less to the diet. The bow and arrow was the primary weapon for hunting on land. The wooden bow was backed with twisted strands of sinew for a strong pull and was strung with a sealskin thong. Along the inner islands of fjords and on the mainland, caribou often were abundant and were hunted during the summer with barbed, bone-pointed arrows. They were driven by women and children toward concealed bowmen, and if there were not enough people to make a sweep, white poles were set up and topped with a piece of turf to look like people and to frighten the caribou in the desired direction (Figure 4-8). Later sources report that caribou sometimes were driven into water and killed with lances by kayakers, and they were driven over precipices or between stone fences toward concealed bowmen. The varied means for taking caribou were well-developed, but the weapons involved were less sophisticated than those for harvesting sea mammals.

The artifacts used for fishing were far less complicated than those used for hunting. An elementary device for taking arctic char was a stone weir (dam) built across a river near its mouth. Char swam up the river and over the weir on an incoming tide, and as

Figure 4-8   A West Greenland caribou hunt. (From Egede, 1818)

the tide ebbed, they were trapped by the barrier. They then were hand collected or impaled on fish spears (leisters) in the shallow water. Some fish, including halibut, were taken at sea by kayakers using baited hooks and lines, while capelin were caught along the shore in dip nets. If many capelin were harvested in the summer, they were sun dried on rocks and stored as food for winter. From Birket-Smith we learn that throughout the year fjord cod and sea scorpions could be taken on jigs with attached lures. Sea scorpions normally were not desirable fare, but their catch was dependable, and in times of food stress a harvest might save people from starvation.

Among most peoples who collected, fished, or hunted, the edibles obtained by women were important and often essential. Eskimos clearly are an exception to this norm because nearly all of their sustenance was obtained by males. One explanation for male domination in food-getting hinges on the importance of kayaks for hunting sea mammals. The accidental death rate for kayakers was high, and for women to hunt from kayaks as well as to raise children probably would have been unrealistic under most conditions. In West Greenland it was presumably the women who most often picked berries and plant greens, dug roots, and gathered bird eggs or mussels that were eaten. Yet here as among most Eskimos the collected food products were few and seldom recognized as important in the diet.

Contrary to what may be expected, in West Greenland south of the Arctic Circle, the area that Egede knew best, travel by dog sled was relatively unimportant. Dogs were expected to forage for food except after many seals were killed, when they were fed boiled blood and intestines. One of Egede's illustrations (Figure 4-5) includes a sled with dogs attached to individual traces, apparently of equal length. As many others have observed, he noted that Eskimo dogs howled but never barked.

Hans Egede devoted more attention to Eskimo religion than to any other aspect of the culture. His missionary zeal may explain the emphasis, although Protestant missionaries often judged aboriginal beliefs too foolish to describe. Egede felt that Eskimos could be called "atheists," but he preferred the more neutral label "naturalists." He could not resist noting that "they are unhappily fallen into many gross Superstitions" and calling the origin myths

ridiculous, but he did attempt an accurate report of their supernatural concepts.

Torngarsuk, identified as the heathen deity of shamans, perplexed Egede because each shaman described him differently.
Some said that he had a large human body and a single arm, others
regarded him as formless, and still others thought he had the
appearance of a bear. His abode was on earth or in the waters
beneath the earth, depending on the person questioned. Egede
interpreted these differences to mean that shamans really did not
know the nature of this deity. Torngarsuk usually is translated as
"the Devil," but Egede and other missionaries may have unknow-
ingly originated this interpretation as they attempted to cast Eskimo religion into the mold of Christianity. The being Egede
attempted to define apparently represents a composite of the
oracle spirits of individual shamans, who had different spirit
helpers and therefore depicted them in different ways. A shaman
sought rapport with a helping spirit or *tornak*, from which the
word Torngarsuk was derived. A tornak might be the spirit or *inua*
of a dead animal, or it could be the essence of an inanimate object
such as a mountain or the sun. Helping spirits served many different functions; one gave advice, another harmed enemies, and
still others rendered aid in dangerous situations. The importance
of the inua or "owner" of things, which ranged from animals and
individual rocks to forces in nature such as the wind, was appreciated by Egede when he noted that "Each Element has its Governor
or President."

Sila was another supernatural concept that Egede appears not to
have understood very well. As a nonpersonified mystical force the
word defies a narrow translation. It may mean "weather,"
"world," or "understanding," or a more fundamental meaning
might be "that which is outside everywhere." Sila was a dangerous, fearful, and all-pervasive spirit of the air that was inherently
neither good nor bad, but could be either. In many respects Sila is
comparable to the idea of "mana" known so well from Polynesia.

Egede designated a specialist in supernatural matters by the
Eskimo word *angekkok* or alternatively as a conjurer, prophet, or
sorcerer. The modern generic term for such a person is *shaman*,
from a Tungus word introduced into Russian and then into English. In southwest Greenland an aspiring shaman obtained supernatural power by visiting a remote locality where he waited near a

special shaman's stone to gain control over a spirit. When a great supernatural force appeared, the tyro was thought to die; after his rebirth three days later, the tyro was in control of a particular spirit. Subsequently, or following additional trials, a shaman acquired sufficient power to cure the ill, advise people about leading successful lives, and divine causes of death. A shaman typically communicated with the spirit world in the evening before an audience. The house in which he performed was darkened, the hands and feet of the shaman were securely bound, and a drum was placed at his side. After the audience sang a song of their ancestors, the shaman began invoking help from another realm. A spirit immediately appeared and talked with the performer as he worked free of his bonds and magically flew to the highest heaven. There he talked with the souls of the greatest shamans, who revealed all that was asked of them. A shaman's journey to the heavens required only a moment, and the ritual was highlighted by the revelations of the shaman about his mystical travels.

Egede identified these Eskimos as descendants of the Skrellings met by old Norse settlers. He felt that as the colony declined some of the Norse may have joined with Eskimos and cited as evidence a few Norwegian words in Eskimo. He reasoned that since some Eskimo customs were similar to those of Jews, Eskimo ancestry might be traced to these people at the time of their dispersal and wanderings. Examples of customs attributed to both Eskimos and Jews included not cutting their hair, bewailing the loss of virginity, and wearing old clothes when they buried the dead. At the same time Egede dismissed Eskimo accounts of their origins as "fables."

Following publication of *A Description of Greenland* in 1741 and the appearance of an English edition in 1745, Eskimos should never again have been judged in the manner of old. This book strips much—but certainly not all—of the mystery away from their life-style. Egede presented a broad range of Eskimo customs with reasonable thoroughness; his biases are honest and transparent. An autopsy of his book would serve no positive purpose, but we might consider the topics that Egede underemphasized or ignored.

Curiously Egede placed little stress on manufactures apart from boats and clothing. The attention devoted to sea-mammal hunting provides unparalleled familiarity with subsistence activities, but the artifacts themselves largely are ignored. Even when Egede described material culture, he did not stress its relative significance. For example, the lamp was of unacknowledged importance. In West Greenland, where wood was scarce, human life would have been difficult without the lamp. It heated houses, cooked food, provided light, and dried clothing. The combination of a clothes-drying rack hanging from the ceiling over a pot suspended above a lamp may be the most elegant of Eskimo cultural achievements, and the lamp was the focal form. But a lamp without oil was useless. The ability of hunters to obtain enough animal fat to keep their lamps burning was as important as lamps themselves. As spring approached, oil reserves were likely low, but seals could be hunted at their breathing holes by the maupok or waiting method. The adaptive chain began with a lamp, and it could not be broken at any point if the population was to survive.

Eskimos did not live in pastoral bliss, but neither did they behave as base and unrestrained savages. In spite of his efforts Egede could not comprehend why these people subscribed to their more esoteric beliefs. As "naturalists" Eskimos had many sterling qualities, not the least of which were their pacific nature, tolerance of others, and tenderness toward children. Egede lamented such practices as wife exchange and plural marriage but felt that the openness of their customs gave them a naive purity all their own. He clearly was sympathetic toward Eskimos, and he died believing that the old Norse Christians who settled Greenland were among the ancestors of these people, a conviction that may have tempered his views and attitudes.

*   *   *

In 1730, just nine years after Egede founded the mission in Greenland, his royal sponsor, King Frederik IV, died. Efforts in 1728 to send soldiers and criminals as new colonists failed because of human dissension and deadly disease. Furthermore, the trade with Eskimos was not profitable. In 1727 Count Nikolaus Ludwig von Zinzendorf of Saxony, the founder of the modern Moravian Church, appears to have attempted to gain Danish support for Moravian missionaries to work in Greenland with the Lutherans, but he was unsuccessful. When Christian VI became king, he decided to withdraw official support of the Lutherans, which was tantamount to abandoning the fledgling colony. In 1731 while in Copenhagen to attend the coronation of Christian VI, as well as to foster Moravian interests, Zinzendorf met two baptized Eskimos and learned that the Lutheran mission to Greenland was to be abandoned. At that point he again entertained the possibility of sending Moravian workers to Greenland.

Moravians in Germany became exercised about heathen Greenlanders, and although poor and oppressed themselves a number of persons were determined to carry their gospel to the far north. Matthew Stach, his cousin Christian Stach, and Christian David accepted what they interpreted as God's will to go forth, and they gained the support of Count Zinzendorf. Egede had planned for years before launching his mission, but the Moravians depended on divine help channeled through sympathetic persons at the last moment. The first three missionaries arrived in Copenhagen with very little money and no provisions or equipment, but their needs were filled through the generosity of the people there. After official permission was gained to found a mission and free passage arranged, they set off for Greenland. In 1733 the Moravians established New Herrnhut a few miles from Godthaab, and before long they were serious competitors with the Lutherans for Greenlandic souls. During the early years of the mission the Moravian who best described Eskimos was David Crantz, who traveled there in 1761. His two-volume work, *The History of Greenland* (1767), stresses the formative years of the Moravian mission, includes a long section about natural history, and describes the Eskimo life-style, especially aboriginal customs. The 100 pages devoted to Eskimos are based on personal observations, conversations with people, and published accounts. The following pages emphasize the findings of Crantz that supplement those of Egede.

Crantz was more successful than Egede in conveying the attitudes and values of Greenlanders. He recognized the multiple dimensions of personality types and struggled admirably to convey their essence. To him the people were simple without silliness, not jovial but good humored, phlegmatic and sanguine, patient, sociable, and concerned with the present; "consequently they are not covetous to scrape a heap of stuff together, but are liberal in giving." Their subdued rustic pride made them feel superior to the more outgoing Europeans. Crantz characterized them as "stoics" and resented the "savage" label. "The Greenlanders are not properly an untractable, fierce, wild, barbarous or cruel people, but rather a gentle, quiet, civil and good-natured generation." Support for these generalizations took many diverse forms. Eskimos did not swear; in fact, there were no abusive terms in their language with the possible exception of humorously conceived nicknames. Since they did not know of intoxicants, there was no drunkenness, nor was their behavior toward one another obscene. The Greenlanders' goodness in the absence of "divine or human laws" perplexed Crantz and led him to conclude that "internal natural instinct" gave rise to their moral order.

A dark side of their behavior was far less admirable, or as Crantz wrote, "The seed of all evil lies in them, and their tendency to it is as natural and strong as in any other of Adam's children." He noted further that they valued their good name above all else, but they aided one another only with the clear prospect of return in kind. Those who had nothing to give received nothing, and if they were cold or starved, no one cared. An orphan without relatives, unless he were taken into a family as a servant, could expect kindness from no one. Children tortured birds to death, seemingly without pity, and a drowning kayaker might not expect rescue unless he had relatives. A man married a number of women for lust, not to perpetuate his kind, and adultery initiated by either sex was shameless.

The notions that Eskimos habitually ate meat and fish raw or drank seal oil were dispelled by Crantz, who stated that they only occasionally ate small pieces of flesh or fat from freshly killed animals. Crantz placed overwhelming emphasis on resources from the sea, especially since caribou were becoming scarce in his time. He described and illustrated weapons for taking aquatic species (Figure 4-9) and also illustrated a man hunting from a kayak with a large harpoon (Figure 4-6). In this 1767 publication, Crantz appears to have introduced the words "kaiak" and "umiak" into English usage.

No small craft in the world equals the seaworthiness of an Eskimo kayak. A man wearing a waterproof parka tied around his face, his wrists, and the manhole was merged with his vessel. Nowhere were men more skilled in handling kayaks than in southwest Greenland. A kayaker could if necessary travel 70 miles a day, and storms held no fears because a paddler could ride atop the waves. If his kayak turned upside down, the man righted it with his paddle. Traveling alone could be dangerous, however, because a man who lost his paddle might drown. The ability to

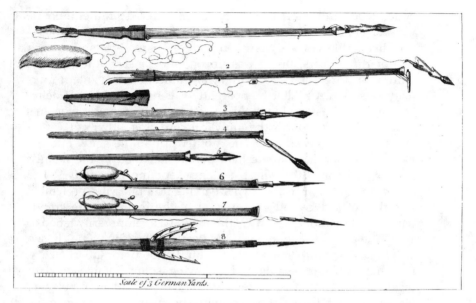

Figure 4-9 Weapons used against aquatic species by West Greenlanders. The toggle-headed harpoon (1, 2) used against large seals
was hurled with the aid of a "hand-board." The detachable-headed
lance (3, 4) wounded an animal, and a smaller thrusting lance (5)
made the kill. The less powerful harpoon dart (6, 7) was for taking
small seals. Birds were impaled with a spear (8) launched with a
throwing-board, and if a bird was not struck with the end point, it
might be wounded by one of the side prongs. (From Crantz, 1767)

right a kayak under varied circumstances was critical, and Crantz
reported 10 different techniques. In some localities men learned to
right a capsized kayak with only a throwing-board or even with
one arm while holding the hand flat. Eskimos tested their skill by
righting a kayak while holding a stone clenched in one fist.

   A comprehensive ethnography includes at least minimal coverage of certain topics. The yearly round of food-getting activities
and the artifacts involved must be presented at some length. Only
then is it possible to understand the economic adjustments of a
people to a particular habitat. A second criterion is the inclusion of
details about the life cycle of an individual. A third subject is
ceremonial activities, but these were so poorly developed in southwestern Greenland that they can be included as a part of the life

cycle. Egede and, more especially, Crantz offered a rather intimate view of family life in normative terms.

In her fertile years a woman reportedly bore an offspring each two or three years, but it was uncommon for a mother to raise more than three or four children, an indication that infant mortality was high. Childbirth apparently was not difficult, but delivery might be hastened by holding a chamber pot over a woman's head. Following a birth the umbilical cord was either cut with a mussel shell or bitten free. The mother put a little snow into the newborn's mouth, and she held part of her food in the infant's mouth and said "thou hast eat and kept me Company." The offspring's name, selected by its parents or a midwife, preferably was that of a deceased grandparent of the infant. If the grandparent had died only recently, the name was temporarily taboo to avoid the constant reminder of the death. Often the name chosen was that of an animal, a part of the human body, or an artifact. A new name might be acquired following some notable deed or misdeed, such as a humorous incident or scandalous episode. Names among Greenlanders obviously meant something quite different from names among Danes or Germans. Since the subject is reported in detail, it is apparent that the social subtleties and their significance were understood.

A mother's love for an infant was great, and most of the time she kept the baby in the back of her parka. A child was nursed for four or more years, and Egede felt that it was not weaned sooner because of the coarse foods. A child rarely was punished physically, scolded, or even corrected. An extremely vexed mother might return a small child's blow, but this brought her husband's disapproval, especially if the child were a son. Parents treated children rather like their friends. If asked to do something against its will, a child did not protest but simply said, "I will not." Parents reasoned with children and hoped that they would obey. The undisciplined behavior of boys was said to have been tolerated because parents hoped their sons would support them in their old age. This does not explain why daughters were treated in much the same way as sons, especially since daughters might leave their natal homes when they married. Presumably children in general were given a great deal of freedom because self-reliance and independence were overwhelmingly important values to adults of both sexes.

A little boy was taught by his father to throw stones, shoot arrows, and carve toys with a knife. By the age of 10 he was given a kayak so that he could hunt birds and fish with other boys. His first test of skill came at about the age of 15 when he hunted with his father. A feast was held to honor the youth after his first major kill. On this occasion he told about the hunt as guests praised his abilities and commented on the superior quality of the meat. Henceforth women speculated about who could be his future wife. A young man of 20 was expected to build his kayak and to own a set of tools and weapons. A few years later he brought a wife to live in his parents' house. Crantz succinctly described the cumulative markers leading to adult responsibilities, and from his record of each major step, we realize the intensity of a hunter's education. A son became an important member of a family after he began hunting at the age of 10.

Until a girl was about 14 years old, she had no responsibilities except to care for a smaller child, but from adolescence onward a girl acquired adult skills. When she married, she not only cared for her children but butchered the animals killed by her husband, processed skins and sewed them into garments, and cooked all the food. Women likewise built and repaired the houses. Only after her sons married and brought their wives into the house were a woman's domestic chores lightened; she then fully controlled the activities of her daughters-in-law.

"Bride capture" fascinated Crantz, and it is difficult to determine how freely his imagination ranged as he described the custom. Marital arrangements were made by the parents of the groom, and apparently by the bride's parents as well. Old women representing the groom's parents then went to the girl's parents and extended the formal request, and hearing it the bride became distraught. She tore her hair and might faint or try to run away, but in the end she was dragged to the groom's home, where she sat looking disheveled and not eating for days. Although modesty partially explained her behavior, she probably feared that she would be mistreated or rejected by her husband. A feast accompanied by gift-giving was hosted by the groom's father, if he had the means, to honor the marriage of his son. An alternative method was to pledge children in marriage while they were small; when the time came for them to wed, the union already was accepted by the participants and villagers alike. These were the proper ways of marrying, but some couples did not seek permission and openly slept together to gain recognition as husband and wife. First-cousin marriages were rare, and an adopted child could not marry a sibling with whom he had been raised. Most men had a single wife, but an outstanding hunter might support as many as four wives and their children. In plural marriages the first wife had the greatest authority, and apparently wives were not jealous of one another. A man some-times married sisters or a mother and her daughter, and it was permissible for him to take a second wife by force.

A woman might abandon her husband, especially if she was oppressed by other women in the house. Harsh treatment by mothers-in-law was notorious. If a woman was discovered to have committed adultery, her husband might blacken her eye, a dra-matic act given the dispositions of these people. It was not unusual for a childless couple to divorce. To end a marriage a man discon-tented with his wife "gives her a sour look, marches forth, and does not return home again for several days." After a couple had children, especially sons, separation was unlikely. When it did occur, the children always went with their mother, and the bio-logical father could never depend on these sons for support in his old age. This realization probably made a man reluctant to leave the mother of his children. If a wife died, the husband did not remarry for a year unless there was a nursing offspring. When a man had two wives and one died, the survivor assumed full responsibility for raising all of the children. She attempted to be more loving with her stepchildren than with her own to win their lasting affection.

In the course of daily living each family was autonomous. A man supervised the activities of his family, and even though a number of families lived in the same house, their obligations toward one another were few. Women cooperated in repairing a house, people attempted to enter and leave a dwelling at the same time to keep it warm, and in times of stress food was shared by all. Additional cooperation did not exist except during certain hunting activities. A man who excelled as a hunter might attract a following, and he occupied the north end of a house, the most honored spot. He was responsible for the cleanliness of the dwelling, but he could neither command nor punish householders. If a family chose to live else-where, they simply moved.

Eskimos are renowned for their congenial nature, and examples of this quality were noted by Egede. Feasts preceded most forms of diversion, and delicacies, including the tail of a whale, were served by the host. After the guests ate, someone picked up a drum and played. The tambourine-like Eskimo drum had a wooden handle attached to a hoop-shaped wooden frame; over the frame the skin from a whale's tongue was stretched and tied in place. A man beat the rim with a stick, singing songs about events in general or his life in particular. As each verse ended, the audience joined in as a chorus. The songster distorted his face and made strange gestures, causing the audience to laugh at his antics. Egede described "a certain illegal Game" that might follow a feast and songfest. A curtain of skins was hung at one end of the sleeping bench in preparation for the game. Only married couples participated in the festivity, which focused on husbands and wives exchanging partners and copulating behind the curtain. Wives were freely lent, and a woman considered herself especially fortunate if chosen by a shaman.

Egede found the etiquette of Greenlanders to be their most deficient behavior. Since manners are defined by the observer's culture, his dismay is not surprising. He considered it strange that they exchanged no formal greetings when they met and more difficult to accept that they scraped sweat from their faces with knives and licked it from the blades. Family members urinated in a common tub, and women washed their hair in urine to make it smell pleasing. Furthermore, people ate from utensils dogs had licked without cleaning the containers, and they consumed lice that they found on themselves or others.

An annual Sun Festival, held at the winter solstice, celebrated the sun's return and the probability that hunting and fishing conditions soon would improve. Large groups of people feasted on the best foods until they were nearly bursting. Later one man after another sang and drummed, as the audience joined in the chorus. Songs were about hunting, the noble achievements of ancestors, and expressions of joy at the sun's return. The celebration lasted through the night and began again the next evening with another round of eating, singing, and dancing. Days later, after all the food was gone or the people exhausted, the festivities ended. Crantz maintained that this was not a religious ceremony, yet the conviviality of the occasion may mask a deeper meaning. Were this a religious ceremony, as later observers also doubted, it was one of only two held annually. Each year, soon after the Sun Festival, a rather clear ritual set was reported by later observers. The principals were youths who dressed in tattered old clothing. Some were outfitted with huge penises, and they went as spirits from one house to another, speaking in an unintelligible manner. One participant concealed a blood-filled bladder next to his chest. When he was stabbed, the blood flowed freely, and he fell down as if dead until one of his companions revived him. The actors did not wear masks until historic times; in fact, masks were unknown in West Greenland until after contact with Europeans.

Crantz felt compelled to call Eskimo supernatural beliefs "superstition," not religion, and elaborated that "it is very hard to say any thing about it, because they are extremely ignorant, unthinking and credulous, and yet are very various in their opinions, forasmuch as every one hath liberty to believe any thing or nothing." He exposed as false the reports that Eskimos worshipped the sun, were idolaters, and made sacrifices; these were misunderstandings. Once missionaries learned to speak Eskimo, they realized that these people had beliefs about souls, spirits, and the fate of the dead, although their concepts sometimes were vague. According to Crantz, Greenlanders once honored a Supreme Being, but after generations of neglect they nearly had lost their association with Him. Crantz studied Eskimo beliefs in search of survivals from the "patriarchal religion" and felt that they had learned something about Christianity from the Norse. It appeared that they vaguely knew about the world's creation and Noah's flood. However, Greenlanders also believed that the souls of men and other animals were the same, and Crantz judged them "stupid brutal creatures" in this respect. He felt that those who purported to believe in the transmigration of souls did so for personal gain; he thought that a poor widow who told a man that his son had the soul of one of her dead children did so only with the hope of benefits from the father.

From accounts by Egede and Crantz we learn that social control was based on individual and family accountability, but more broadly based political action was practically nonexistent. If one person murdered another in anger, the male kin closest to the deceased was duty bound to kill the murderer; there the matter reportedly ended. The only other murders were of persons, usually old women, accused of practicing sorcery. The killing of a witch was universally approved, and the death was not avenged.

These Greenlanders had developed a mechanism to defuse potential violence between individuals. The social value of their "singing-combat" or performance of ridicule songs was emphasized by both observers. As a means for social control ridicule songs were highly effective. A debtor, liar, or thief usually reformed if it seemed that he might be exposed in song because people were ashamed to have their failings revealed in this manner. If a man's behavior remained blatantly offensive, he was challenged to a song duel. Beforehand the two contestants composed songs, and these were sung before an eager audience. The challenger first presented his "taunting Ditties" to the beat of his drum, and the challenged responded in kind. To the delight of the assembled listeners songs were exchanged until one man's inventory was exhausted and he lost the duel. After a dispute was settled in this manner, the loser could not overtly express any ill feelings. The aim of a song duel was the prevention of serious antisocial behavior, the essence of many legal systems. The humaneness of this means for deterring disharmony was consistent with the Eskimo ideal of avoiding violence. In the words of Crantz, "they live as we may imagine our ancestors lived immediately after the Flood."

Old age, after a life of labor, brought no rewards. An old woman might be branded a witch and stoned to death, thrown into the sea, or cut to pieces. If not accused of sorcery, she might be buried alive or might throw herself into the sea when she realized that she was a burden to her housemates. Death came sooner to most men. Numerous hunters drowned at sea, and those who did not meet this fate usually died in middle age. After a well-regarded person died, the body was clothed in his or her best garments and the death lamented with tears and "ghastly Howlings." The legs of the deceased were then flexed and the body wrapped in skins for close relatives to carry to a grave site. Stones were piled over the corpse and the person's earthly possessions were placed near the grave. These artifacts were not for the use of the dead in another realm but were placed there so that the living would not be reminded of the dead. A woman in mourning went about in a very unkempt condition, and she wore her parka hood up when outdoors to prevent her death. After a small child had been buried, the head of a dog was placed near the grave; the dog guided the child's soul to the land of the dead since so small a soul could not find its way alone. The souls of women who died in labor, those of great hunters, and those of men who died at sea journeyed to a pleasant land in the underworld. All other souls went to a cold and desolate abode in the sky; here they lived in tents, and by playing ball with a walrus head they caused the northern lights.

*   *   *

An account of Eskimo life in southwest Greenland cannot justly conclude without at least mentioning a disease reported most often from this region. It is called kayak fear or "kayak angst," which translates as kayak phobia or as kayak dizziness. I am somewhat hesitant to discuss the syndrome because it is not identified during the earliest historic times. Yet kayak fear was termed a "national disease" among West Greenlanders by the turn of the present century, and it probably prevailed there in aboriginal times.

In a textbook case kayak fear occurs among men hunting alone at sea in kayaks. When the sun is at its zenith, the sea calm with a mirrorlike quality, and a kayaker either still in the water or paddling and staring at the seascape, he may be overcome with a set of fearful sensations. The first symptom is a sense of confusion and dizziness accompanied by a difficulty in estimating distances, even how far it is to the bow of the kayak. He begins to feel alternately hot and cold; he sweats and wants to squirm about but fears doing so and attempts to sit even more quietly than before. By staring ahead he tries to gain self-control. The lower part of his body seems cold, and he thinks that this sensation is caused by water flooding the kayak. To break the spell he may paddle slowly toward shore or ruffle the glassy surface of the water with his paddle. These efforts at times suffice to break the trance. If they do not, however, the attack continues, and the hunter fears that he will capsize and drown. His arms may become paralyzed, and he may imagine that the kayak is sinking. If help arrives or the spell is otherwise broken, he will paddle ashore, and this phase of the attack will pass. On reaching land he may have the urge to urinate or defecate; his feeling of nausea and a headache may last for days. For many kayakers the experience intensifies until at some point they either drown or abandon hunting from kayaks. The cases on which this summary is based were reported by a physician in 1905.

At about this time it was estimated that in the Julianehaab district 10 percent of the men older than 18 suffered from kayak fear.

The disease stems from a form of sensory deprivation and was reported as early as 1806. In 1761 Crantz made a number of observations about kayaking that may be related to this malady. He reported that some men never learned to handle kayaks skillfully and were forced to depend on fish and shellfish for food. He also noted that after the husband and the elder son of a woman drowned in kayaks, she refused to allow her surviving son to hunt in this manner, and he was forced to serve as a "maid" to others. Thus in reasonably early historic times there existed humble alternatives to hunting sea mammals from kayaks. The disease of kayak phobia is reported only among Greenlandic Eskimos and is confined primarily to those in the western sector. For all of Greenland between 1901 and 1930 there were about 750 drownings as a result of kayak accidents.

The citations from Crantz suggest that the disease may have been known in aboriginal times. In early historic times as caribou herds were depleted in the west, sea-mammal hunting presumably became more vital, with greater risks taken by kayakers. As Danish intervention into the lives of the people led to abandonment of fully aboriginal patterns, economic alternatives to hunting from kayaks slowly began to emerge, and we know that by 1913 men who were afflicted with kayak fear could earn a living at a coal mine.

*   *   *

West Greenland customs as described by Egede and Crantz did not emerge as the norm against which other Eskimos were compared, at least not in any chainlike sequence. When Henry Ellis (1748) wrote about his voyage to Hudson Bay in 1746-7, his observation that the Hudson Strait Eskimos "are believed to be the same People with the *Groenlanders*" was in reference to Egede's work. Ellis hesitated to accept this grouping, however, because Greenlanders were described as placid, and he found the Hudson Strait Eskimos fierce. In 1767 Crantz wrote that Eskimos in Labrador and Greenland spoke the same language, basing his statement on the experience of an Eskimo-speaking Moravian missionary who visited Labrador in 1764. Crantz had read the account by Ellis of his visit to Hudson Bay and concluded that the Eskimos there and Greenlanders were very similar. In my presentation West Greenlanders are the ethnographic point of departure because they were the first Eskimos described well and in detail. It was not until about 1800 that sufficient information about aboriginal life from northern Canada to Siberia prevailed to render trustworthy judgments about Eskimo cultural continuity across the American arctic.

*   *   *

Eskimos often, if not typically, are characterized as a peaceful, fun-loving people who abhorred violent behavior against other persons. Egede described them in this manner as did many others, but the stereotype seems erroneous. In many early Eskimo and explorer encounters, conflict and physical violence occurred. How much resulted from the overbearing attitudes of explorers and their confidence in superior weapons is not clear. Certainly the practice of seizing people and sailing off with them, as was commonly done by explorers, caused ill feelings among the victimized groups. The amount of normal physical aggression in Eskimo life is not difficult to establish, but again the underlying reasons for it are not readily apparent.

When evaluating violence among Eskimos, we first may consider the essence of their life-style. Foremost, Eskimos survived by killing; all, or nearly all, of their food was obtained by hunting and fishing. Whether the quarry was a caribou, duck, or seal, blood was likely shed at the kill, and fish might be clubbed to death. Thus the death—or murder—of animals literally gave life to Eskimos and was a part of their normal routine. Furthermore, their survival depended on their teaching children, especially boys, to kill from a tender age. As Crantz recorded in southwest Greenland and as numerous others have noted throughout the Eskimo area, children tortured birds to death and apparently did so without pity. Birds probably were singled out because children could capture small ones with comparative ease. As has been noted, a dominant characteristic of Eskimo society was the emphasis on self-reliance and independence for individuals, especially men. Convention fostered permissive attitudes toward children with the intent of creating self-sufficient adults. Thus we have a milieu in which people's survival depended on killing animals by employing personal skills developed from childhood.

Under most circumstances gossip, informal ridicule, and ridicule songs were effective means of social control. Yet under certain conditions these methods of inducing conformity did not suffice. If a person was accused of sorcery and was widely thought of as a witch, he or she usually was killed for what was perceived as the common good. We must also keep in mind that suicides were not uncommon, and the same was true for infanticide and senilicide in some sectors. Thus ample precedent prevailed for taking human lives as a patterned means for coping with certain conditions likely to recur in their society.

Murders committed because of a stressful climax in a personal situation seem best labeled as "crimes of passion." In the heat of anger one man might kill another over a relatively trifling matter. Disputes over women also loomed large as a cause of murder. After a person had been killed, revenge was expected, and the murderer or a close male kinsman was marked for death by relatives of the deceased. In some sectors the Eskimos butchered the bodies of murder victims, in the manner of animals killed for food, to prevent the soul from seeking revenge. Possibly because men took strong aggressive action to survive as hunters it was not difficult for some to cross a narrow barrier to kill a person in anger or during other emotional trauma. Homicide not only was accepted but was a common means for resolving individual differences.

*   *   *

To a modern American reader the ethnographic sketch for West Greenland may seem curiously wanting in certain essential elements. True, these people hunted for a living, wore skin clothing, sometimes drove dog teams, had skin boats, and followed many quaint customs. But where are the snowhouses, dependence on dog-sled travel, or most of all, perhaps, an emphasis on polar-bear hunts? These and other cultural ways often considered to typify Eskimos existed in another sector of Greenland but were not to be found in the southwest.

NOTES

WEST GREENLAND ESKIMO CONTACTS WITH EUROPEANS FROM 1605 TO 1656. The background information about Danish Norwegian voyages to Greenland is drawn from Finn Gad (1971, 217-58). The same source and Adam Olearius (1656, 163-79) provide information about captive Eskimos. The 1656 voyage of Nicholas Tunes is described in a book by Louis de Poincy, revised and published by Charles de Rochefort, presumably in 1667. Gad (1973, 11-2) stresses that shortly before the resettlement of Greenland by the Danes in 1721, the trade for metal products from Dutch whalers was intensive in the northern sector of West Greenland.

PRIMARY ETHNOGRAPHIC SOURCES. The 1745 English edition of Hans P. Egede's work *A Description of Greenland* conveys most of the baseline information, and important elaborations are drawn from David Crantz (1767). The illustrations reproduced from the study by Egede are from the 1818 English edition. These and later sources about West Greenlanders are summarized by Birket-Smith (1924), who includes information from his fieldwork just south of Disko Island in 1918.

LUTHERAN AND MORAVIAN MISSIONARY ACTIVITIES. The sketch of Egede's early endeavors as a Lutheran missionary is from Louis Bobé (1952) and Gad (1973, 13-50). The background information about Moravian missionary efforts in Greenland is based on Crantz (1767, v. 1, 257-92; v. 2), Gad (1973, 163 ff), John T. Hamilton (1900, 49-50), and H. Ostermann (1929, v. 3, 280-1).

SECONDARY ELABORATIONS. George Nellemann (1969-70) described West Greenland caribou-hunting techniques, some of which were not mentioned in early historic sources. Included were driving animals along stone fences, over cliffs, and down steep slopes. It seems likely that these techniques were employed in early historic times.

The Danish anthropologist Erik Holtved (1963) evaluated ethnographic accounts about the deity Torngarsuk. He concluded, largely on the basis of a comparative study of myths, that Torngarsuk was not a supreme supernatural at the time of historic contact but that in earlier times he was more powerful and possibly occupied such a position.

The information about kayak fear is based primarily on the analysis by Zachary Gussow (1963), supplemented by the works of M. Ch. Ehrström (1951) and Edward F. Foulks (1972). Peter Freuchen (1935, 241-2) described the opportunity for men with the kayak disease to work in a coal mine, and kayaking in 1761 is mentioned by Crantz (1767, v. 1, 163 fn).

CHAPTER

5

Polar Eskimos

The Polar Eskimos lived farther north than any other people, but no one really knows whether they thought of themselves as the only human beings, as John Ross reported in 1818. The coast to the south of their homeland is dominated by glaciers, and the nearest Greenlandic Eskimos lived about 250 miles away. Although Canadian Eskimos were equally far off, small groups of them occasionally ventured to northwestern Greenland soon after 1850. Before the arrival of Ross, the Polar group may have known of other Eskimos only in legendary terms, and they might have considered themselves the world's only people.

The Arctic Highlanders, so named by John Ross, are now called the Polar Eskimos or less often the Smith Sound Eskimos. They lived along a comparatively narrow coastal zone bounded on three sides by immense glaciers and are unique among Eskimos because they lacked the typical summer side of Eskimo life. The Polar Eskimo year was dominated by a long winter, "the season of fast ice," and their "season of no ice," relatively speaking, spanned little more than four weeks in August and September. With such a short period of open water it is understandable that the kayak was known only in memory and the umiak had been forgotten. Unlike most Eskimos they did not make bird spears, bows and arrows, fishhooks, or leisters, nor did they use the throwing-board with weapons. Fishing was unknown, as was hunting sea mammals in open water; caribou, the major land-dwelling species, were not hunted. In yet another respect the Polar Eskimos stand as unique among aboriginal Americans: they alone systematically exploited a local source of iron. To learn more about these people we must begin with the year 1853 and the arctic adventures of a very remarkable man, Elisha Kent Kane.

The firstborn son of a strong-willed lawyer, Elisha Kane attended the University of Virginia until rheumatic fever forced him to return home to Philadelphia. After recovering he earned a medical degree from the University of Pennsylvania in 1842, and he took the qualifying examination for a United States Navy surgeon. Before obtaining his commission he traveled around the world. He made a precarious descent into a live volcano in the Philippines, he practiced medicine at a Canton River port before being taken ill, presumably with cholera, and he made a venturesome trip up the Nile River. After traveling nearly 40,000 miles, he returned to Philadelphia, received his commission, and sailed for West Africa in 1846. His stay in Africa ended when he was stricken with "coast fever" and was forced to return home. Kane soon arranged an assignment as special messenger for President James K. Polk to Winfield Scott, the commanding general of United States troops in Mexico. Before long Kane was fighting his way through Mexico, but by the time he reached Scott, later instructions from the President had arrived. Since Kane had typhus and was unfit for further service in Mexico, he returned to Philadelphia, where he was received as a local hero. After recovering his health, Kane was assigned to a supply ship on an uneventful cruise (1849), but he longed for more challenging duty. The ongoing search for a lost English explorer in the American arctic provided Kane with the opportunity that he so eagerly sought.

John Franklin was an English naval officer and experienced explorer who had mapped the Coronation Gulf area of the Canadian arctic (1821) and a sector of the arctic coast west of the Mackenzie River mouth (1826). On his third expedition, organized to search for the Northwest Passage, two vessels, the *Erebus* and *Terror*, were under his command. The combined crews of 129 wintered at Beechey Island in 1845-6 and spent two additional winters in Victoria Strait. Franklin died in June 1847, and the ships were abandoned in April 1848. All the survivors appear to have died on a trek south to the Back River. However, the fate of this third Franklin expedition would not be known, even partially, until 1853-4, and even then hope prevailed that survivors were alive somewhere in the arctic. Between 1847 and 1855 nearly 40 separate parties searched for Franklin and his men. Ten rescue efforts were launched in 1850, of which nine were organized by the English. Kane was a member of the only American searching party to set forth in that year. Two vessels from the United States participated, largely because of the interest and financial backing of a wealthy New York merchant, Henry Grinnell. President Zachary Taylor was sympathetic to a Federally sponsored search but Congress only reluctantly cooperated in the humanitarian effort, authorizing the use of Navy personnel and equipment. Lieutenant Edwin J. De Haven was given command of the brig *Advance*, and it was accompanied by the brigantine *Rescue*. Although the vessels were reinforced to withstand arctic ice, even the enthusiastic Kane was startled by their diminutive size and poor equipment. Furthermore, none of the officers or crew had previous experience in arctic waters.

They sailed for Lancaster Sound and Barrow Strait in late May 1850, following the route of Franklin. De Haven's orders permitted him to search anywhere except to the south toward the mainland since that region had been investigated. At Lancaster Sound, the Americans joined numerous English vessels combing the region. While Kane and De Haven were on Beechey Island, off the southwestern sector of Devon Island, the site of Franklin's winter quarters in 1845-6 was discovered by the English. They found temporary buildings, three graves, and many artifacts, including over 600 empty meat cans. The would-be rescuers looked in vain for a written record of the route that Franklin and his men planned to follow from the camp. The searchers decided to probe in different directions, with De Haven sailing north along Wellington Channel. After weathering a storm and being temporarily frozen in the ice, De Haven decided to begin the homeward voyage. Before they could leave, however, the ships froze in the ice and drifted into Wellington Channel. Later the pack ice carried them east along Lancaster Sound, and when ice badly damaged the *Rescue*, its crew was transferred to the already overcrowded *Advance*. By Christmas many men had scurvy. Fortunately the vessels continued to drift east along Lancaster Sound, and in early March the *Rescue* was repaired in an improvised drydock cut into its icy encasement. By mid-April the crew returned to the *Rescue*, and the men began to regain their health. When the ice finally broke away from the ships, they sailed toward Greenland, where the crews could recuperate before resuming the search. Ice prevented the vessels from reaching Lancaster Sound, however, and so they sailed back to New York.

Kane soon convinced himself that after Franklin had wintered at Beechey Island, he had sailed north through Wellington Channel toward the North Pole and reached the "Open Polar Sea" whose existence still was supported by some reputable geographers. Kane assumed that the *Erebus* and *Terror* were trapped there but that the crews were surviving on the rich animal life presumed to exist in the sea. Smith Sound, at the head of Baffin Bay, was an obvious approach to the Open Polar Sea. Kane was determined to sail there in search of Franklin as well as to satisfy his desire for adventure and geographical discovery. In 1852, Edward A. Inglefield had piloted the steamer *Isabel* a short distance north of Smith Sound before he was forced back by a storm, and Kane knew that Inglefield had sighted open water north of the sound. Who could say how far north this expanse of open water led?

Grinnell placed the *Advance* at Kane's disposal, other persons contributed money, and Federal agencies as well as private institutions provided men, money, or equipment. The crew was composed of Navy and civilian personnel. One civilian member, Isaac I. Hayes, deserves special mention because he later led his own arctic adventures. A young medical doctor, Hayes had received his degree just before the *Advance* sailed in May 1853. The vessel anchored first at St. John's, Newfoundland, where sleds were purchased and six Newfoundland dogs and barrels of dog food were given to Kane by the governor. At Upernivik, Carl Petersen, a Dane who spoke Eskimo and English, was recruited as a sled driver and interpreter. At the first landing in south Greenland, Kane attempted to enlist two Eskimos as hunters. The only person he was able to recruit, a youth of 18 named Hans C. Hendrik, proved a remarkably capable individual. He was nearly indispensable to Kane, and he later joined three other arctic expeditions. In 1878 Hendrik published an account of his adventures with white explorers.

After being battered by ice the *Advance* finally entered Smith Sound and limped into a small harbor from which the brig was never to sail. A small party reconnoitering northward found ice as far as they could see, a very disheartening sight. The crew settled in to winter farther north in Greenland than had any other white explorers. The winter of 1853-4 included such problems as an accidental fire and a proliferation of rats on the brig, but none were unmanageable. Future mobility, however, was in jeopardy because by late winter most of the sled dogs had died. Men were forced to pull the heavily loaded sleds to advance bases for a dash to the Open Polar Sea. One party attempting to set out caches suffered incredible hardship and was in desperate condition when saved, only to have the rescuers and rescued nearly perish together on their return to the ship.

In early April, as despair deepened, a man on watch yelled out, "People hollaing ashore!" When Kane and the others appeared topside, they saw and heard people across the ice calling out repeatedly and gesturing wildly. Kane realized at once that these were "natives of the country." They approached unarmed, and after calling for Petersen to interpret, Kane went forth without weapons (Figure 5-1). The first Eskimo he met was a tall, powerfully built man wearing a fox-skin parka and trousers of polar bear skin. His boots were made from the lower part of a bear's legs with the soles and claws of the feet intact. This was Metek, who never before had seen a white man but approached Kane fearlessly. The peaceful intentions of Metek and his seven companions soon were obvious, and Kane invited them aboard. These Eskimos were from Etah, the northernmost permanent settlement in the world, located some 70 miles south of the ice-bound *Advance*. Hendrik and Petersen could understand most of what the Eskimos said despite dialect differences from the language of south Greenland. The behavior of the Eskimos aboard ship almost overwhelmed Kane and the others. Three or four of them spoke at once, laughing when they could not be understood, and moved about constantly, looking at and handling everything in sight. They asked for all that they saw and attempted to steal as many novelties as possible. Before long they were running back and forth to their sleds with their gifts and loot. By late afternoon the wonders of the day had exhausted them, and they slept near the galley stove. The next day before they left Kane bartered barrel staves, beads, and needles for

Figure 5-1 Elisha K. Kane's first meeting with the Polar Eskimos. The weapons carried by Kane and the Eskimos were added by the artist, since a description of the meeting noted that all were unarmed. (From Kane, 1856)

four dogs and all the walrus meat the men could spare. The Eskimos agreed to return in a few days and permit Kane to borrow their dogs, but they did not appear. Later a smaller party of ''incorrigible scamps'' arrived and stole what they could, yet in his precarious position Kane dared not become angry.

The year 1854 brought death, near-disaster, and very few rewards to Kane and his party. In April two men died, one from tetanus and another following the amputation of a frozen foot. A plan to travel north to reach a food cache set out the previous year and then cross to Ellesmere Island failed. Polar bears had raided the cache and the eight men who had struggled to reach it were in no condition to travel on. Kane concluded that only smaller, more mobile parties could explore the region successfully. Hayes and another man crossed to Ellesmere Island by dog sled and reached 79°45', thus charting 200 miles of unknown coastline. Hendrik and William Morton, a former member of the De Haven expedition who was with Kane on this trip, made a final probe north of

Greenland and reached 81°22'. They saw water to the north and speculated that this was the gateway to the Open Polar Sea, but they could proceed no farther. In early July, Kane and Hendrik sledded from the still icebound *Advance* to Smith Sound and realized that they could not free themselves from the ice that summer. In desperation Kane set off with a few men in a whaleboat, hoping to meet the English along Lancaster Sound and obtain aid from them. In northern Baffin Bay, however, they were stopped by an unbroken field of ice to the south. They returned to the *Advance*, and it was apparent to all that without some desperate action they would be forced to spend a second winter on the brig. Eight men, including Petersen, defied Kane's judgment and attempted a dash south before winter. The nine others, including Hendrik, remained with Kane and prepared for the winter by converting a portion of the brig into a small but snug moss-lined compartment.

In the fall Eskimo visitors took two buffalo robes, along with Kane's best dog and cooking utensils. Kane was angry and sent two of the crew in pursuit of the thieves. After walking 30 miles they caught up with the Eskimos, one of whom was Metek's wife; the women already had converted the robes into garments. A boy was sent to Etah to tell Metek that the women were being led back to the ship as prisoners. A few days later Metek arrived with a sled loaded with "the sinful prizes of many covetings," which he regretfully restored to Kane. Kane and Metek negotiated a "treaty." The Eskimos were not to steal; they were to bring fresh meat whenever they could, sell dogs or lend them, and show the whites where to find game. Kane promised in return to not harm the Etah people, give them presents, trade for meat, welcome them aboard the brig, and kill game on joint hunts. The pact was not seriously broken by either party.

Life on the *Advance* became alarmingly difficult in the fall and desperate during the winter of 1854-5. In spite of the snug quarters it was clear that nonessential wood from the vessel would not provide sufficient fuel. Meat supplies were low, and mental depression as well as physical illness became routine among the men. In early December, Petersen and another man who had abandoned Kane were brought back by Eskimos, and finally the six others, ill and starving, were returned by kind-hearted Eskimos. The "secession party" certainly was not welcomed; at first they were barely tolerated by those who had remained with Kane. In time, how-

Figure 5-2 A Polar Eskimo dressed in polar-bear skin clothing. The man is wearing boots made from the lower legs of a polar bear with the soles and claws intact. (From Kane, 1856)

ever, common privation made most of them equals again. The need for fresh meat to ward off scurvy was desperate, and Hendrik attempted to reach Etah. He succeeded but found that these Eskimos were starving and no food was available. On his return he managed to kill a walrus and seals, which revived the crew temporarily. Later in the spring Hendrik asked permission to walk to a Polar Eskimo community south of Etah, to obtain walrus hide for boot soles, and with misgivings Kane granted him permission. Hendrik arrived at the village and stayed there, eventually marrying a girl who had nursed him back to health when he had been ill during a trip there in the winter. The desertion by Hendrik was a severe blow to Kane because this young Eskimo was a reliable hunter and a knowledgeable traveler.

In April new sleds were built and old ones refitted for carrying three boats to the open water of Baffin Bay. Late in May the *Advance* was abandoned, but progress toward Baffin Bay was pathetically slow. One man died from internal injuries received in a desperate effort to save a boat at the edge of an ice floe. At Etah, with open water near, Kane said good-bye to the Polar Eskimos who were so helpful. The boat trip south proved to be nearly as hazardous as the time spent on the northern ice. Finally near Upernivik they met a Danish vessel, and Kane learned that artifacts from the Franklin expedition had been found near Victoria Strait, far, far from where Kane and his men had endured so much in their vain attempt to find the lost explorer.

Kane returned a hero to Philadelphia and labored hard on a book for a general audience. As soon as it was finished, he left for England despite his failing health. His purpose was to help the very persistent Lady Franklin to launch yet another search for her now long-lost husband. Kane became very ill and soon left England for the warmth of Cuba, only to die at Havana early in 1857. His body was taken to New Orleans by ship, up the Mississippi River by steamboat to Cincinnati, and by train to Philadelphia for burial. Along the route tens of thousands of people stood waiting to honor the man who for a brief moment was the hero of the nation.

*   *   *

In the multiple exposures of Europeans to the arctic no explorer encountered thus far depended as heavily on the Eskimos as Kane. The Eskimo Hans Hendrik was recruited as a hunter, and the game he killed was crucial for the survival of the Kane party. Hendrik served Kane well as a sled driver, traveling companion, and effective intermediary in dealing with the Polar Eskimos. Numerous travelers appreciated Eskimo adjustments to their habitat but Kane was the first to draw heavily on Eskimo technology for survival. Like the Eskimos he traveled by dog team, and a sled he had built for the expedition was the Eskimo type. Kane and his men wore Eskimo-style garments and they converted a portion of the *Advance* into an Eskimo-like dwelling for the winter of 1854-5. When they had used the last of their fuel to heat these quarters, they relied on Eskimo lamps for heat. Finally, Kane, like Eskimos, was not especially particular about what he ate. Rats aboard the ship were a terrible nuisance and Hendrik, to pass the time, shot them with arrows. The idea of eating rats was repugnant to the others, but when meat was scarce Kane ate, and seemed to enjoy, meat soup made from these "small deer."

In his autobiography, Hans Hendrik briefly recounted his experiences with Kane. Having grown up in south Greenland, Hendrik was not prepared for the long arctic night. In translation he wrote, "Then it really grew winter and dreadfully cold, and the sky speedily darkened. Never had I seen the dark season like this, to be sure it was awful, I thought we should have no daylight any more. I was seized with fright, and fell a weeping, I never in my life saw such darkness at noon time. As the darkness continued for three months, I really believed we should have no daylight more." Hendrik observed that the following spring, when the "succession party" attempted to flee to the south, Kane forbade him to accompany them, although Kane gave the impression that Hendrik remained largely by choice. Hendrik felt that the explorers could not reach Upernivik by small boat, and this was one reason that he deserted Kane to live with the Polar Eskimos.

Elisha Kent Kane's *Arctic Explorations* is eminently readable and was vigorously promoted by the publisher, who sold nearly 20,000 copies before publication. Many children's books and articles about Kane appeared. As a child Robert E. Peary read a story about Kane in a Sunday-school paper, and the clipping was among Peary's possessions when he died. Kane's two-volume work appears to have introduced a generation of American readers to the lifeway of Eskimos and was partially responsible for the Polar Eskimos becoming the stereotype as the only "real" ones.

Kane died believing in the existence of the Open Polar Sea, and Isaac I. Hayes, the medical doctor who accompanied Kane in 1853-5, shared his conviction. Hayes organized a voyage of discovery in 1860, and Henry Grinnell again was among the sponsors. The plan was to sail along the western shore of Smith Sound in a schooner reinforced for the voyage and renamed the *United States*. Hayes set off early in July, and at Upernivik he obtained dogs as well as skin clothing. Here he recruited Eskimo hunters, additional sailors, and an interpreter. They landed near Cape York and met Hans Hendrik, who gladly joined the expedition with his wife and baby.

The *United States* rode out a fierce storm in Smith Sound, but before long the schooner was damaged badly by ice and was leaking at an alarming rate. The crew managed to reach an anchorage near Etah, where they wintered. With caribou numerous in the vicinity, fresh meat was readily available. Unfortunately most of their dogs died from disease, a serious blow to Hayes' plans. He sent Hendrik and August Sonntag, who also had been with Kane, south to obtain dogs from the Polar Eskimos. On the trip Sonntag fell through the thin ice over a tidal crack, and although rescued by Hendrik he soon died. When Hendrik returned, he had only five dogs, although he had left with nine. Along the way he made lavish gifts to people, thinking that they would provide dogs later, but this proved to be an unsuccessful technique. Although Eskimos visited the schooner, they would not part with a single dog. Hayes recognized and accepted the logic in their explanation that dogs were nearly indispensable to feed themselves and their families.

Toward spring Hayes was able to obtain enough dogs to push north by sled. He and a few men set out to cross the jumbled mass of ice on Smith Sound leading to Ellesmere Island. Traveling conditions were so extraordinarily difficult that they averaged only about two miles a day, and a month was required for the crossing. After reaching Ellesmere Island, Hayes and one other man pushed on to about 81°35', which was nearer the Pole than any other person had ventured in this region of the world. By mid-May they were forced to turn back because the sea ice was beginning to rot and lanes of open water delayed their progress. Hayes sailed homeward in mid-July, 1861, convinced that a polar sea existed still farther north. Whether or not it was "open" would be for others to determine.

For the English the most compelling goal of arctic exploration was to find a Northwest Passage, but in the United States the purpose for adventuring far north was largely to reach the North Pole. Kane and Hayes, among others, found the most feasible access route to the Pole. Robert E. Peary, a civil engineer for the United States Navy, devoted years of his life to discovering the North Pole. Between 1886 and 1909 he made seven voyages to Greenland and claimed to have reached the North Pole in 1909. Although Kane deserves credit for first popularizing the Polar Eskimos, Peary made them famous, not so much because of his information about them but because their importance to him during his arctic travels was conveyed to the many readers of his books.

When Kane was among the Polar Eskimos in 1853-5, they numbered about 140 persons at eight widely scattered villages along the coast from Cape York to Etah. Although hundreds of miles separated the most distant families, they thought of themselves as one people, and a birth or death in any village was of interest to all. Kane's account of this expedition includes nearly 750 pages of text and figures, with about 80 pages devoted to the Polar Eskimos. His narrative is presented essentially as a diary and Eskimos are mentioned only as they were met by Kane or others of his party.

When Kane encountered these people for the first time, he noted in a terse sentence, "They had no wood." A simple statement of comparable import probably could not be made for any other aboriginal people. Bone was substituted for wood. For weapon shafts narwhal tusks were used, and alternatively bear or walrus bones were fitted and lashed together. Sled runners made from the bones of whales were mortised, tied with thongs, and shod with strips of ivory. The absence of wood helps to explain why the Polar Eskimos made neither kayaks nor umiaks.

Weapon points and knife blades were fashioned from metal the Polar Eskimos received in trade from the south, according to Kane. This may be correct, but some metal possibly was obtained as jetsam from ships or more directly from whalers. In prehistoric times the Polar Eskimos, unlike any other aboriginal Americans, used meteoritic iron for blades. John Ross was told by these Eskimos that their metal came from "Iron Mountains." An analysis of it indicated a high nickel content and a meteorite as the source. In 1894 Peary visited the source of the iron, about 35 miles east of

Cape York, and found that it consisted of three meteorites named "Woman," "Dog," and "Tent" by the Eskimos. These were the "great irons" thought by the Polar Eskimos to have originally been a woman, her dog, and her tent hurled from the sky by a supernatural. By the time Peary saw the trio, the Woman did not have a human appearance. The upper portion of her body had been chipped away and the head long ago removed. The sled carrying the head fell through the ice, taking down the dogs and nearly drowning the people with the sled. After that time the Polar Eskimos chipped only small pieces from the Woman's body when in need of iron. According to Peary, by the mid-1850s or even earlier iron was obtained in trade from ships' crews, and Eskimos stopped using the meteorites. For some curious reason Peary expended a vast amount of effort to remove the 1000-pound Dog, the 6000-pound Woman, and 100-ton Tent, which were taken to New York.

Kane's most vivid ethnographic account was of a walrus hunt by Hendrik, Morton, and two Polar Eskimos. In the late fall these men sledded to a spot where new ice was forming at leads in old floes. Walrus, unlike seals, do not maintain breathing holes but seek open water or places where they can break newly formed ice with their thick skulls. When the hunters finally heard sounds "between the mooing of a cow and the deepest baying of a mastiff," they cautiously approached a pool where groups of walrus were repeatedly surfacing for air. Each hunter crawled closer and closer but was motionless whenever a walrus surfaced, inching nearer only after the animal sounded. When one hunter reached the edge of a pool used by five walrus, he fitted a toggle harpoon head on a shaft made from a narwhal tusk. A long walrus-hide line attached to the harpoon head was held taut by tucking a section under another line attached to the shaft (Figure 5-3, upper left). The Eskimo stood upright with the harpoon poised in his right hand and his left arm at his side. The water boiled as a walrus neared the surface, and when it appeared the hunter lifted his left arm. The startled animal thrust itself high out of the water for a better view of this strange sight, and the Eskimo immediately launched his harpoon. The harpoon head cut into the hide of the animal beneath one flipper, and it sounded at once. The hunter ran quickly across the ice and paid out the line but held onto the loop at the end. He grabbed a short-handled ice pick, drove the point into the ice, and wrapped the line around it. As the walrus thrashed about, the line was alternately slackened and tightened. The wounded animal and its companions surfaced, looked around, and dove again. While they were submerged, the hunter removed the ice pick and dashed to another spot, where he implanted it again and attached the line. The walrus knew where the man had been a few moments before and crashed upward through the ice at that spot, missing the hunter only because he had moved. This evasion was repeated until another harpoon could be launched into the wounded prey. The walrus repeatedly crashed against the edge of the ice in a vain effort to reach its tormentors. By the time it died four hours later this walrus had more than 60 lance wounds (Figure 5-3, upper right). Another set of skills was required to pull the 700-pound animal onto the ice. The hunters made two sets of parallel cuts, each set some six inches apart, in the neck of the walrus where the hide was very thick. A line was passed through one opening and on through a thong loop attached to a stake driven into the ice. The line then was passed back again through the other opening in the neck, and both ends of the line were pulled simultaneously to lift the animal onto the ice for butchering.

Later sources, especially an ethnography by Erik Holtved, convey what probably were long-standing features of walrus hunts. Hunters usually sledded together close to the thin ice where walrus could be taken. The men dared not drive their dogs too near because noise made by the sleds was enough to frighten the animals away. As in Kane's time the hunters walked across the ice in a single file, each one following in the footprints of the lead man to make as little noise as possible when crushing the snow cover. As very thin ice was approached, they walked with special caution, testing the ice with their harpoon foreshafts and seeking a new path if it was dangerously thin. Once they located a pool of crushed ice where walrus had been breathing, the hunters surrounded it and thrust harpoons into the animals when they surfaced. The hide of the walrus is thinnest just beneath its front flippers, and it was here that they attempted to strike. As soon as a walrus was harpooned, an ice pick was thrust into the ice at a distance from the hole to hold the harpoon line. Each hunter was careful to drive his pick just far enough into the ice for it to hold without cracking the ice, which would make the ice pick unstable. If a number of hunters struck an animal at nearly the same time, the man whose

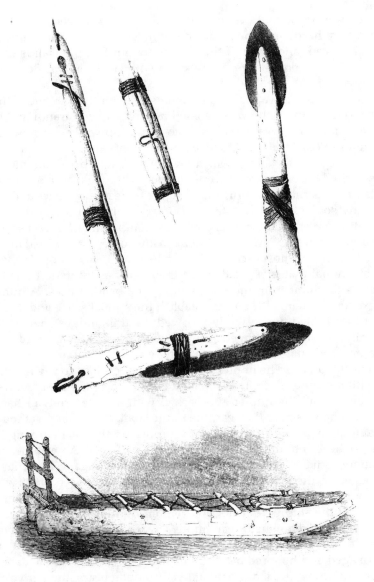

Figure 5-3 Polar Eskimo manufactures: upper left, harpoon head and shaft with detail of the line loop to keep the head taut; upper right, metal-bladed lance head; middle, metal-bladed knife; lower, sled made of bones lashed together. (From Kane, 1856)

line was most taut when the walrus dove was considered the primary harpooner; he received the most desirable parts, the entrails, head, and heart. If the ice was so thin that the walrus could not be lifted onto it after being killed with lances, it was flensed in the water.

In the spring walrus sunned themselves on the ice, and if they basked too long, the water sometimes froze over, stranding them on the surface. Walrus are able to thrust upward with powerful blows to crush relatively stable ice, but they cannot break through moderately thick ice from above. Walrus trapped on the ice searched for open water, were pursued with dogs, and killed with lances. A stranded walrus might starve to death on the ice and be a ready source of food. A favored Polar Eskimo food was decayed walrus meat, but this delicacy was comparatively rare because summer temperatures were often too low to permit the meat to rot.

To men the most exciting word to hear was *nanook* or polar bear, the animal that most challenged their skills as hunters. Kane described a hunt from the first sighting of a bear's tracks. A hunter examined them with care to establish the animal's size and its rate of travel. Sled dogs eagerly followed the trail and, as soon as the bear was sighted, lunged forward with even greater speed. The bear stood on its hind legs for a better view of its pursuers and then quickly ran off. The hunter freed a number of dogs to bay the bear until he could reach it. Tormented by the dogs, the bear stood its ground, and the hunter approached with a lance firmly in hand. When he was near the bear, the hunter took a few steps as though running away and then abruptly turned on the bear, driving his lance head into the left side beneath the shoulder. An experienced hunter quickly withdrew his lance to thrust it again; if the lance lodged in the animal's body, he fled for his life. Men often were wounded by bears; Kane reported that of the seven men who once visited the ship, five had scars from encounters with polar bears.

Old and renowned bear hunters were reluctant to talk about their exploits according to an account by Knud Rasmussen in 1903. An aged and honored bear hunter said, "One must not talk about bear-hunting, . . . if one's thoughts turn upon bears, then drive out and kill some. But sit inside and prate about them? no, leave that to old women."

Seals and walrus were the primary staples. Men did not eat plant foods, but women cooked and ate a species of small flower.

Figure 5-4 A Polar Eskimo netting birds on a cliff. (From Kane, 1856)

Even among these people where starvation was common, food taboos prevailed. They apparently did not eat hares, and women were prohibited from eating eggs. As in south Greenland, seals were taken with harpoons at their breathing holes in the winter and were hunted as they basked on the ice. Important food from the land included auks and guillemots taken from cliffs with long-handled nets (Figure 5-4).

The Polar Eskimo food quest necessitated a high degree of mobility for exploiting the widely scattered resources. Polar-bear hunting was best during the spring in the northern sector of their country, and auks were taken from cliffs in the fall. Conditions for hunting narwhal, seals, or walrus were far more favorable in some localities than others, and seasonal differences were important. People ranged over hundreds of miles in search of food, and a hunt might last for months. Dog-sled travel was vital; it is difficult to conceive of human survival on the existing resources without dog traction. Only in times of extreme need were dogs killed for food.

Although Kane and Hayes traveled extensively by dog team, the best information about sledding is from Holtved. He notes that bone crosspieces formed the bed of a sled. These were attached to the runners by thongs passed through drilled holes near the runner tops. At the rear, uprights were lashed. The bone runners were shod with ivory strips lashed on through countersunk holes (Figure 5-3, bottom). This type of sled was admirably adapted to rough terrain or broken fields of ice because the flexible bindings stretched and gave when the runners were forced out of parallel. At extremely low temperatures the snow surface became grainy and ivory sled shoes created too much friction. Under these conditions, a man melted snow in his mouth, spit the water into one hand, and spread it over the shoes to form a thin film of ice. The coating produced far less friction but wore away quickly and required frequent replacement.

From a thong loop at the front of a sled were fitted a series of traces, each about six feet long, leading to the harness of a dog. This, the fan-shaped hitch, had many merits. Each dog was able to pick its own trail over rough ice, and the weight of a team was distributed widely, decreasing the likelihood that an entire team would fall through thin ice. When descending a steep grade, the dogs were spread out as far as possible to break the sled's speed, or they might be hitched at the rear of a sled for the same purpose.

Success as a hunter was only partly a product of a man's skills and weapons. Of equal importance was his ability to maintain a dog team and to travel for long periods in search of food. The number of dogs in a team depended on the owner's ability to feed them, and a large team consisted of seven dogs. With dogs so economically important, considerable energy was expended in their behalf. In the spring boots sometimes were used to protect the dogs' feet from sharp ice crystals. A bitch with a litter stayed in a house tunnel, or a small snowhouse was built for her. In the winter when a bitch with nursing pups was used to pull a sled, her teats might be protected from freezing with a piece of skin tied beneath her body. Pups were playthings for children, and they roamed freely until they were old enough to be included in a team. To help pups mature as useful animals, amulets were tied about their necks. To make a small pup grow quickly into a large animal the head, legs, and body were pulled, and air was blown into its anus. The sharp points of a dog's teeth were knocked off with a stone so that it would not bite through its traces; if the dog was fierce, it was half strangled before the operation. If a dog was savage toward those in other teams, a dog duel was arranged. The vicious dog was held with thongs by two men, and a dog from a different team was held in front of him by other men. The dogs were swung together face-to-face to provoke an attack and were allowed to bite each other. One dog after another took a turn facing the aggressor to subdue him at least temporarily. Dog-baiting also was a sport. When a young dog was added to a team, it was called by name and soon learned to obey commands. A team was guided, encouraged, and punished with the long lash of a bone-handled whip. A great deal of skill was required to handle a whip with authority, and children practiced using little whips by the hour.

The Eskimo attitude toward dogs was a perplexing combination of concern and cruelty. Almost everywhere dogs had supernatural associations; a widespread myth associates human origins with the mating of a dog and a woman. While dogs were whipped and often underfed, Eskimos usually were reluctant to kill them. By and large a man took a very pragmatic view toward the animals of a team. When food was abundant they ate well, but when it was scarce they starved with the people. A bitch with pups was treated best because her owner knew that he must have a good team to hunt and thus survive. Yet old and worthless dogs, like old people, usually were a liability and were treated accordingly.

People from temperate regions often romanticize dog-team travel. The image of an Eskimo wrapped in furs and sitting comfortably on his sled, mushing home to his igloo in the arctic twilight, is an idyllic but not realistic picture. Usually the trail is rough and the load heavy, forcing the man to run with his team or even bolt ahead to make certain that a runner does not strike a rock or piece of ice that could break the sled. Some dogs are too lazy to

Figure 5-5 An idealized interior view of a winter house. (From Kane, 1856)

pull their share, old males stop to urinate on any object along the trail, and a dog dislikes evacuating while on the run, which means the team may be dragged to one side or the other. With a fan-shaped hitch, the dogs jump over each other's traces, producing a knotted mass of lines coated with feces and urine that must sooner or later be untangled with bare hands and sometimes with one's teeth. Then there is always the possibility that a team will upset the sled or suddenly run off after a fox or other game and leave the driver alone and miles from a village. The ethnographer Birket-Smith was assured by a missionary who lived in the arctic that anything one might say when handling dogs would not be held against him on Judgment Day.

Kane described a typical winter house after he and his Eskimo hunting companions took refuge in an abandoned dwelling. The low-roofed, cave-like structure in which Kane found himself was built of stones and covered with turf. He called it an igloo, a generalized Eskimo word for house; in English igloo has come to mean a dome-shaped snowhouse, which is not quite correct terminology. From Kane and later sources we know that the typical Polar Eskimo house was pear-shaped, had higher walls at the front than at the back, and was made from stone. A house was built partially beneath the ground, and above the walls large flat stones formed a low roof (Figure 5-5). The roof was of cantilever design, with one end of each stone slab set on top of a wall and the other counterweighted with a heavy rock. A low tunnel led into a house, and above the inner end of the tunnel was a window made from sewn strips of seal intestine fitted onto a frame of skin. Because it was not possible to see through the intestine, in each window was a peephole for a clear view outside. At the rear of a house was a sleeping platform made from stones. After Kane and those with him entered the empty dwelling, one Eskimo lit a fire by striking a

Figure 5-6 A Polar Eskimo lamp, which is made from a walrus shoulder blade, resting on a rock and partially supporting a flat stone from which melted snow drips into a sealskin container. (From Kane, 1856)

piece of quartz against iron pyrites. The sparks ignited willow-catkin tinder and then dry moss. The flames were transferred to fat-soaked moss set in blubber on a walrus shoulder blade that served as a lamp. Above the lamp two rocks supported a stone on which snow melted, the water dripping into a sealskin vessel, their only utensil. This simple but efficient arrangement is illustrated in Figure 5-6. Later at another settlement and in a bigger house with heat from two lamps and the bodies of the family members and guests from the ship, the temperature in the room rose to 90°F, even though it was −30°F outdoors.

A dome-shaped house of snow blocks was called an "iglooyah," not an igloo. Snowhouses built from a spiral of snow blocks may have been introduced to the Polar Eskimos in the mid-1800s by Eskimos from central Canada, where these structures were typical winter dwellings. In northern Greenland two men usually cooperated in their construction. One man cut the blocks with a broad-bladed bone knife as a second man trimmed and fitted the blocks together in an ever-higher spiral inclined inward. After the man inside placed the final block in the center of the rooftop, he cut an opening at the base as the entrance. A large snowhouse was about 12 feet across and 6 feet high, and was entered through two small snow domes connected by a short passage. A window frame with a seal-intestine cover was placed above the entrance where a snow block had been removed, and at the back was a wide platform for sleeping and lounging. Along the sides were two narrow platforms on which meat was stored and lamps were set. A small snowhouse was built as an overnight stopping place for travelers or served as the base from which hunters ranged for a week or more. However, a larger snowhouse might be occupied for months on end. For example, in the spring of 1895 many families gathered at one locality to hunt large herds of walrus. The settlement included over 40 snowhouses and housed two-thirds of all the Polar Eskimos. One of these large houses was illustrated by Peary (Figure 5-7), who noted it was 12 feet across and had a sealskin ceiling to help prevent the roof from melting. A ventilation hole at the apex served to let excess heat out.

During the brief summer season people abandoned their houses of snow or stone and turf to live in tents. These structures were framed with poles made from narwhal tusks, and the cover of sewn sealskins was held down at the edges with rocks. Over the entrance was hung a curtain made from sewn strips of gut; it admitted light but kept out insects.

The manufactures of Polar Eskimos were highly specialized and few in number because of portability requirements. Hayes called these people "Arctic nomads" and not without cause. His inventory of the property owned by a successful hunter and his family illustrates the limited number of possessions, all of which could be carried on a single sled. In addition to the dog team, sled, and

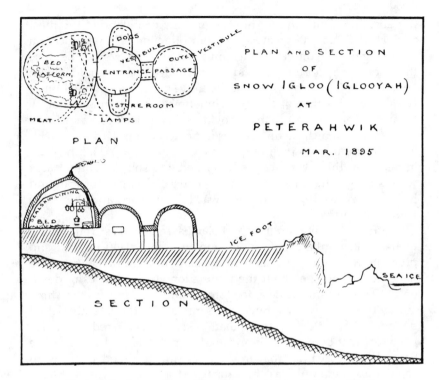

Figure 5-7 A snowhouse illustration by Robert E. Peary. (1914)

sledding equipment the family owned two polar-bear skins used as bedding, six sealskins for making a summer tent, two lances and two harpoons with extra harpoon lines, soapstone cooking pots and lamps, some materials and tools to repair the sled, clothing, a sewing and mending kit for clothing, dry grass for boot insoles, and dry moss for lamp wicks. No doubt there were additional small items, such as knives, fire-making equipment, and some stored property used seasonally, such as a net for taking cliff birds, but the list suggests a use of comparatively few portable artifacts, none of which could be termed luxury items.

A Polar Eskimo man and his wife were fully self-sufficient because they literally made everything that they or their children required, and an egalitarian quality prevailed in many aspects of family life. For example, children called their parents by name, rather than by a kinship term. Individual freedom was great but not absolute. Outstanding hunters usually commanded the most respect and had the greatest freedom of action. They attracted a following of less competent men, might marry two women because they could support them and their children, and could obtain another man's wife by wrestling for her. The success of one hunter compared with that of another sometimes was dramatic; not all Polar Eskimos were capable providers living well-ordered lives. Hayes conveyed these differences in an account of two men arriving at his camp with their dog teams. One man owned all the dogs in his team, they were well fed, his sled was solid, and the traces were strong. The other man's team consisted largely of lean and hungry borrowed dogs, the sled was falling apart, and the traces were in disarray.

The travail of life among the Polar Eskimos is best reflected in their small number. The population was about 140 in 1855 and probably was nearly the same in the early nineteenth century. We have no knowledge about the population size or causes of death until Kane began living among them in 1853, but at that time mortality probably was much the same as for the late aboriginal period. The most dramatic population statistic is offered by Hayes. He wrote that between 1855 and 1861 34 persons died and 19 were born. Violent deaths from mishaps during the food quest were sometimes mentioned as the cause of death. Clements R. Markham wrote that in 1850 several men had died while netting birds at cliffs; presumably they fell to their deaths. Peary reported that a man was drowned while trying to take a bearded seal and another died of wounds inflicted by a polar bear. He also generalized that a man was much more likely to die from an accident than from old age.

Eskimos have the reputation of being friendly and nonviolent people, but this stereotype does not fit the Polar Eskimos. Of the 140 persons known to Kane three adult males were murdered within a two-year span, and Hayes wrote that a "very unpopular" man was stabbed and buried alive beneath stones and snow. Men apparently were murder victims more often than women, and sorcery seems to have been the most important factor contributing to these deaths.

Experience apparently taught the Polar Eskimos that a motherless or fatherless child was doomed to death by starvation, and this attitude led to infanticides. When the mother of an infant or small child died, the offspring was buried with her. Similarly, if a woman with an infant lost her husband, she exposed or strangled the offspring, and on at least one occasion it was buried with the dead husband. Around the turn of the century when the father of a motherless 10-year-old boy died, another man offered to kill the boy. A woman born about this time said that after her mother died, leaving two young daughters, she watched as her sister was choked to death with a piece of string. She too was partially strangled but managed to pull the string free before she suffocated and was then allowed to live.

Any child with both parents living was treated with great kindness in the well-known Eskimo pattern. An indulgent mother might even carry a six-year-old child in the back of her parka and occasionally nurse it. Emil Bessels observed, "The little ones grow up like lap-dogs." He also wrote, however, that if a baby cried a great deal it might be placed naked on the snow, even at low temperatures, until it stopped. In the 1930s when Holtved lived among these people, he found that children were threatened far more often than punished. A crying child might be told, "Don't cry or the big raven will come and hack out your eyes!" Children also were warned that when they misbehaved a spirit might harm them.

We are poorly informed about the details of aboriginal social life among these Eskimos and are able to set forth only the general patterning. We know that the betrothal of children was common and that unmarried youths lived in a "young people's house" where couples slept together but had no mutual responsibilities. When a pair cared for one another and the respective parents did not object, a marriage resulted. No formal marriage ceremony existed, but a man was expected to take his bride by force, even though she might be willing to accompany him. A couple lived with either set of parents or established a separate household. It was relatively common for a person to have a number of partners before settling down with a more permanent spouse. Men might decide to exchange wives, and the women involved were expected to comply. If a woman refused to cooperate in an exchange, she was beaten by her husband. One man even said that the only time he was ever forced to beat his wife was when she refused to sleep with other men. The desire for variety in sexual partnerships might have been significant in such exchanges, but there clearly were other considerations. When a man's pregnant wife could not accompany him on a hunting trip, he might take along another woman who could better withstand the rigors of the journey. In a strained domestic situation a man might exchange his wife for another on an indefinite basis. This arrangement often was sufficient to bring the original couple back together.

The aspect of Polar Eskimo behavior that has commanded the most attention is a pathological condition called *pibloktoq*, a form of "arctic hysteria." While not confined exclusively to these Eskimos, it most often has been reported among them. Adults, especially women, were subject to attacks. Although the symptoms varied, in general a person might seem tired and depressingly silent beforehand. The attack itself seldom lasted more than a few minutes. A victim commonly tore off all or most of her clothing, irrespective of the weather. She was likely to run across the snow, roll in it, "speak in tongues," or imitate the sounds of animals. Bizarre actions and superhuman strength were typical, and while property might be damaged, other people never were harmed. Afterwards the victim was exhausted and might sleep for a long time, not remembering the attack or her actions at a later time. The response of observers to attacks, which were reported as frequent, was one of mild interest but no great concern. In fact, pibloktoq was considered normal and even expectable.

The cause or causes of pibloktoq have been pondered for many years. The reason most often cited has been the severe strain caused by the arctic climate with its long, cold, and dark winters. Yet ethnographic evidence suggests that Polar Eskimos did not regard the winters as oppressive; quite to the contrary, they looked forward to them with anticipation. Furthermore, attacks occurred throughout the year. One related explanation rests on the stresses associated with their life-style. The fear of starvation or death of oneself or of a close relative, or some other culturally common source of anxiety, often precipitated attacks. Another suggestion is that pibloktoq had a physiological basis and was caused by vitamin and mineral deficiencies, especially of calcium. Thus far the pertinent studies have proved inconclusive and the cause remains elusive.

Beliefs about supernaturals were similar to those described for West Greenlanders. The focus was on spirits controlled by shamans, and numerous persons had supernatural power. Constraints on the activities of individuals were relatively few; the Polar Eskimos had great personal freedom, albeit the females had considerably less than the males. The feeling of unity among kindred, which included the entire tribe, was reflected in many ways. Families visited one another frequently and for long periods of time. They shared food not only with persons in their hamlet but also with those from other settlements. The right to local resources or to an unoccupied dwelling belonged to everyone on an equal basis. Personal property consisted only of clothing, weapons, tools, and utensils, and when a person died, his or her belongings were placed next to the stone-covered grave.

Clements R. Markham, a midshipman on the *Assistance* during the Franklin searches in 1850-1, made one of the first attempts to establish Polar Eskimo ties with other peoples. In 1865 and 1866 he argued that their language was similar to that spoken by all other Eskimos and unrelated to American Indian languages. He went on to maintain that the Polar Eskimos, or Arctic Highlanders as he preferred to call them, were culturally distinct from other Eskimos. The absences of the kayak, bow and arrow, and snowhouses among the Polar Eskimos were significant differences he cited, and to this list he might have added the umiak and fishing equipment. However, the Polar Eskimos shared so many core features of Eskimo culture that they really could not be classed separately. Their extreme dependence on specialized ice hunting methods had resulted in the loss of artifact types commonly used by other Eskimos and gave their lifeway its somewhat distinctive cast.

The most notable aspect of the Polar Eskimo economy was its extreme dependence on sea mammals taken on sea ice; the only important food source from the land was the population of cliff birds. This adaptation had a striking effect on the food-getting technology. The only weapons were a harpoon, knife, and lance; the only facilities were a pole net for taking birds and possibly traps for foxes and hares. How strange it is that the Polar people did not hunt the caribou reported by early explorers as present and even plentiful. Their ancestors had used bows and arrows, which are highly effective against caribou, but the form had passed from existence. It seems that these people soon would have died out if they had continued to live as they were in the early 1800s, especially since accidental death was reasonably common and homicide not infrequent. They may have been saved from extinction by

Eskimo migrants from Canada who reintroduced forgotten artifacts, thereby adding greater versatility to the food quest. Their
food-getting specialization sustained them, but it reduced their
variability and flexibility to a point that their existence was precarious. We may praise the adaptive perfection of their technology
and at the same time recognize that left alone it might have led to
their doom.

NOTES

FRANKLIN SEARCH EXPEDITIONS.   Jeannette Mirsky's book (1934, 1970) is
an accessible source that summarizes the last voyage of John Franklin and
subsequent rescue efforts; for a detailed account the study by Leslie H.
Neatby (1970) should be consulted. Mirsky (1970, 322-4) also lists all
search parties. The most detailed report of Franklin's last voyage is by
Richard J. Cyriax (1939); G. F. Lamb (1956) wrote a useful biography about
Franklin.

KANE'S LIFE AND ADVENTURES.   Kane (1854) in his book about the First
Grinnell Expedition does not add to our knowledge about Eskimos, but
his two-volume work concerning the Second Grinnell Expedition (Kane,
1856) includes more information about the Polar Eskimos than had any
previous source. Biographies about Kane were written by William Elder
(1858), Mirsky (1954), and George W. Corner (1972); the latter source was
consulted for most of the information about Kane's life.

PRIMARY ETHNOGRAPHIC SOURCES.   The standard works are by Erik
Holtved (1967) based on fieldwork in 1935-7 and 1946-7 and by Alfred L.
Kroeber (1900) based on a literature search, interviews with Polar Eskimos
taken to New York by Robert E. Peary in 1897-8, and artifacts collected by
Peary. A major difficulty with these sources is that they do not specify
which artifacts were introduced by Canadian Eskimos or were brought
from south Greenland, after about 1850. These accounts do not represent
aboriginal conditions as they existed at the times of Ross (1818), Kane
(1853-5), or to a lesser extent Hayes (1860-1). The spiral dome-shaped
snowhouses may not have existed in aboriginal times (see Holtved, 1967,
31), but Knud Rasmussen (1908, 23-6) recorded in a tale about migrants
from Canada a statement that the Polar Eskimos built snowhouses, of a
form without cold traps and long tunnels (p. 32). On the same page, the
Canadian Eskimos are credited with the introduction of the bow and
arrow, leister, and kayak; they may have introduced the open-water
sealing harpoon.

SECONDARY ETHNOGRAPHIC ACCOUNTS.   Supplementary material is drawn from the writings of Emil Bessels (1884), Josephine Diebitsch-Peary (1894), Clements R. Markham (1865, 1866), Robert E. Peary (1907, 1910, 1914), Knud Rasmussen (1908, n.d.) and James W. VanStone (1972b). Few useful data are included in the report by C. H. Davis (1876) based on first-hand accounts by members of the expedition led by Charles F. Hall in 1871.

CENSUS DATA. Kane (1856, v. 2, 108) gave the figure of about 140 persons for 1853-5 and added that "there are more, perhaps, but certainly not many." Elsewhere Kane (1856, v. 2, 211) wrote that there were 140, "exactly confirmed by three separate informants." For 1860-1, Isaac Hayes (1867, 386, 431) reported about 100 persons. Emil Bessels (1884, 863) wrote that he saw 102 persons in 1871-3 but doubted that there were as many as 10 others, although a separate account from the same expedition (Davis, 1876, 483) cited the figure of about 150. In 1895 Peary (1914, v. 1, 511-4) counted 253 persons, 140 males and 113 females.

POLAR ESKIMO CONTACTS WITH OTHER ESKIMOS. According to Polar Eskimo tradition Eskimos once had lived north and south of Smith Sound, but they became separated by glacial ice, presumably when it reached the sea (Hayes, 1867, 384-5). In the official report of the *Polaris* expedition organized by Hall in 1871, the editor C. H. Davis (1876, 451) reported that near Etah in 1872 the expedition members met Canadian Eskimos who had arrived four or five years earlier by umiak and kayak; they had brought with them the bow and arrow. Hendrik (1878, 33) reported that according to Polar Eskimo lore their ancestors had traded walrus ivory for wood at Upernivik, and they still referred to more southerly Eskimos in Greenland as "Southlanders." The migrants from Baffin Island are mentioned or discussed by several observers, including Peary (1914, v. 1, 488-9) and Rasmussen (1908, 23-6). A detailed analysis of the last migration of Canadian Eskimos to northwest Greenland was written by Robert Petersen (1962).

HANS C. HENDRIK. The autobiographical account by Hendrik was translated from Eskimo by Henry Rink and appeared in 1878. Ethnographic information is nearly nonexistent in Hendrik's book, but he did mention that the Polar Eskimos had four different kinds of fox traps and captured hares in nets made from thongs (Hendrik, 1878, 35). These details appear to have escaped other early observers.

Hendrik's most remarkable adventure with white explorers was as a member of the Polaris Expedition (1871-3) under the command of Hall, who died late in 1871 under strange circumstances (*see* Chauncey C. Loomis, 1971). The following spring, when the *Polaris* was in grave danger of being crushed by ice, boats and food were placed on the ice. At this point, on October 15, 1872, the ship suddenly drifted off, leaving Hendrik, his wife and 4 children, another Eskimo and his wife and daughter, and

10 persons from the *Polaris* on the ice. After drifting about 1500 miles they were rescued nearly six months later off southern Labrador. They had stayed alive by killing seals and burning the oil in lamps. After their rescue, they were taken to the United States, and the Hendriks finally were returned to West Greenland.

PIBLOKTOQ.   The monograph about arctic hysterias by Edward F. Foulks (1972) and an article by Zachary Gussow (1960) include extended quotations from persons who had witnessed pibloktoq attacks. Explicit reports about cases among the Polar Eskimos appear to date from around 1900 and later; it is curious that neither Kane nor Hayes recorded instances. Foulks made a field study of pibloktoq in northern Alaska in 1969-70, but the people he studied had abandoned their aboriginal life-style long ago. Foulks (1972, 114) found that hysterias still existed and concluded "that abnormalities in the physiological functioning of calcium are capable of producing a variety of mental disorders including hysteria-like behavior."

DETAILS.   In their comparative study of North American Indians, Harold E. Driver and William C. Massey (1957, 345) report that only the Polar Eskimos cold-hammered meteoritic iron into blades. Dennis Rawlins (1970) reviews the evidence for Peary's claim of having reached the North Pole and rejects it. A less convincing recent article supporting Peary's claim was written by Guy R. L. Potter (1970).

CHAPTER

6

East Greenlanders

East Greenland was unfamiliar to early explorers because great masses of ice drifted southward along the coast from the polar sea to create a nearly impenetrable barrier for their ships. The medieval Norse skirted the region in their search for a hospitable land. When Danish-Norwegian colonization began in 1721, the area of interest was southwest Greenland. Within 50 years outposts were founded along the west coast, but the east coast was a vast region that had not yielded to exploration. The 1800s brought the first successful effort to penetrate the ice-choked area.

A modest but eminently practical plan to explore east Greenland was formulated by Wilhelm A. Graah in 1828. Under the authority of Graah, a lieutenant in the Danish Royal Navy, umiaks and kayaks left Julianehaab on the southwest coast, rounded Cape Farewell, and ventured north in 1829. Geographical discovery was the primary purpose, but to find traces of early Norse colonists also was a major concern. Fortunately Graah was able to hire a guide who had come from the east to trade, and in late March 1829 they set forth. The main party included 4 Danish men, 5 Eskimo men, and 10 Eskimo women hired to row the umiaks. In addition a number of kayakers were recruited to reconnoiter ice conditions

Figure 6-1 Greenlandic women rowing an umiak as another steers with a paddle. (From Graah, 1932)

and to hunt. After several delays the boats rounded Cape Farewell and landed on a small island where great masses of sea ice surrounded them, causing nearly a month's delay. When the umiaks were launched again, they nearly were crushed by ice before they could reach open water and hoist their sails for the first time. Adverse ice conditions soon caused a three-week delay and then a second delay of more than two weeks. By mid-June the travelers were only about 125 miles north of Cape Farewell, and the provisions were being depleted at an alarming rate. Graah decided to send most of the men back in one of the umiaks. With his guide, female crew, and one kayaker he ventured from one village to the next. He found that no one had heard of Norse settlements or runic stones, nor had any of these Eskimos seen a ship. At Kemisak he was able to replace two of his rowers, who had burdensome children, with three unmarried girls who willingly accompanied him in return for beads and kerchiefs.

When Graah approached the community of Kemisak, young and old alike helped beach the umiak and carry supplies ashore. Very few of the 100 villagers had ever seen a European, which meant that he was at the southern fringe of the unknown. The old people were especially forward and inquisitive. When Graah felt overwhelmed by the barrage of questions and the persistent inspection of his possessions, he fired a gun in the air to disperse the crowd, at least temporarily. As the journey continued, Graah was awed by the size and appearance of the icebergs. Some glittered like silver in the sun, and others seemed to be hills of marble. He now understood why mariners mistook some bergs for land. By the wait and rush technique the voyagers managed to reach what are now known as the Graah Islands, but in mid-August they were turned back by impenetrable masses of ice. In addition, the seas were increasingly unsettled, and his oarswomen, while not openly mutinous, did not wish to continue. By early October they had turned back to Nukarbik, where he planned to winter. On the trip north arrangements were made for the construction of a winter house, but it had not been completed. With winter at hand, they improvised as best they could and moved in at the end of the month. The house was divided into three compartments, one for Graah and the other two for his rowers. His remaining kayaker was the "gallant" of one rower.

For the next five months Nukarbik was their humble home, and the women settled down to their routine. They "laughed, cried, jested, scolded, arranged their beads, put on and took off their finery, and ever and anon anointed their hair with their urinary unguent." Graah passed his time learning the language and preparing charts of areas he had mapped, while his kayaker was content to beat a drum and sing one song after another day after day (Figure 6-2). When Graah was traveling, his account stressed human and navigational trials of the journey, but when he settled at Nukarbik, he described the people at length and included informative accounts of specific episodes.

About 500 Eastlanders lived along the explored section of coast, and Graah vividly conveyed the privation that they faced. In the fall of 1829 little food was on hand, and the people of Nukarbik faced a bleak winter. Graah offered to buy anything edible at any price but obtained practically no food. For these Eskimos life and death hinged largely on the harvest of seals. They were the prime source of meat, and their blubber was the fuel for lamps used not only to cook food but to provide light and heat. Sealskins were essential for clothing, as were intestines for windows, sinews for thread, and bones for artifacts. By January 1830 adverse ice and weather conditions made seal hunting impossible. In February the visitors and villagers had eaten the last rotten seal meat and began eating skins that had been saved for boat and tent covers. At this

Figure 6-2 In Graah's winter quarters at Nukarbik. The kayaker performs as his lady friend cooks a meal and the rower without a lover sulks. (From Graah, 1932)

point most Nukarbik people sledded to neighboring communities in the hope of obtaining food.

The marginal existence of East Greenlanders was poignantly described by Graah. Just before his arrival at Nukarbik, over 100 persons had left the southeastern sector for a Moravian mission on the west coast; many other Eastlanders planned to forsake their homeland as soon as possible. In the recent past people were murdered and eaten in times of privation, and when Graah saw few old people along the coast, he suspected that most of them had been killed for food. In spite of the specter of starvation, to beg for food was disgraceful. These were an immensely proud people who valued their independence above all else. Adult males answered to no one and commanded no other men. Children learned self-sufficiency early, and even as infants they might scratch or hit their parents without fear of punishment. Boys especially were indulged because as adults they would be the only insurance of their aged parents against privation. As soon as a male child could "creep about alone," his father made him a spear and taught him how to use it. A youth was given a kayak, and when he killed his first seal, a feast was held to honor him and acknowledge his new status as a marriageable male.

From a later report by Gustav Holm about this area we learn that one settlement consisted of 21 people; 5 were males, and the 16 females were mostly children. With this sexual imbalance some girls were trained as hunters. One woman of about 20 hunted in a kayak but was even more skilled at ice hunting. She and other females who assumed the male role dressed and were treated as men. Here is an excellent example of flexibility in Eskimo culture and a clear illustration that women were as capable as men of becoming specialized sea-mammal hunters and supporting the group.

Graah was attentive to details. He noted, for example, that if a man borrowed hunting equipment and something happened to it, the borrower was not responsible provided the damage or destruction was accidental. Yet a careless borrower was obligated to make good the loss. We also learn that when a man died, his tent and umiak went to the eldest son if that person was a responsible adult. Everything else was divided by the widow and younger sons; daughters received nothing. When a girl married, her only possessions were clothing and possibly a few tools and utensils.

Instead of discussing attitudes and beliefs in the abstract, Graah described actual events at length, thereby conveying the values of these people as they affected daily life. The most dramatic episode began to unfold in early December. A man at Nukarbik accidentally cut himself severely above the wrist, and after binding the wound, he continued to work as usual. Before long the arm swelled, and a large, extremely painful tumor formed. Graah applied a gum plaster to the wound but feared that he would be held responsible if the man died. The following day the man's wife, the only rational person in the house, held the delirious patient in her arms. His friends sobbed and cried as the children squalled. In the absence of more appropriate medication Graah gave him a mixture of wine and lemon juice, and when he felt somewhat better the victim tore off the gum plaster. For the next three weeks the man suffered horribly, and a woman seer was consulted about the case. She raised the man's head by means of a cord fastened around it, and when the head proved "heavy," she announced that he would die. The patient refused all offers of food to shorten his period of misery, and since everyone had accepted his decision to die, the wife grew angry when Graah brought him food. Later the wound opened, and as blood gushed from it, all the people in the house cried, shrieked, and threw everything portable out of the house so that the possessions would not be tainted by death. The hemorrhaging man was determined that his son throw him into the sea, but his wife tried to convince him that being buried alive in the snow was preferable. Finally the blood ceased to flow, and the man went into convulsions. A few hours later he regained his senses, and before long he was eating, only to have a relapse and a repetition of the near-death scene, but with a difference. When his wife began to arrange his burial clothing, the patient, who was fully conscious of what these preparations meant, fainted. The skin shroud was ready and the window open for removing his body. At this juncture he regained consciousness and told them to stop since he felt better. He gradually recovered his strength, and he was still alive seven months later when Graah saw him last. An account such as this reveals far more about Eastlander life and death than could be conveyed by a host of generalizations.

Graah wintered along the east coast so that he could make another assault on the ice farther north during the following summer, but he was unable to reach as far as he had the previous year. His travels among the Eastlanders did not add a great deal to the understanding of Eskimos, but he did obtain new data and demonstrated the feasibility for a lone European to live among these people along an unknown fringe of the arctic. Nearly 50 years would pass before another attempt was made to penetrate farther north than Graah had gone, and this trip led to the discovery of a new group of Eskimos.

*   *   *

In 1883 Captain Gustav Holm of the Danish Navy was instructed to explore the east coast north to the vicinity of 66° latitude and, if possible, to find evidence of early Norse colonists. Eastlanders visiting the west coast reported that far to the north was a place called Angmagsalik and people from there once had visited southwest Greenland. Holm felt that by traveling in umiaks with Eskimo guides he could reach Angmagsalik. The first summer, 1883, the Holm party provisioned a depot along the east coast. In May 1884 they started for Angmagsalik, but about halfway there most of the party turned back. Holm and 10 others reached their destination toward the end of August.

When the Holm party arrived at Angmagsalik, the people kept their distance and gazed in amazement, without offering to help unload the boats, an indication that the visitors were not entirely welcome. Some said, "It must surely be a dream that I should see *Kavdlunaks*" or Europeans. Their astonishment was tempered because they had heard shamans tell of seeing strange things in supernatural realms, yet ordinary people were now experiencing a wondrous event. The Eastlanders were not afraid after they realized that some of the people with Holm were Angmagsalik Eskimos who had met him in the south and had guided his northward journey. Eskimos in surrounding communities soon learned about the newcomers and brought gifts for them. Holm wrote, "The mutual hospitality of the natives knows no bounds. It is not counted as a virtue by them, but as a stern duty."

During Holm's early months at Angmagsalik, the people refused to answer questions about any previous visits by whites. They thought that their ancestors had burned a European house, and they feared revenge. This belief apparently arose from the Eskimo destruction of Norse settlements in southwest Greenland. In the years immediately preceding the arrival of Holm strange artifacts had washed ashore, and shamans had predicted that Europeans would appear. A clever shaman insisted to Holm that a few years earlier he had helped Europeans travel south after their umiak was destroyed. They reportedly had promised that when Europeans returned he would be rewarded. These Eskimos were astounded by all the undreamed-of artifacts owned by the Holm party, and they could not resist inspecting everything with care; each person sought a personal explanation about the novel forms. Tobacco was the most popular trade item because some Eastlanders had learned to take snuff in the west and they told of its benefits. Everyone soon acquired a craving for snuff, especially when they were hungry or tired. After tobacco they desired cloth for garments because fur clothing was hot during the summer and bulky, especially when traveling by boat.

For these Eskimos the world's creation, mythology, and history all focused where they lived. They thought Greenland was an island, but beyond that they concerned themselves very little with their origins or history. The people living along the east and west coasts of south Greenland were known to them, and they thought the interior glacial ice was inhabited by supernatural beings, including a group called the "Ingaliliks." Ethnologists have reasoned that these mythological inlanders represented the Indian enemies known to them when they lived in Alaska and Canada before migrating to Greenland. Eskimos along the Alaskan Bering Sea coast call one group of adjacent Indians "Ingalik."

The steep and rocky Angmagsalik coastline is deeply indented with fjords, and mountains lead to the inland ice. Numerous glaciers feed into the sea, and the coastal region includes a host of islands. Few spots suitable for habitation are found along the coast or among the islands. Heaths and mosses are the predominant plant cover, and sheltered localities support growths of dwarf birch and willows. Terrestrial plants were unimportant foods, but foxes, polar bears, and ptarmigan could be hunted seasonally on the land. Caribou, hares, and musk-oxen were locally extinct, but aquatic resources were diverse. Human survival depended too on the conditions with respect to *storis* or drift ice. The coast was relatively ice-free from September until massive floes from the polar sea froze along the shore in November and winter ice formed in the fjords. This coastal ice often broke free and drifted back and forth during violent storms, sometimes leaving a band of open water between the land and the pack ice. However, when the storis pressed into the fjords and froze in place, hunting was impossible and starvation predictable. Seal harvests were essential for human survival, with fish and sea birds necessary supplements. The most important fish was the small but abundant capelin. The pack ice brought driftwood and other debris from the other side of the top of the world, and on rare occasions an entire ship drifting by provided a wealth of materials.

In 1884 the Angmagsalik Eskimos numbered 413, and they lived in three settlement clusters. Each community consisted of one large rectangular dwelling that housed from 12 to 58 people. A stone and turf house designed to accommodate many resident families was about 14 feet wide and up to 50 feet in length. At the center of one long side was a low tunnel that joined the house below the floor level and thus served to trap cold air. Along this side of a house were three openings for translucent gut windows; narrow platforms beneath the windows were built for young males, unmarried men, and guests. The rear wall, facing the tun-

Figure 6-3 An interior portion of a house as sketched by an Angmagsalik Eskimo. Lying beneath a sealskin, a shaman is consulting a familiar spirit in an attempt to cure an ill person in an adjacent compartment. In front of each compartment a cooking pot and a drying rack are suspended over a lamp set on a platform. (From Thalbitzer, 1941; redrawn by Patrick Finnerty)

nel, was dominated by a six-foot-wide bench, with skin curtains hung at intervals to separate family living areas. A four-foot length of bench was sufficient for a man, two wives, and six children. Each wife had a blubber-burning lamp of stone on a stone platform at one side of the family compartment, and a drying rack hung above each lamp (Figure 6-3). The low roof was supported by a ridgepole atop vertical posts and was covered with driftwood, sod, dirt, and finally old skins held in place with stones. Among the most important household furnishings were water tubs, cooking pots, eating utensils, and urine containers. Lamps burned continually, not only cooking the food but making the low-roofed houses very hot.

In the summer and early fall closely related families lived in skin-covered tents and boated from one locality to another hunting seals and fishing for arctic char or capelin (Figure 6-4). Families sometimes ranged north or south on extended hunting trips that might last a year or two. When they traveled afar and were forced to build a winter house in the late fall, it was small, made from stone, and weatherproofed with a cover of snow.

Tattoos were popular among women. This may seem surprising for a fur-clad people, but much of a woman's life was spent in a house or tent where her only garment was a small pubic apron. Shortly before puberty a girl was tattooed by her mother. Tattoos

Figure 6-4 An Angmagsalik Eskimo drawing of summer tents between cliffs, kayakers, and women rowing umiaks. (From Thalbitzer, 1941; redrawn and rearranged by Patrick Finnerty)

were pleasing to look at, and it was thought that the designs somehow made their owner more skillful at domestic tasks and protected her from evil. Lines were made by sewing through the skin with soot-covered thread; most women had a vertical line just below the root of the nose and others across the bridge of the nose and on the chin. Additional patterns of dots and lines often adorned their arms, breasts, and lower legs. Out-of-door clothing for women included short pants and boots that reached the knees. In cold weather a woman's thighs were protected by wrappings of skin. She wore a short parka, with the hair facing in, beneath a second parka of the same cut with the hair outward; women with small children had large pouches in the backs of their parkas. In most respects the clothing of men was similar to that of women. A man customarily wore short drawers, even in cold weather, but when hunting he put on knee-length breeches and boots. A man's summer parka was hip length with the hair facing in; for cold weather a second parka was worn with the hair facing out. When it was cold or stormy, a kayaker wore an overparka made from intestines.

Summer travel by families was in wide, flat-bottomed umiaks rowed, not paddled, by women. A woman often steered an umiak with a paddle while the man of the household paddled along in his kayak. Sails were unknown among these people. Winter travel was by short wooden sleds with pegged-on bone runners and upstanders. Three to eight dogs pulled a sled and were guided by a thong whip flicked precisely at an ear or flank of a laggard. The fan-hitch trace lines were of nearly equal length, but knowledge-able animals were put on somewhat longer traces. When a sled stopped, a paw of each dog was wedged in its harness to prevent the team from running off with it. During the summer dogs fended for themselves on unoccupied islands; when food was scarce dogs were killed and eaten.

Seals, as an essential staple, were most successfully hunted from kayaks. One of the two similar types of open-water sealing har-poons is termed a "feather" harpoon because basal projections have the appearance of feathers. A sophisticated weapon such as this had many different kinds of parts. As was indicated pre-viously, most Eskimo harpoons are complicated weapons, and the ones made at Angmagsalik were among the most complex. Appar-ently their open-water sealing harpoons were highly developed because they depended heavily on harvesting seals from kayaks. Thus specialized sealing weapons were a highly adaptive techno-logical response to a food-getting situation.

The complexity of the feather harpoon is more fully appreciated after its most important parts are detailed (Figure 6-5). The stone blade (a) is pegged to the bone harpoon head (b), which has a hole at the base for receiving the ivory foreshaft (c) that fits into a hole in a short bone socketpiece (d) at the end of the wooden shaft (e). The foreshaft is held to the shaft with thongs. The throwing-board (f) is attached to the shaft by two pegs (g), and two bone "feathers" (h) at the base of the shaft serve as counterweights to the heavy

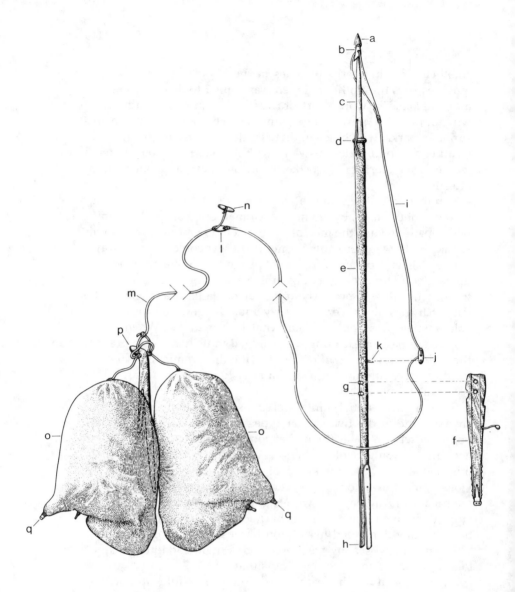

Figure 6-5 Angmagsalik toggle-headed "feather" harpoon and throwing-board for hunting large seals from a kayak. (Drawn by Patrick Finnerty)

forward end. The harpoon line (i) passes through a hole in the harpoon head and extends to a bone clasp (j) with a hole in it that fits over a tension peg (k) on the shaft; the clasp-peg arrangement on the line is designed to hold the head in place. The line extends to another bone clasp (l) to which the float line (m) is attached by a toggle (n). The double sealskin floats (o) are attached to a wooden fork (p), one prong of which fits beneath a strap behind the kayak manhole. The floats are inflated through bone nozzles (q) and plugged with wooden stoppers.

The head of a feather harpoon was attached to about 40 feet of line coiled in a special holder fastened in front of the kayak manhole (Figure 6-6). As a harpoon was hurled, the line uncoiled from the holder, and as soon as a seal was struck the kayaker pulled the floats free and tossed them overboard. The floats were so buoyant that a seal could not pull them beneath the water, and the hunter followed the floats until the seal surfaced. He launched a retrievable lance repeatedly to inflict additional wounds until the seal could be killed with a knife or small lance. Seals also were hunted on the ice at their breathing holes, by the peep technique, and stalked as they sunned themselves in the spring by using essentially the same techniques as those found in West Greenland.

Fish probably were second in importance as food. During the winter large holes were cut in the ice and baited with blubber and bloody meat to lure sharks. The sharks were harpooned at night when they surfaced and remained motionless at these openings. In the summer arctic char were taken with leisters at stone weirs in rivers or with special double-headed toggle harpoons at holes in river ice. In the early summer capelin were abundant in some

Figure 6-6 A hunter launching a "feather" sealing harpoon. (Drawn by Patrick Finnerty)

localities and were dipped from the water in large scoops by people in umiaks.

Angmagsalik Eskimos did not have a sense of tribal identity; quite to the contrary, people in adjacent hamlets were mutually antagonistic, although in face-to-face situations they were courteous and hospitable. They contrasted with most other Eskimos in having one communal dwelling per hamlet. Angmagsalik housemates were expected to extend mutual aid in the same manner that they would to blood relatives. Social cohesion prevailed because most people respected customary law, in which the first tenet was that everyone cooperate throughout the year in subsistence activities. The titular head of a dwelling was an older and respected hunter who allotted space to families and could refuse to accept persons as new housemates. He also decided when festivities were held and when people would move into tents during the summer or return in the fall.

The most approved means for dealing with antisocial behavior was to do or say nothing. To make fun of someone was the next step, and if this was not effective the antagonists usually turned to songs of ridicule. Dueling songs composed by adversaries were sung over long periods of time, often for years. The duelists, women or men, visited one another after they had composed and practiced new songs of contempt. They stood facing each other in the open before an audience. Real offenses were exaggerated, the sins of ancestors recounted, and accusations made about uncommitted crimes. Male opponents might strike each other on the forehead during an exchange and mock one another, to the delight of the audience. In at least some exchanges it appears that a duelist who outlived his opposite was the winner.

Alternatives to song duels included stealing from a rival, destroying his property, or harming him by sorcery. The ultimate act of hostility was to openly murder the enemy, and the homicide rate was high considering the small population. If everyone agreed that a person had been truly evil, his murder was not avenged. In most cases of homicide the son or a close relative of the victim was expected to take revenge by killing the original murderer. This form of retribution, however, was less feared than the revenge sought by the victim's soul, especially if the corpse was intact when buried or cast into the sea. One means to prevent soul revenge was to cut up the body in the same way that a seal is butchered and distribute the pieces in different places. Alternatively the dead person might be scalped and the body sunk into the sea. The scalp was kept as a trophy and later produced as evidence of the murder. Women often were said to be the reason behind a murder. In one example a woman was lazy and unfaithful to her husband, who beat her. She had a son by a previous marriage who went hunting with his stepfather and his cousin. First the stepson and then the cousin harpooned the man and sank his kayak. The son acted to protect his mother, and the cousin cooperated from fear.

With the high mortality rate, infanticide was practiced only under extenuating circumstances. When the mother of a nursing child died, the live baby was buried with her if there was no one to care for it. Suicide was not uncommon among these people. One girl was so ashamed after her husband, a shaman, took her mother as an additional wife that she drowned herself. The aged or diseased were those most likely to throw themselves into the sea, the customary means of suicide.

A prevailing opinion holds that Eskimos were "communistic" or at least lacking in a strong sense of private ownership. This view is partially substantiated among the Angmagsalik since hamlet residents lived in a common dwelling and shared their food. Each person was free to exploit natural resources as an individual, however. A hunter who located a polar bear or a seal's breathing hole was its "owner" by right of discovery, although he would distribute his kill among relatives following an accepted pattern. Traps set for animals were individually owned; in fact, a strong sense of private property existed for any artifacts that protected people or were used to make a living. A man made and owned a kayak and umiak, his tool kit and weapons, plus his clothing sewn by his wife. A woman owned her clothes, sewing equipment, skin bags, and other clearly personal belongings, but people rarely owned more artifacts than they actually used. Like most Eskimos they felt that possessions had a spirit essence or soul, possibly even a part of the owner's soul, which is a far more personal concept of property than that prevailing among Euro-Americans. They felt that to barter, lose, or have something stolen was to give up a bit of oneself, and this also applied to game killed. Thus when the Danes bought a seal, the owner usually cut off and kept a small piece in an effort not to offend the soul of the animal. Personal

property intimately associated with an individual during life became grave goods when he or she died.

Ownership applied also to certain kinds of information that were
revealed only for a fee. Among males the only organized body of
knowledge freely conveyed from one generation to the next was a
father's instructions to his son about the basic skills of hunting and
kayaking. Specialized training was provided by different persons,
each recognized as an authority on a particular topic. One man
listed seven major categories of specialized knowledge: hunting,
kayaking, feats of strength, drum singing, magic prayers, witch-
craft, and shamanistic practices. Each included subdivisions; for
example, hunting instructions were for specific species and were
offered by the persons most adept at taking them. It appears that
the teacher always was an older person, and he usually offered
individual instruction. A tyro might have numerous instructors
about the same subject, especially for dealing with the supernatural, and pupils compensated their teachers in proportion to
the value placed on the information. The longest period of instruction was in shamanistic skills, and it spanned years.

A young hunter first learned to kill land species and then seals
on sea ice before hunting from a kayak. By age 12 a youth had a
kayak of his own and began acquiring skill as a hunter at sea.
Practical instructions, precise rules, and ritual constraints were
integrated in his education. After a boy harpooned his first bearded
seal, his hair was cut for the first time; the seal's claws and the hair
were thrown into the sea.

Precise rules for dividing large sea mammals or polar bears were
observed. When a large seal was harpooned, the first five hunters
who helped to make the kill or who touched the animal before it
was ready to be towed ashore received a captor's share. Even
when a man killed a seal and brought it ashore unaided, only the
breast, head, heart, and skin belonged to him. The remainder was
distributed to relatives in a precise manner; his children received
the entrails, his mother's brother the neck, his wife and children
the loins, and so on, to the tail, which belonged to his wife's
father's father. Alternatives encumbered these allocations. For
example, if a man discovered a bear with a cub, the cub's head
belonged to his child, but if he were childless the discoverer kept
the head. Other requirements pertained to the treatment of the
animal; the killer of a seal smeared its head with urine, and after

three days he threw the skull into the sea.

The life-giving sea was the home of beneficial supernaturals, but on the inland ice lived beings that usually were harmful. The most important spirit of the sea was a woman who had sea mammals in her hair. Spirits controlled by shamans visited her and combed her hair to release seals and narwhals as food for people. The inland ice supported the progeny of the mating between a woman and a dog. These included man-like giants who hunted land animals with bows and arrows in the winter. During the spring they came down to the sea, but since they did not have kayaks, they netted seals or harpooned narwhals from the land. Sometimes they were seen by shamans at this time of the year. These giants occasionally captured people, but they could be friendly, even to the point of exchanging wives with humans. Other supernaturals from the dog-woman mating had upper bodies of human form but lower extremities of dogs; they always were dangerous to people. Still others, of different origin, were called "Ingaliliks"; in their large cooking pots an entire seal could be boiled.

The mating of a young woman and a dog also gave rise to Europeans. This woman rejected one man after another as a husband and finally married a dog. She gave birth to different kinds of progeny that in time were a burden for her parents. Her father placed the woman and her children on an island and paddled there periodically to take them food. Before one visit the woman told her children to eat her father, and on his next visit they consumed him and his kayak. The mother then put the children, who were to become the ancestors of Europeans, in a boot sole and pushed it out to sea, saying, "Your father cannot make anything for you, and so you must learn yourselves to make things." When these children found land, they learned to make houses, iron, and ships, which explains why Europeans returned by ship from across the sea.

These people believed that the essence of a person was embodied in his name and souls. The names of the dead, beginning with that of the last person to die locally, were called out by a mother as she placed a wet finger on the mouth of her newborn. These became the individual's names, but they were never used or even mentioned aloud. The water used by the mother symbolized the sea and food, and the ritual transferred the knowledge of the dead to the newborn. People were called by nicknames, and a person was prohibited from saying his own name. At death a name remained in the body until the naming ritual, when it entered the body of a newborn.

A human soul was thought to have many parts, or perhaps more accurately, multiple souls existed in the body of a person. An individual's well-being depended on the condition of his souls. When someone was sick, a soul was ill; if a soul was lost, the person became ill or would die unless it could be restored by a shaman. For personal protection against potentially harmful spirits or for dispelling sickness and famine, amulets were worn. Women placed them in their hair topknots, men wore them on cords tied about their bodies, and both sexes sewed them to the garments they wore. The tongue of a loon, small wooden carvings of humans, the snout of a fox, or red lichens are examples of amulets used by ordinary people.

Shamans learned to control spirits from practitioners of the previous generation, who usually trained novices in pairs. A pupil went to a lonely spot and rubbed a small stone against a large rock until his arms ached. The process was repeated for three days, and a spirit finally emerged from the rock. When the spirit appeared, the seeker of power reportedly died a terrible death and was reborn later in the day with the spirit ready to serve him. The stone-rubbing ritual was repeated time and again over a number of years until an apprentice controlled spirits with many qualities. The most powerful spirit, that of a huge bear, was acquired near the end of his training. The bear reportedly swallowed the shaman and vomited forth one bone at a time; his skeleton then articulated and his flesh came back to life. The individual spirits of shamans had the capacity to change weather, capture a soul, restore the soul of a sick person, or serve as oracles. At the end of his training period a shaman called forth his varied spirits in a public performance. He later used his powers for the good of mankind. Shamans interceded with spirits of the nether world in public performances only during the winter. At times of crisis during the summer they went into a trance and communicated with a spirit after being covered with a skin. Ceremonies were not held on a calendrical basis, and masks, said to have been used to frighten children, were nearly unknown among them. Thus the more formal ritualistic aspects of religious life with community-wide participation were absent.

0 ⊢———————⊣ 5 cm.
0 ⊢———————⊣ 2 in.

Figure 6-7 Supernatural aids of shamans: *a*, shaman's bear; *b*, tupilak. (From Thalbitzer, 1914; redrawn by Patrick Finnerty)

Persons dealing in misery and death by sorcery, either male or female, possessed varied means to achieve their evil goals. One method of displaced murder was for a sorcerer to fashion human ligaments into a snare and place it around his kneecap, with small human ribs held in place within the cord. By pronouncing a victim's name while he drew the snare tight, the sorcerer was able to cause the person's death. The most powerful weapon of a sorcerer was a *tupilak* (Figure 6-7). A tupilak often was made from parts of animals but also included something that belonged to the potential victim. A male sorcerer might put his parka on backward, with the hood covering his face, sit near a river mouth, and recite a magical formula. The tupilak was placed at the sorcerer's penis where it grew large and then disappeared into the water to bring death or disaster to the victim.

One of the most important functions of a shaman was to establish whether a sorcerer had released a tupilak to harm or kill someone. The shaman's task was to summon a familiar spirit to catch or consume the malevolent force. A shaman could practice the black arts, but if he assumed this dual role, he ran the risk of becoming a wild talker, an indication that he was insane. A mad shaman was bound, gagged, and left to die or thrown into the sea. His escape from death was possible only if he confessed old transgressions and apparently gave assurances that he would abstain from sorcery.

Tension and uncertainty appear to have loomed large in Angmagsalik life. The sense of harmony and the joy of living associated with most Eskimos were not absent but were far less apparent. Accidental death, trauma, hunger, the fear of hunger, and starvation were specters from which relief was illusionary. When men were unable to hunt, they appear to have devoted a great deal of time to making or embellishing artifacts in ways unrelated to utilitarian needs. Small carvings of animals or people were common, and low-relief figures frequently adorned manufactures. Bone or ivory carvings often were pegged to wooden vessels and to the wooden eyeshades of hunters (Figure 6-8). Stylized carvings occur of animals, people, and less often of mythological creatures, with seals dominating. The most common geometric form was an oval figure, a shape almost certainly derived from the outline of a seal. Women shared in this artistic tradition by using strips of skin in contrasting colors to elaborately decorate skin bags

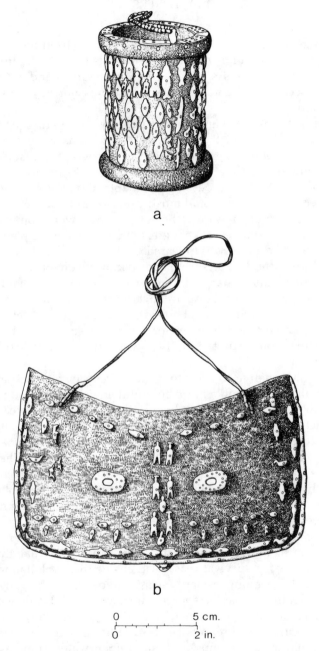

a

b

| 0 | | | | | 5 cm. |
| 0 | | | | 2 in. |

Figure 6-8 Wooden drinking cup, *a*, and eyeshade, *b*, with bone or ivory figures attached. (From Thalbitzer, 1914; redrawn by Patrick Finnerty)

with geometric patterns or less often with stylized figures of people. Among Eskimos no similar emphasis on relief figures adorning utilitarian forms is found elsewhere in Greenland or Canada; it does occur again among Alaskan Eskimos but in a less stylized fashion.

Angmagsalik Eskimos are especially fascinating because so many details about their aboriginal conditions were recorded by Holm and others. Furthermore, their geographical isolation and the limited area they were able to exploit make them something of a test case for human ecological adaptability. As was mentioned earlier, caribou, hares, and musk-oxen were extinct before contact, and we do not know whether or not they were abundant originally. Tradition records that great whales once were plentiful, but they too had nearly disappeared by 1884. Men said that caribou, musk-oxen, and whales were gone because women were jealous of their husbands for having intercourse with the wives of other men. Women, however, appear to have felt that the situation resulted from the fact that men cohabited so frequently with other men's wives. These rationalizations for depleted resources probably were not very comforting, but they were an effort to explain the situation.

One alternative to accepting the scarcity of food around Angmagsalik was to find a more bountiful environment. Judging from Graah's description of conditions to the south, this area held no attraction for Angmagsalik Eskimos. Their only other alternative was to range north, and they were familiar with the coastline in that direction as far as about 250 miles. Although families sometimes traveled north for a summer or winter, no one lived permanently in that sector, and transients sometimes starved there. Thus there was no accessible region known to them in aboriginal times where they might live more fruitfully.

The local scarcity of land-dwelling species, the lean areas north and south, and the great inland ice cap meant that their only alternative for survival was to intensify the exploitation of sea mammals, meaning primarily seals. It appears that hunting seals at their breathing holes was largely unrewarding, and they could be taken as they basked on the ice only during a relatively brief period in the spring. The reports seem to indicate that most seals were harvested in the summer and fall in open water from kayaks. To appreciate the magnitude of the difficulties faced by hunters from kayaks, this method is compared with the land hunting techniques practiced by most aboriginal hunters, including Eskimos elsewhere.

Hunting by its nature means to seek out, to find, and to kill. In obtaining a solitary land-dwelling animal such as the arctic hare, this means to sight the animal, which may require considerable skill, stalk or pursue it, and then use a weapon to take it. The escape capacity of a hare is limited to concealing itself or running away. In either case it may be tracked, and it can run only where a hunter can walk. Gregarious land animals such as caribou, less capable of concealment because of their size and number, may be driven as well as stalked. For caribou and hares alike the only escape dimension through movement is across the landscape. The contrast between hunting on land and in water obviously is great. The sea hunter must own a vessel that can be maneuvered in heavy seas, and the boatman must possess special skills just to pursue his quarry. Furthermore, after a hunter sights a seal and positions himself to launch a weapon, his target is elusive because it surfaces only briefly for a breath before diving. Even after a weapon is launched and strikes home, the seal attempts to escape by swimming back and forth as well as up and down, making close pursuit difficult. The cultural response of Eskimos, and many other people, was to develop drags to impede the seal's escape and to indicate its movements. Although a harpoon wounds and restrains an animal, another weapon usually is required to make the kill. Even this brief contrast between land and sea hunting points up the intensity of the survival problem faced by the Angmagsalik. In the absence of substantial food resources on the land they had no realistic means for survival except as specialized seal hunters.

Despite the sophistication of their sealing harpoons, the extinction of the Angmagsalik appears to have been near at hand had not the Europeans appeared. When Holm arrived in 1884, the regional population was 413. In the two preceding years an estimated 16 percent of the people had died. When the Danes began exercising local control in 1892, the population was only 293; 118 persons had migrated to southwest Greenland in 1891. Starvation or suicides resulting from food scarcity accounted for most deaths in eastern Greenland. In addition hunters often died in kayaking accidents; three such deaths were noted during Holm's stay in 1884-5.

To explain the decline of the Angmagsalik in terms of the over-exploitation of seals is tempting and possibly valid. Yet this may not have been the case, although the evidence is not the best. We know that when Angmagsalik men dared not hunt in rough seas, a West Greenlander with the Holm party did not hesitate to hunt, killing 40 seals during a winter when Angmagsalik hunters went hungry. They were accustomed to launching their kayaks only in relatively calm weather because some men were unable to right a capsized kayak. Yet West Greenland Eskimos knew of many different ways for righting a kayak. It appears that the Angmagsalik had never acquired the essential—and learnable—techniques to make the best use of their kayaks. This meant that no matter how effective their harpoons might be they often could not be used. The viability of the Angmagsalik may not have rested on the size of the seal population nor on the sophistication of their weaponry but rather on their ability to use to full advantage the equipment available to them. A lack of kayaking skills may have contributed significantly to their near extinction.

NOTES

PRIMARY SOURCES.   The account of travel to the east coast by Wilhelm A. Graah was consulted in the 1837 English edition. The 1932 Danish edition was the source for the illustrations. Almost everything of substance about the aboriginal Angmagsalik Eskimos appears in volumes 39 and 40 of *Meddelelser om Grønland*, edited by William Thalbitzer. Volume 39, which appeared in 1914, includes an English translation of Gustav Holm's report, based on his 1884-5 expedition, that was originally published in 1888-9. The bulk of the text, however, is devoted to descriptions of the material culture collected by Holm, G. Amdrup in 1898-1900, and Thalbitzer in 1905-6. Also included are anthropometric measurements of these Eskimos, excellent demographic data, myths, and linguistic information. The four parts of volume 40, published between 1911 and 1941, are devoted largely to the Angmagsalik language, literary traditions, music, and songs.

SECONDARY SOURCE.   Information about scalping practices and other ritual aspects of murders has been drawn largely from an article by Jens Rosing (1961).

CHAPTER

7

Canadian Inuit

One of the most remarkable aspects of Eskimo culture is that from northern Alaska to Greenland all Eskimos speak similar dialects of the same language. For a single aboriginal language to span such a vast region is unprecedented but it was a reasonable development in this area. Northern Eskimos not only shared a common lifeway but also were great travelers and lived along coasts that posed few barriers to movement by boat or dog team. Their close linguistic ties suggest that Eskimos spread rapidly from one sector of the far north to all others; this they could do because their culture was well fitted to movement into the region. The migration was within the Christian era, and earlier populations, such as the bearers of Dorset culture, were either assimilated by these people or were extinct. The language that spread across northern North America is termed Inupik by its speakers, who usually call themselves Inuit. The distinctive aspects of Greenlandic Eskimo life resulted from their relative isolation after they left the mainland. By contrast the Inuit of Alaska were subject to influences from Asia as well as from other Eskimos and Indians to the south. The Inuit of central Canada, called the Central Eskimos, were spread more widely than any other cluster of tribes that shared a broadly similar

Figure 7-1 An illustration of a European meeting "savages," and the houses of "savages," in the northern Canadian portion of the 1550 world map by Desceliers. (Reproduced by permission of The British Library)

way of life. These Eskimos characteristically ranged long distances by dog team, lived in snowhouses most of the year, and subsisted primarily on seals. The information about them is very uneven. They were encountered early in the east and much later in the west, but most accounts from these contacts are poor. For the core area, reports about some Eskimos are both relatively recent and very good.

Renaissance explorations in eastern Canada effectively began with the 1497 voyage of John Cabot, and in 1501 or 1502 Sebastian Cabot reportedly presented three savage men to the English court of King Henry VII. The captives almost certainly came from coastal Labrador, and the descriptions by Richard Hakluyt may qualify

Figure 7-2 An illustration of pygmies hunting large birds in the northern Canadian portion of the 1550 Desceliers map. (Reproduced by permission of The British Library)

them as Eskimos. The three "were clothed in beastes skinnes and ate raw flesh, and spake such speeche that no man coulde understand them, and in their demeanour like to bruite beastes, whom the King kept a time after. Of the which upon two years past I saw apparelled after the manner of Englishmen in Westminister Pallace, which at that time I could not distinguish from Englishmen, till I was learned what they were." No additional information is available about the trio.

A possible early reference to Eskimos on the mainland of northern Canada occurs as a map notation. The 1550 world map by Pierres Desceliers includes numerous illustrations as well as an acceptable rendering of Labrador, Newfoundland, and the lower

St. Lawrence River, clear evidence that this region was well known to cartographers of the time. In the northern extreme a cluster of dome-shaped "houses of savages" is shown (Figure 7-1), and nearby "pygmies" are illustrated hunting large birds close to similar dwellings (Figure 7-2). Perhaps the pygmies represent Eskimos, and the dome-shaped structures are snowhouses. The caption beneath the pygmy illustration reads as follows in translation: "Pygmies, above is the representation of a people called pygmies, people of small stature and similarly small ideas. At the age of three they procreate, at eight years they die without having before their eyes shame, justice or honesty. For this reason they are called brutes, not men. It is said that they are constantly at war with the birds called cranes."

The earliest accepted illustration of living Eskimos was produced at Augsburg, Germany, probably in 1567 (Figure 7-3). According to the text accompanying the print a French ship "in search of strange adventures" sailed to "Terra Nova" in 1566. Upon meeting a man with his wife and child, the sailors appear to have attempted to capture the trio. The man was shot in the body with an arrow and wounded on one side with a sword. He wiped blood from his side on one hand, licked it, and fought with increased fury. Finally he was killed but not until after he had slain 12 French and Portuguese whom he hoped would serve as food "for they prefer to eat human flesh to any other meat." The sailors captured the woman, who was permitted to retrieve her child from hiding. The woman's clothing was described as made from sealskin, and her face was tattooed. "The men tattoo their wives for identification, for otherwise they would run around like cattle." The missionary spirit of the writer of the text is indicated by the closing sentences. "Let us thank God the Almighty for his blessings, that he has enlightened us with his words, that we are not such entirely wild people and cannibals as live in the country where this woman was caught, and from where she was brought, where they do not know anything about the right God, but live even worse than cattle. May God convert them to his wisdom. Amen." The illustration was printed as a single sheet, and how it came to be issued in Germany is not known. Apparently the print was a broadsheet advertising an exhibit of the woman and her child. The mother's clothing and tattoos are characteristically Eskimo, and "Terra Nova" probably was Labrador.

Figure 7-3 The earliest known illustration of Eskimos was printed in Germany, probably in 1567. The caption and text are deleted in the reproduction. (From Sixel, 1967)

By the mid-1500s the Newfoundland Banks and the coast of Labrador attracted innumerable cod fishermen from England, France, and Spain. Roman Catholic Europe and, to a lesser extent, Protestant England depended on cod for food during the numerous days of fasting. Fishermen did not write about the peoples encountered, and the early explorers contributed little. As described in Chapter 3, John Knight and three others apparently were killed by Labrador Eskimos in 1606, and shortly thereafter the remainder of his crew also was attacked. After Henry Hudson discovered Hudson Bay in 1610, searchers for a passage concentrated their efforts on finding a western outlet for this great inland sea. When the Hudson's Bay Company was founded in 1670 by Médard C. Groseilliers and Pierre E. Radison, the charter identified the region of control as all the drainages of Hudson Bay, including the ill-defined western sector of Labrador.

From the time of Cartier the French controlled the St. Lawrence drainages, and they founded Fort Pontchartrain in 1702 near modern Bradore in southeastern Quebec. The fort operated as a trading, trapping, and fishing center for about 60 years. Throughout its existence residents were harassed by Eskimo raiders from the north. Little of substance was reported about these Labrador Eskimos because of the usually hostile nature of the contacts. Ethnologists have studied the sketchy evidence and have written numerous rather labored interpretive articles about the distribution of Eskimos in Labrador. The early historic southern limit of Eskimos was at or reasonably near Hamilton Inlet, the place where they attacked the Knight expedition in 1606. During the next century Eskimos ranged farther south, beyond the Strait of Belle Isle, and became the mobile marauders encountered by the French. If Eskimos had lived along the Strait of Belle Isle in the early 1500s, it is strange that they were not mentioned by Cartier; he clearly met Indians, not Eskimos, in 1534 and on subsequent voyages. Reasonably detailed and early accounts about Eskimos within the modern boundaries of Labrador do not exist. We search in vain for a Hans Egede, Gustav Holm, or even an Elisha Kane reporting on the region. The Moravians established a lasting mission at Nain, Labrador, in 1771, but they did not have a David Crantz documenting the old ways contrasted with the new.

Eskimo ethnography and arctic explorations entered a new era when explorers purposefully and successfully wintered in the

Figure 7-4 An Eskimo man and woman from the islands in Hudson Strait. (From Lyon, 1824)

north. In 1819, the ships commanded by William E. Parry wintered off Melville Island and proved that the long arctic night could be endured without great hardship. The knowledge gained on Parry's first voyage also suggested that negotiating a northwest passage might require more than a single year. Thus the feasibility of plying the passage for commercial gain was greatly diminished. Future searches for a westward waterway were largely responses to the navigational challenge and the furtherance of knowledge. By this time, too, recording the customs of far-off peoples was an increasingly respectable goal.

Parry had no sooner returned to England in 1820 than he began preparations for a passage attempt concentrated to the northwest of Hudson Bay. As captain of the *Fury*, Parry was in charge of the expedition; he was accompanied by George F. Lyon commanding the *Hecla*. Each man later published an account of the voyage. They sailed in May 1821, and after brief encounters with Eskimos in Hudson Strait, they headed northwest. The coast was examined with considerable thoroughness, and no westward waterway was

Figure 7-5   An Iglulik snowhouse settlement on Winter Island in 1822. Kayaks are resting on columns of snow in the background, and long, ladderlike sleds are to the left. The dog in the right foreground had one leg tied up to prevent it from straying. (From Lyon, 1824)

found in this sector. As new ice formed in early October, they found a sheltered anchorage near what came to be known as Winter Island. They settled in until spring, and to break the monotony theatricals were performed, foxes were trapped, a school was organized, and the men hunted. The most exciting day, however, was February 1, 1822, when men pacing the decks for exercise cried out, "Eskimaux! Eskimaux!" Lyon, Parry, and four others went out to meet the unarmed Eskimo men who approached along with a few women and children. After an exchange of gifts the Eskimos invited the English to their coastal settlement about two miles distant.

When the English arrived at the village (Figure 7-5), Lyon was charmed by what he saw. "Our astonishment was unbounded, when, after creeping through some long low passages of snow, to enter the different dwellings, we found ourselves in a cluster of dome-shaped edifices, entirely constructed of snow, which, from their recent erection, had not been sullied by the smoke of the numerous lamps that were burning, but admitted the light in most delicate hues of verdigris green and blue, according to the thickness of the slab through which it passed. The natives were evidently in their best apparel, and made a very neat appearance; the darkness of their deer-skin dresses affording a strong contrast to the brilliancy of their habitations. To attempt giving a description of all we saw in one visit would be ridiculous; suffice it to say, we were much pleased." Lyon soon learned that the five-house cluster, with from one to three domes per house, sheltered 64 persons from 13 families.

Snowhouses typically are identified with the Central Eskimos, and because of their uniqueness these structures deserve further attention. A man preparing to build a snowhouse used a thin wooden rod to probe snowdrifts as he looked for snow of a uniform consistency that was neither hard, soft, nor layered. Soft snow crumbled, hard snow was difficult to work, and layered snow tended to break apart. The blocks were cut with an ivory snowknife, and the better the quality of snow the larger the blocks that could be removed. Blocks cut from superior snow were about 30 inches long, 18 inches high, and 7 inches thick. For a house 10 feet in diameter about 35 blocks were used, and one man could build it in an hour and a half. Under favorable conditions two men could build a similar snowhouse in about 45 minutes. After about 10 blocks had been cut, construction was begun. The foundation blocks were arranged in a circle and were shaped to fit together as well as to lean slightly toward the interior. All of the remaining blocks often could be cut from within the circle. They were set in place and shaped with a snowknife to fit on an ever-increasing incline until the topmost block was shaped and dropped into place. After the dome was completed, the openings between blocks were chinked with snow, and if a dwelling was to be used for very long, snow was shoveled over the structure with a special shovel. Finishing touches included a window of freshwater ice, a vent hole in the roof, and an entrance passage. Household furnishings were meager: stone lamps, lamp stands, stone cooking pots, a rack to dry clothing, and various containers. The people in a dwelling such as this attempted to keep the temperature slightly below freezing to prevent the roof from melting and dripping on the inside. A temporary remedy for a drip was to cover it with a piece of snow to absorb the moisture.

When a number of families were establishing a relatively permanent camp, they built numerous separate and interlocking snow domes for living areas, storage, and dog shelters. One large snowhouse complex visited by Lyon was entered through a long tunnel wide enough for two persons to pass but so low that it was necessary to stoop when walking along. A dome-shaped anteroom was entered by stepping up through a hole in its floor. Off this room were three dome-shaped dwellings, each about 15 feet in diameter and as much as 7 feet high. If two families lived under one dome, they each had a bench on one side of the entrance. Benches were covered with baleen strips or pieces of sealskin and with skin blankets.

From the outside a snowhouse was a glistening dome, but on the inside the snow soon lost its whiteness. Smoke from lamps blackened the interior, and since seals were butchered inside, the floor was covered with blood and oil. During warm spells the dome might thaw, dripping water on everything. If this happened, a new dome might be built over the old one during the next cold spell and the former snowhouse removed from the inside. As the top of a snowhouse began melting in the spring, skins replaced the upper part of the dome as roofing. This was a very uncomfortable period because the house floor was always wet from the thaw.

These people appear to have had no direct European contacts before the visit by Lyon and Parry. Families owned European beads, copper kettles, and imported knives, but they were obtained in trade from Eskimos to the south. The people whom Lyon and Parry discovered came to be called the Iglulik. They lived on Melville Peninsula and adjacent sectors to the north and south. At midcentury the region often was visited by Franklin search expeditions, but their writings about the Iglulik, or adjacent Eskimos, contribute relatively little. The descriptions by Lyon and Parry, supplemented by the later works of the anthropologists Therkel Mathiassen and Knud Rasmussen, make the Iglulik the best-known Eskimos of central Canada.

Lyon's receptiveness to learning Eskimo customs is delightful. After he saw the tattoos of women, he wondered how the designs were made. To find out he indicated that he would like to be tattooed, and one woman willingly obliged. She drew figures on one of his arms and prepared a soot-covered thread for the operation. With a needle and thread she operated with short, deep stitches, pressing her thumb on each puncture as the needle was withdrawn. Each stitch began in the last hole of the previous stitch. After Lyon had about 40 stitches on his arm, she rubbed the wounds with oil to stop the bleeding. Although Lyon had already learned the process, he later was tattooed repeatedly by women.

When the Eskimos arrived, they were accompanied by a pack of 13 ravenous wolves that proved troublesome to the English and Eskimos alike. The wolves did not attack people, but they were adept at seizing anything edible, including unguarded dogs. It is curious that the Eskimos did not attempt to rid themselves of the wolves by using spring-bait traps, which the Iglulik reportedly had in aboriginal times. A spring-bait trap is a form based on the elastic qualities of baleen. A strip of baleen was coiled, tied with sinew thread, and covered with blubber or meat. The set was placed where it would be found by a wolf, who swallowed it whole. As the sinew was digested in the wolf's stomach, the coiled baleen sprang back into a straight position, piercing the animal's stomach and causing internal bleeding that led to its death.

The Iglulik who settled near the English ships began hunting seals at their breathing holes (Figure 7-6) and at leads in the locally stable ice in early February. The presence of the ice-bound ships apparently did not influence their choice of hunting sites. Parry related that these Eskimos had eaten all their surplus food and depended entirely on day-to-day seal harvests. Although the Eskimo men hunted persistently, they had little success, and all were fed by the English during these lean periods. As Parry noted, unless seals were killed, the people had no food or fuel for their lamps. Without heat from lamps they not only were cold but could not melt snow for water and were forced to eat the snow, which, as Parry wrote, "is not only a comfortless but an ineffectual resource." In stressful times these Eskimos ate sealskins or raw and frozen wolf meat. In early April about half of the Eskimos abandoned their settlement to search for more productive hunting grounds. The men who remained hunted walrus on the loose floes and killed two, to the great relief of the women. About two weeks later these Eskimos abandoned their snowhouses on Winter Island.

By late spring the English had begun to realize that these Eskimos were a reliable source of geographical information. They were most excited by an Eskimo woman's map and her report that a sea existed three days' travel to the west from the base of Melville Peninsula. After talking with the Eskimos further, Lyon and Parry

Figure 7-6   An Iglulik man in the shelter of a snow-block wall as he waits for a seal to appear at a breathing hole. (From Parry, 1824)

became convinced that a narrow strait existed not far away, and "This little North-West Passage set us all castle-building, and we already fancied the worst part of our voyage over."

After nearly nine months of confinement the *Fury* and *Hecla* worked free of the ice on July 2, 1822. Sailing north, they battled ice floes, winds, and tides to reach the village of Igloolik on the island of the same name. Here there were many houses or igloos of stone and bone. A short distance beyond, unbroken sea ice stopped their westward progress, but in early August an Eskimo man drew them a map showing that a passage existed to the northwest.

Sailing through the strait was doubtful because in early August the ice was thin but firm and by mid-August more ice formed on calm nights. When some open water was sighted, they proceeded cautiously through a narrow westward passage but were soon confronted by an unbroken field of ice to the west; this strait was known to Eskimos as "The Closed." In spite of their endeavors the ships had gone only about 40 miles west of Igloolik. They turned east and prepared to winter off Igloolik Island near the Eskimo community they had found. On December 2 they saw the last of the sun and settled in for their second winter. The months of forced inactivity offered Lyon and Parry an excellent opportunity to learn more about local Eskimos, an appealing prospect for them both.

These Eskimos built a number of different types of dwellings, as Lyon and Parry had noted in part. When the snowhouses thawed in May, they moved into more substantial structures, which they occupied again in early fall before snowhouses could be built. If existing house foundations were nearby, they were refurbished

Figure 7-7   Iglulik women in typical winter clothing, including their extremely bulky boots. (From Lyon, 1824)

and occupied. These ruins, as well as new structures built, had stone and turf foundations with walls made from sea-mammal bones. The top was covered with tent skins and later with snow. Alternatively the walls of fall houses might be made from blocks of ice set on end; these formed an octagon, which was covered with a roof of skins. A European inside this type of dwelling felt that he was in a house of ground glass. The summer housing form was a double lean-to. These were framed with poles and covered with sewn seal or walrus skins held down along the edges with heavy stones.

As Lyon and Parry knew so well, ice dominated the sea throughout the year in the Iglulik area, and travel by boat or ship was severely limited. The Iglulik did not use umiaks, and the same was true for other historic Eskimos living westward to Coronation Gulf. Kayaks may not have been made by some Iglulik bands, although others depended on them for killing caribou as they swam across lakes or other bodies of water.

When European mariners met Eskimos, kayaks were, as has been noted, a likely topic of interest. Parry found that when he paddled an Iglulik kayak, it was not as "crank" as he had expected. By keeping his body erect and in a central position he could maintain his balance. He learned not to lean against the manhole ring since pressure on it served as a lever to upset the paddler. He found that to prevent foundering when coming into the wind was difficult, and "catching a crab," or having a paddle take a wave, was most likely to upset a kayak. Parry thought that after a few months of practice a seaman could handle a kayak with the confidence of an Eskimo.

Dog-team travel provided the high degree of mobility required in the food quest. A band or family camped at a locality as long as animals could be killed locally, then moved elsewhere. The land was covered with snow for about nine months of the year, and sleds could be used for 10 months across sea ice and even longer over the ice adjacent to the shore. Dog teams pulled sleds loaded with household goods from one camp to the next or hauled sleds loaded with meat from a kill site to camp. In this region where wood was so scarce, sled runners sometimes were made in remarkable ways. Typically the runners were cut from the jawbones of whales and were shod with strips of whale bone. Alternatively runners were fashioned from pieces of sealskin molded to the proper form and filled with moss and earth, over which water was poured to freeze and set the form. The runners were from 4 to 14 feet long and were connected across the top with pieces of antler, bone, or wood placed at regular intervals. Dogs were broken to the harness when they were as young as two months, and a typical team had about eight animals. The dogs were hitched to a sled in a fan-shaped arrangement by using individual trace lines. During the summer, dogs carried household items in skin packs when the people went inland on hunting and fishing trips.

Sled dogs had sharp ears, bushy tails that turned up, furry winter coats with the hair as much as four inches long, and soft wool near the skin. Their coats were black, white, reddish, or a mixture of colors. Like wolves they howled but never barked; unlike wolves they carried their heads high and their tails up. Each dog was named, and the most intelligent animal, irrespective of age or sex, was chosen as the lead dog. The lead dog responded to the driver's commands, and the others followed its example. The trace of the lead dog extended as much as 20 feet, and the traces of the other dogs were about 10 feet each. Shorter traces were used for the less diligent dogs so that they could be whipped with ease. The driver sat toward the front of a sled with his feet hanging over one side so that he could jump off quickly to maneuver the sled around obstacles or prevent it from upsetting. He carried a whip with an 18-foot lash that trailed behind the sled, and he could flick it to chastise any laggard. A disadvantage of the fan-shaped hitch was that about a third of the team pulled ineffectively at an angle to the sled's movement. Furthermore as the dogs ran they jumped over each other's traces, and the lines became so badly tangled that periodic stops were required to untangle the knotted mass.

A team of about seven dogs with a 900-pound load on a good trail could cover about 55 miles a day, but if the trail was poor, a day's journey might be only about 25 miles. As an inducement for dogs to pull a very heavy load a woman might walk ahead of the team and periodically pretend that she was cutting meat. She also might throw a mitten in the snow to deceive the dogs into thinking that she had dropped something edible, which made them lunge forward. Another trick to encourage a team to run with renewed vigor was for the driver to shout "polar bear" or "seal."

Caribou hunts provided essential food for some of the Iglulik during much of the year, and whether food was scarce or not, the cry of *tugto* or caribou was enough to make men set off eagerly on a hunt. Barren Ground caribou wandered north into the Iglulik area during the spring, summered near the northern fringe of the continent, and returned south in the fall, although some animals might winter in the north. Caribou usually are curious, and this characteristic was exploited by hunters. As long as they were not openly approached, caribou often could be attracted to a hunter who imitated their sounds or wore a caribou-skin disguise. An inquisitive caribou slowly wandered toward a hunter; it required great patience to wait for the animal to come within effective arrow range. An arrow was not shot until a caribou was very near, within 12 paces according to Lyon. A different method was followed by men hunting as a team. In full view of a caribou they approached walking closely together; after they had been seen, the men veered away from the animal, which eventually followed out of curiosity. As they wandered off, one man quickly hid behind a rock as the other walked on. When the caribou passed near the concealed man, he shot it with an arrow.

The greatest number of caribou were taken during cooperative hunts as the animals migrated in large herds. These hunts were most intensive in the late summer and fall when the caribou skins were best for clothing, the meat prime, and the fat layer thickest. Family groups walked inland to intercept caribou along their migratory routes. As a herd approached an entrapment site, such as a small valley leading to a lake, women and children appeared behind the animals to drive them through the valley and into the water. Here men were hiding in kayaks, and as the caribou swam across the lake, they speared as many as possible.

The natural history of arctic animals seldom attracted the attention of Lyon or Parry, but an extraordinary account of a polar bear hunting a walrus was recorded by Lyon and deserves mention. An Iglulik hunter told that he once saw a polar bear swim cautiously to a large piece of rough ice where two female walrus were sleeping near their calves. Unknown to the walrus the bear climbed onto the ice and loosened a large chunk of ice with its front paws and nose. The bear lifted the ice block over the head of one adult walrus and let it fall, killing her instantly. Since the calf belonging to this female did not swim away with the others, the bear killed it as well. Similar instances of polar bears killing walrus with pieces of ice, or even with rocks, have been reported by other observers.

Figure 7-8   Iglulik men in typical winter garments. All three are wearing trousers of caribou skin and sealskin boots. The parkas of the two men in the foreground are made from caribou skin, and the man in the background is wearing a sealskin parka. (From Lyon, 1824)

Another polar-bear hunting technique also deserves mention in this context. The bear's white coat blends imperceptibly into the landscape, but its black muzzle is very conspicuous against the ice. Some Eskimos, and a few reputable scientists, report that a bear may camouflage its nose with a paw when hunting a seal.

Lyon introduced his discussion of Iglulik honesty as follows: "I verily believe that there does not exist a more honest set of people than the tribe with whom we had so long an acquaintance." He could excuse occasional thefts by noting that these Eskimos had neither iron nor wood, which were esteemed as much as gold or jewels by the English. Yet the Iglulik were faulted as being envious and slanderous toward each other, for begging, and for showing a lack of gratitude. As deplorable as these characteristics may have seemed to Lyon, they were adaptive among the people themselves. With no effective means to control the behavior of others, slander —or perhaps more appropriately gossip—exposed the failings of individuals. "Begging" served to equalize the distribution of scarce resources, and a lack of gratitude suggests the obligatory nature of sharing. Lyon had unbounded praise for the hospitality of the Iglulik, especially in times of adversity. They freely shared their food and took the clothes from their backs to comfort cold and wet visitors.

The quality of life was much the same for women as for men among the Iglulik. Young couples often rubbed noses as a sign of affection, and in household affairs a wife's voice equaled that of her husband. Couples "seem most fond of each other," according to Lyon, but he did not choose to call it "love." A woman freely discussed her affairs with her husband or in public, yet despite this "deplorable state of morals and common decency," in most conversations adults were modest in word and gesture. Wives seldom were abused, but a husband's ire sometimes found dramatic expression, as in the following instance. The two wives of this man often quarreled over him, and once when he was sitting between them, they began to scratch each other and pull one another's hair. The man became so angry that he seized a knife, cut one wife severely on the back of the hand, and wounded the other on the forehead. His anger soon passed, and when he realized what he had done, he broke the knife into pieces.

Adults judged each other largely on the basis of hunting or housekeeping skills and shamanistic abilities. No one ranked higher than any other on an absolute scale of authority. After Parry had wintered with the Iglulik for two years and had acquired considerable understanding of their language, he wrote, "It was with extreme difficulty that these people had imbibed any correct idea of the superiority of rank possessed by some individuals among us." Violence against persons and property or overt expressions of anger were rare, and the tendency was for a disgruntled individual to sulk rather than act. Furthermore Parry wrote, "War is not their trade; ferocity forms no part of the disposition of the Esquimaux."

Later accounts about Iglulik social control suggest that it may not have been quite as amorphous as suggested by Parry. The Danish archaeologist and ethnographer Therkel Mathiassen studied Iglulik life in the early 1920s. He found that in each settlement there usually was an older man, the capable head of a large family or an especially skilled hunter, who determined when to move from one hunting site to another and how food was distributed. He was called *isumaitoq*, "he who thinks," and while he did not command or control the activities of others, his advice was followed because he was considered wise.

Lyon and Parry never could accept Iglulik attitudes toward the desperately ill, the dying, and the dead. If a sick person's recovery was a reasonable expectation, relatives attending the invalid were solicitous, but people were indifferent to the suffering of dying persons and ignored them or were callous toward them. A dying woman often was provided with some food and oil for a lamp and put in a small snowhouse that then was blocked shut. The aged and senile were left behind when people moved camp. If such a person could catch up with the travelers, he was accepted, but in all likelihood he would die alone.

After a death those preparing the corpse wore mittens and stuffed caribou hair in their nostrils. The body was dressed with care and was taken from the house through a window. It was dragged along the ground to a nearby place of burial and was covered with a few stones or with snow. What most disturbed the English was that the debris around a village included not only dog carcasses, rotten meat, and blubber, but human remains, usually partially torn apart by hungry dogs, foxes, or wolves. Remembrances of the dead could, however, be very touching. Parry noted that when a man and his wife visited the spot where their tent had stood, the woman went to the sleeping place of her adopted son who recently had died and wailed in mourning.

From intermittent remarks by early observers we know that privation commonly followed adverse hunting conditions. A dramatic instance was reported by John Rae, who wintered among the Iglulik in 1846-7 and 1853-4. In general his account does not effectively expand on those of Lyon and Parry, but he does mention a terrible famine. A few years before 1853 about 50 people died of starvation. In desperation one man strangled himself, and another took off his clothes to freeze to death. Only two women in the group apparently survived, and they did so by turning to cannibalism.

After spending two winters among the Iglulik both Lyon and Parry spoke Eskimo with sufficient ease to understand and describe the belief system of these people reasonably well. Yet their accounts pale when compared with the description of Iglulik religion and world view compiled by Knud Rasmussen in the early

1920s. Rasmussen, of Greenlandic and Danish ancestry, spent his youth in Greenland and spoke Inupik before learning Danish. He became a largely self-trained anthropologist and soon established himself as the foremost Eskimo ethnographer of modern times in the humanistic tradition of reporting. Even though his Iglulik study was made nearly 100 years after those of Lyon and Parry, the life-style of these Eskimos does not appear to have changed a great deal, no doubt because they had remained isolated from the rest of the world.

In a snowhouse late one winter day Rasmussen talked with people about their religion. After recording innumerable statements about their taboos, he tried to find out the principles behind them. No one could offer an answer, and they thought it unreasonable for him to take this line of questioning. The most knowing man present, Aua, asked Rasmussen to go outside with him. As they looked across the cold and windswept ice, Aua gazed at Rasmussen and asked, "Why?" Why did one blizzard follow the next when people could best hunt in calm weather? At this moment men appeared across the ice, bending forward as they struggled back to camp against the wind; they had hunted seals at their breathing holes all day but did not make a kill. Aua led Rasmussen into a house where a small lamp burned with a tiny, heatless flame as a couple and their children shivered in the cold. Aua asked "why" and explained that the man had hunted all day without success. They next visited a tiny snowhouse where an old woman lived alone because she was ill and apparently near death. Yet she had done no wrong in her long life. Aua again asked "why" of Rasmussen. After they returned to their snowhouse Aua said, "You are equally unable to give any reason when we ask you why life is as it is. And so it must be. All our customs come from life and turn toward life; we explain nothing, we believe nothing, but in what I have just shown you lies our answer to all you ask." Aua and other men went on to explain that they did not believe, *they feared*. They feared the weather spirit of the earth, hunger, sickness, the souls of people, the souls of animals killed, Takanaluk, and Sila. The primary purpose behind their taboo system, which was based on experience and wisdom, was to avoid offending the souls of food animals, even though the animals had to be killed since "human food consists entirely of souls."

The forces that controlled the Iglulik universe were neither good nor bad, and while they often were personified, they were not worshipped in the manner of gods. The major task of the people in dealing with these supernaturals was to pacify them by observing traditional rules of behavior. The most awesome force was Takanaluk, "The Terrible One Down There," the spirit that lived at the bottom of the sea and was the mother of sea mammals. She once was a human, a girl, who in her pride rejected all suitors. In his anger her father said, "May she have my dog!" Then one evening as the family was settling down for the night, a strange man arrived and slept with the girl as his wife. He had the canine teeth of a dog hanging from his chest as amulets and was actually the father's dog in human form. The girl's father took her away to a nearby island, but the dog swam there to join his wife. The girl bore some human offspring and others that were dogs. Her dog husband swam to the mainland regularly to get food for his family. Once the girl's father tricked him into carrying stones back to the island, and he drowned. In retaliation the girl told her children to kill their grandfather when he arrived with food, but he managed to escape. Since she was without food, the girl sent her children away, using boot soles as boats. When they reached other places, some of the children became whites, and others Indians. She then returned to the mainland to live with her father, only to be lured away by a deformed man who was really a bird, a storm-petrel, in human form. The girl's father found her and took her away while her husband was out hunting. The husband changed into a storm-petrel and pursued their boat. When he could not obtain the girl, he caused a terrible storm by beating his wings. As the height of the waves increased, the man grew fearful and threw his daughter into the sea for her husband to retrieve, but she clung to the gunwale with her hands. Her father hacked off the first joints of her fingers, and after they fell into the sea, they became common seals. She still held on, and the father cut off the middle joints, which became bearded seals. He cut again, and the last joints became walrus. She could hold on no longer and slipped into the sea, sinking to the bottom to become the spirit Takanaluk. She joined her dead dog husband, whose spirit guarded the passage to her house, and only fearless shamans dared attempt to reach her. In his remorse the girl's father lay down at the edge of the sea, and when the high tide took him to his daughter, he became the Father of the Woman of the Deep. As a spirit he was always angry, especially at those who broke the rules. Takanaluk was accorded great respect by the Iglulik since seals and walrus, their mainstay, came from her.

The constraints placed by these people on themselves in relation to the animals killed were legion. A fundamental dichotomy prevailed between edibles from the sea and those from the land; they were kept physically separate except under prescribed circumstances. One of the strongest prohibitions concerned working immediately after a bearded seal, polar bear, or whale had been killed. In each instance adults were not allowed to perform ordinary activities for three days. Each animal also had its own particular set of taboos. For example, when a seal was brought into a snowhouse for butchering, a lump of snow was dipped into water, and the water was dripped into the seal's mouth to quench the thirst of its soul. Until the seal was actually cut up, women were prohibited from sewing or doing any other work. For the first night after a seal was killed, its soul was in the harpoon that killed it. This harpoon was placed next to a lighted lamp to keep the soul warm during the night. Many more demanding restrictions were connected with caribou. Walrus hide or anything made from it could not be taken on a caribou hunt. After a caribou had been killed, a small piece of meat or suet was placed under a stone as a sacrifice to the dead. Allowing dogs to gnaw bones would harm the souls of caribou, and these animals would disappear. When a woman butchered a caribou, she left small sections of skin around the eyes and genitals because caribou souls were offended if women touched these parts. From the time a family started inland in search of caribou until late fall after they had returned to the coast and moved into a snowhouse to hunt seals, women could not sew new garments. Minor repairs on existing items could be made but only at a distance from the camp. This sewing taboo was observed because it was thought that an evil spirit would be drawn to the locality by the thread. New caribou-skin clothing was made at the first snowhouses built in the fall, but when they moved into snowhouses on the sea ice, women could sew only sealskins. Rituals were performed to offset the potential ill effects of having items derived from the land, meaning primarily caribou-skin garments, on the sea ice.

The Sea Goddess, previously referred to as Takanaluk, was the most important deity among coastal Eskimos in central Canada.

She was known by different names in the east and west, but in these areas she was far less important. In central Canada shamans typically visited the Sea Goddess during public performances to persuade her to release animals for human food, to calm stormy weather, or to desist from sending illness abroad. A shaman "drops down to the bottom of the sea" on his miraculous journey to the home of the Sea Goddess. On his return he customarily reported that all would be right in the world again if the taboos were obeyed. The people then freely confessed their transgressions; the women's breaches of those taboos related to menstruation and miscarriages were considered especially serious. A feeling of relief followed the confessions because it was felt that harmony had been restored to the universe.

*   *   *

The ships of Lyon and Parry worked free from the winter ice off Igloolik in early August 1823. It seemed prudent to sail for England rather than attempt a third wintering because the crews were not in the best of health and there was not enough food aboard for another year. Lyon returned to the arctic the following year in command of the *Griper* and under orders to winter at the base of Melville Peninsula. In the spring he was to cross the peninsula with a small party and trace the northern shore of North America to Coronation Gulf and the most eastern point reached by John Franklin on his travels from the interior in 1821. The *Griper* arrived in Hudson Strait without incident, but off Southampton Island a terrible gale badly battered the ship. A few days later another storm struck and lasted for days, to be followed by still another gale. The *Griper* lost its anchors, and in such unsettled weather they dared not approach the coast without adequate anchors. Only a change of winds and slack water at the turn of the tides saved the vessel from certain destruction on coastal shoals. The only reasonable action was to return to England, which Lyon did but with a sense of failure. On Southampton Island they met Eskimos who apparently had had few if any previous contacts with Europeans, but Lyon reported very little about them. Parry's voyage of 1824 was equally unsuccessful.

Numerous other English ships wintered among the high arctic islands of Canada between 1825 and 1859 as the search for a northwest passage continued. The crews usually became icebound north of the region where historic Canadian Eskimos lived, and therefore few if any intimate contacts were established. Between 1771 and 1851 a small number of explorers ventured overland through the Canadian northwest to the arctic coast. Foremost among these explorers was Samuel Hearne, who with the aid of a Chipewyan Indian guide reached the arctic coast at the Copper-mine River in 1771. Hearne and most others faced so many perils as they struggled to the coast that any reconnoitering was done in haste. Thus whether the travels were by boat, dog team, on foot, or by ship, the accounts of Lyon and Parry remain the most rewarding descriptions of Central Eskimos.

*   *   *

The most enduring name associated with explorations in the Canadian arctic is that of John Franklin. He was introduced as a lost explorer in Chapter 5, and we now turn back to his early travels in the north. Franklin went to sea in 1800 at the age of 14, and the next year he was on one of Lord Nelson's ships fighting the battle of Copenhagen. He signed as a midshipman on a vessel mapping the Australian coast in 1801, and on this voyage he became a skillful surveyor. Franklin took part in the Battle of Trafalgar (1805) and the attack on New Orleans (1815) before he became a polar discoverer. When the northern sea ice was open as never before, Franklin participated in John Barrow's plan to find a northwest passage. He was placed in command of the *Trent* and instructed to sail over the North Pole to Bering Strait. The *Trent* and the *Dorothea*, commanded by David Buchan, sailed in 1818 and crossed the Arctic Circle near Spitzbergen, where pack ice was encountered. Repeated attempts to penetrate the pack failed, but Franklin gained valuable experience in ice navigation.

By 1819 only two rivers in the northernmost region of North America had been traced to the sea: the Coppermine, explored by Hearne in 1771, and the Mackenzie, descended by Alexander Mac-kenzie in 1789. In 1819 Parry was to make a passage search by sea along Lancaster Sound, as related earlier, and Franklin was placed in charge of a land expedition to trace the continental limit from the Coppermine River mouth eastward. Those accompanying Franklin to Hudson Bay included George Back and Robert Hood, both midshipmen, John Richardson as the naturalist and surgeon, and a seaman. They landed at York Factory along western Hudson Bay and set off to the northwest in early September of 1819. Their travail was immense before they reached the arctic coast in mid-July 1821. The only Eskimos they met, a crippled old man who could not flee with the others and his wife, were seen near the mouth of the Coppermine River. The expedition then pushed east along the coast by canoe, carefully mapping about 675 miles of coastline before they turned back to the west. It was nearly a year before Franklin reached Hudson Bay and the end of his journey. Their trip was marred by the specter of death from starvation, the murder of Hood, and cannibalism. One of the two Eskimos accompanying Franklin wandered off on the return from the coast and presumably died. The second Eskimo, Augustus or Tattannoeuck, served Franklin well and survived the ordeals of the trip. A new species of butterfly, the brown elfin or *Callophrys augustinus*, was named after him, probably by Richardson.

The privation and limited success of his first overland expedition did not deter Franklin from planning a new assault on the arctic coast. He hoped to descend the Mackenzie River and then send exploring parties both east and west. This goal proved acceptable to the Admiralty, and if all went well Franklin would meet Parry, who again in 1824 was to seek a northwest passage by ship from the east. Alternatively Franklin could meet Frederick W. Beechey, who was to sail around Cape Horn, north through Bering Strait, and east to Kotzebue Sound. Richardson and Back again accompanied Franklin, along with E. N. Kendall and British seamen. After landing in New York, they made their way to the Canadian northwest, where they were joined by Augustus and another Eskimo. They reached the Mackenzie River in early August 1825, and after reconnoitering during the fall they wintered at Fort Franklin, a settlement they built at the western end of Great Bear Lake. On July 4, 1826, they reached the Mackenzie delta in their boats. At Point Separation the two boats of Franklin and Back set off to the west, while those of Richardson and Kendall started east.

Franklin first met Mackenzie Eskimos just to the west of the river delta. Expecting a hostile reception, he negotiated the shallows with care but nonetheless was grounded about a mile from the shore. Many kayaks and numerous umiaks, containing a total of about 275 people, soon drew near. Augustus assured them of

Figure 7-9   The attack by Mackenzie Eskimos on the boats of John
Franklin and George Back in 1826. (From Franklin, 1828)

Franklin's good intentions, and a brisk trade in artifacts ensued. As
Franklin prepared to leave, the tide ebbed and the boat was
stranded. A kayaker who had accidentally capsized was taken into
the boat while his kayak was emptied of water; he discovered a
vast amount of trade goods and other artifacts hidden beneath a
canvas cover. Other Eskimos soon attempted to get into the boat,
and two "chiefs" were permitted to board under the condition that
they keep all the others out. As the tide ebbed further, the Eskimos
began dragging Back's boat ashore, and when Franklin attempted
to stay with Back, the Eskimos also helped pull his boat across the
mud. Back's boat was beached first, and Eskimos with knives in
hand began pillaging it as the English attempted to retrieve the
stolen property in good humor. Smaller numbers surrounded
Franklin's boat, and the crew prevented them from boarding with
blows from their gun butts. Franklin and Augustus rushed to the
aid of Back's crew with Augustus shouting himself hoarse as he
attempted to stop the assault (Figure 7-9). The English remained

determined not to fire on the raiders, and a few Eskimos encouraged their comrades to desist. Back finally had had enough, and after he ordered his crew to aim their muskets at the Eskimos, they quickly hid behind beached kayaks and driftwood. By this time the tide was rising, and the boats were launched. The Eskimos followed in kayaks but withdrew after Augustus warned that Franklin would shoot the first person to come within musket range.

Franklin and his crew would almost certainly have been killed if they had fired on the Eskimos, given their number. When the boats became grounded again, Augustus waded ashore to reprove the people for their behavior. The Eskimo response was that they had never before seen whites, and they could not resist taking all the things that they saw for the first time. They pledged friendship in the future, and as a gesture of good faith they returned some items that Franklin requested. Soon after midnight there was enough water to float the boats, and the English sailed off, only to be approached again by many kayakers the next day. They were dissuaded from coming near when a shot was fired near the lead kayak.

The eastern party under Richardson had a less dramatic but somewhat similar encounter with Mackenzie Eskimos at the river mouth. Richardson's party reached the Coppermine River and ascended it a short distance before abandoning the boats. The men walked to Great Bear Lake, where they were met by boats that took them back to Fort Franklin.

Both Franklin and Richardson traveled as rapidly as possible and therefore had only brief trading encounters with Eskimos. Franklin boated as far as the Return Islands without incident. Occasionally he met Eskimos along the way and recorded fragments of ethnographic information, but he was pleased when Eskimos were not seen since they delayed his progress. Franklin and his men returned to Fort Franklin without undue difficulties, and the English members of the expedition, all except two who died, returned to England the next fall. Franklin predictably concluded his published account of the second overland expedition with new thoughts about negotiating a northwest passage.

*   *   *

From the Coppermine River to Hudson Bay and Baffin Island the cultural adaptations of Eskimos in the Canadian arctic were similar.

At the Mackenzie River mouth, a more varied resource base prevailed, and along the river delta and adjacent coast, where edibles were both diverse and highly localized, five different Eskimo subgroups had emerged. They all built substantial wooden houses that they occupied year after year, and comparatively large aggregates of people clustered in permanent villages. These observations alone indicate far more dependable and abundant food resources than those available to the Eskimos immediately to the east. Mackenzie Eskimos were actually more closely akin to the Eskimos of northern Alaska than to the others in northwestern Canada.

The Mackenzie Eskimos were encountered by Franklin and Richardson in 1826 and were again observed by Richardson in 1848 during his search for the lost Franklin expedition. Most other early reports about them were made by the Roman Catholic priest Émile Petitot, a member of the Oblate Missionaries of Mary Immaculate. He is best known for his ethnographic and linguistic studies of Athapaskan Indians in northwestern Canada, where he worked from 1863 to 1878. Petitot spent little time among Mackenzie Eskimos, and yet we are most grateful to him for his notations about them. The only other author to make significant observations about aboriginal Mackenzie Eskimo life was the anthropologist and explorer Vilhjalmur Stefansson. When he visited the Mackenzie delta in 1906-7, the old ways were beginning to pass out of existence.

Mackenzie Eskimos followed the general Eskimo patterning in their clothing, but their hair styles, especially those of women, were somewhat different. A woman wore her hair in two large buns high on her head; into these were woven her discarded hair and that of the men in her life. Beside each cheek hung a long, full curl tied at the end with a string of glass beads. Most men wore their hair long, but some shaved the top of their heads in a tonsured style. Each man had a hole in his nasal septum through which either a dentalium shell or an ivory rod was inserted. When a male reached puberty, a small hole was made in each cheek near the outer corner of his mouth, and into these openings small labrets were fitted. An adult male wore large labrets of stone or ivory, each set with a large blue glass bead (Figure 7-10). A man who murdered an enemy in anger, not in seeking blood revenge, tattooed blue lines from ear to ear across his nose and was known as a "great man." On one shoulder a man had a cross tattooed for

Figure 7-10 A Mackenzie Eskimo man in characteristic clothing and showing a pair of the lateral labrets that were common. (From Petitot, 1887)

each bowhead whale killed and retrieved, while women had vertical blue lines on their chins.

Typical Mackenzie Eskimo winter houses were cross-shaped and built from driftwood (Figure 7-11, 12). Each log or plank was leaned against and supported by the next, so that no fastenings were required. The spaces between logs were chinked, and the

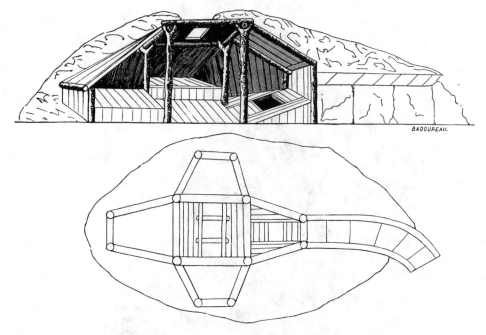

BADOUREAU.

Figure 7-11   The cross-shaped log house of Mackenzie Eskimos.
(From Petitot, 1876)

structure was topped with dirt, snow, and a coating of water
frozen in place. A long underground tunnel framed with slabs of
ice served as an entry and a cold trap. At the center of the ceiling, a
window opening was fitted with a block of ice. Two families lived
in each of the three alcoves, and each woman used her own lamp
for cooking and providing light and heat. Homes such as these
were occupied from late fall until all stored food had been consumed at some time during the winter. The families then moved to
separate camps and lived in dome-shaped snowhouses; here they
fished through the ice or hunted seals at their breathing holes.
With the arrival of spring, families moved into pole-framed skin
tents, and in the fall they intensively hunted or fished before
returning to their winter quarters.

Among these people the principal food varied by locality. During the summer the westernmost bands netted fish along the coast,
but east of the delta the men hunted caribou intensively. The

members of the easternmost bands hunted bowhead whales from umiaks. Most people, however, lived along the delta, and here they hunted white whales (beluga). As many as 1000 persons camped together, which probably is a record for the Canadian arctic. Beluga are small, toothed whales that frequent shallow waters in the summer but move into deep water for the winter. They are slow swimmers, traveling only at about six knots, and their shallow dives keep them underwater up to 15 minutes. As many as 200 kayakers participated in a coordinated hunt. As beluga swam toward the shoals, kayaks were launched and formed a line behind them. The men drove the whales by beating on the water with paddles; the terrified animals swam into the shallows in a vain effort to escape. As the whales floundered, the oldest hunter was called by name. He launched the first harpoon at a large beluga, and then the other hunters began harpooning. An able hunter might kill seven whales during a sweep. To make them more buoyant for towing ashore a man blew air through a tube into their lungs. Beluga meat was either cut into thin strips and hung over driftwood logs to dry or was buried in pits so that it would decay. Rotten meat would be eaten either thawed or frozen. The blubber was rendered over wood fires and stored in skin bags.

For each cooperative beluga hunt a leader was chosen, and a different person might supervise each hunt. There may have been permanent leaders among the group hunting bowhead whales from umiaks, but the information is not complete. More formal authority appears to have been vested in a settlement "chief," but again the data are not the best. The role of chief appears to have been inherited along the male line, but his rights and duties are not known.

Here for the first time we encounter the men's house or *karigi* that is known in parts of Alaska as a *kashim*. Although Central Canadian Eskimos built especially large snowhouses for festive occasions, a special structure occupied by men was not known to the east of the Mackenzie. Mackenzie delta Eskimos sometimes built two or three karigis in a settlement, and they were used from early summer through part of the winter. These square structures, measuring about 30 feet on each side, were log-framed and covered with earth. They had wooden floors except at the center, where there was an earthen fireplace with a smokehole in the roof above. Along the walls were plank benches on which men slept or

Figure 7-12 Interior view of the living area for one family in a
Mackenzie house. The men on the left and right are wearing
labrets. In front of the platform, at each end, are drying racks
above lamps on stands. (From Petitot, 1887)

sat while they made and repaired artifacts or lounged and ate.
When a man beached his kayak after a hunt, he went directly to his
karigi, and his wife was expected to appear promptly with his
meal.

Mackenzie Eskimo life conformed largely to that of other Canadian Eskimos. A man, his wife or wives, and their children formed
the basic unit. Both childhood betrothal and bride capture were
sometimes practiced, and spouse exchange was a part of married
life. Conflicts between unrelated persons were vengeful and perhaps more widespread and intensive than among the Eskimos

described previously. Murders committed in anger were relatively common, and blood revenge led to further retaliatory murders and family feuds. In one instance a woman's rejected suitor killed her as she slept. In another a man who refused to sell his belt was stabbed in the back and killed by a person who hoped to buy the belt.

A feud that erupted about 1860, soon after intensive historic contact, was recorded by Nuligak, a Mackenzie Eskimo. One man hoped to marry the daughter of another, but the father of the girl refused to permit the match. The rejected suitor took a valuable steel-bladed knife from one of the father's younger sons, and the father was furious. At the first opportunity he killed not only the thief but one of his companions. As the feud spread, a cousin of the original murderer allied himself with the thief's relatives, and more people were killed. Finally the father of the girl and the betraying cousin killed each other, but the feud continued on. As Nuligak wrote, "In the olden days the Inuit slew those who killed their kinsmen. One vengeance followed another like links in a chain."

Terrible feuds have been reported among most Eskimos, and they often spanned a number of generations because there was no effective political means to control ingroup violence. Charismatic leaders emerged from time to time and often attracted a voluntary following, but no socially established mechanism was followed to educate new leaders in the case of the death or decline in popularity of former ones. That this was so is most readily explained by the nature of economic activities. Men most often hunted alone or in small groups. Even in large cooperative hunts men usually participated as equals. When cooperative hunts were important, as among Mackenzie Eskimos in pursuit of beluga, some coordination was required, but apparently any able hunter could provide the necessary guidance. Yet hereditary chiefs were beginning to emerge among them, and one reason was that they lived in comparatively large, stable communities for part of the year and apparently were unable to deal with each other effectively on the basis of kinship ties alone.

The Mackenzie Eskimos consistently were bellicose in their early contacts with Europeans; thus they belie the stereotype of Eskimos as peaceful people. In 1799 the North West Company sent a canoe party down the Mackenzie with a Mr. Livingston, his interpreter

James Sutherland, and six others to establish trade relations with these people. They first met a lone Eskimo, and from his kayak he shot an arrow through the side of the large canoe. The man refused their presents, and after instructing them to put ashore he left and returned a short time later with five other kayakers. They too refused gifts and stealthily took the canoe paddles. As the trading party went back to its canoe, Livingston and one other man were killed with arrows. Two others, both Indians, escaped through the woods, while Sutherland and the remaining men drifted downstream in the canoe. They managed to kill five of the Eskimos before Sutherland's companions were slain and the canoe began to sink. As he drifted near an Eskimo camp, Sutherland swam ashore and went to an elderly man for protection. The Eskimos there gathered to determine Sutherland's fate. Since he had not been wounded in the previous fights, they decided that he was invulnerable to weapons, and so after a rock was tied around his neck, he was thrown into the river to drown.

Until the 1850s Mackenzie Eskimos either harassed or openly attacked most explorers and were restrained only because they feared the effectiveness of European guns. The explorer John Rae, who had considerable firsthand knowledge of Eskimos, felt that the Mackenzie group differed from the others because they lived so near the aggressive Athapaskan Indians. These Indians obtained guns from trading posts and thus had an effective advantage over adjacent Eskimos. Rae felt that the Eskimos were able to survive only because they were warlike and had access to enough food so that they could live in comparatively large defensible settlements.

Eskimos and Indians usually were bitter enemies, and their expressions of animosity to each other contributed to their designation as distinct peoples. From Hudson Bay to Alaska the word that Eskimos applied to Indians usually meant "Lousy People." A no-man's-land separated most Eskimos and Indians who would otherwise have shared a common boundary. Trade relations were strained, they did not often learn each other's languages, and a sign language for communication did not develop. Furthermore, they seldom borrowed ideas from each other.

In 1851 John Richardson published *Arctic Searching Expedition*, which includes a section devoted to Eskimos. He was an explorer, physician, and naturalist familiar with Canadian Eskimos; hence his comparative statements about them provide an informed overview for the early 1850s. Richardson classed Eskimos as a littoral group extending from Greenland and Labrador to eastern Siberia and the Pacific coast of Alaska. He felt that they were similar to the Chukchee of eastern Siberia, but he did not elaborate on these ties. Richardson observed that from Bering Strait eastward Eskimos spoke essentially the same language and had a similar mode of life. He termed northern Canadian tribes, with which he was most familiar, the "Central Eskimos," and his most developed ethnological statement was a comparison of Eskimos with adjacent Indians. Eskimos looked different from Indians because their eyes were "narrow and more or less oblique," they had more facial hair, and their complexions were whiter than those of Indians. He noted that Eskimo women were attentive to their appearance while Indian women were not. Eskimos were more provident because they could obtain comparatively little food during the winter whereas Indians could hunt and fish throughout the year and were more mobile in their food quest. Eskimos were more courageous than Indians and had unique manufactures such as kayaks, umiaks, waterproof boots, and waterproof parkas for kayakers. Richardson also thought that Eskimos were superior to Indians in "intelligence and susceptibility to civilization." This effort by Richardson to distinguish Eskimos from Northern Athapaskan Indians was based on certain clearly objective criteria and others that were impressionistic.

Eskimos living in the central arctic were the first Canadian Eskimos described fully, and they often are regarded as the most "typical" Eskimos. More accurately, they were the most widespread group of Eskimos with a highly specialized way of life. They literally depended on snowhouses as winter dwellings and on seals hunted at breathing holes as food; they usually were unable to take enough sea mammals by other means or harvest enough caribou or fish to see themselves through the long winters. To the east and west the food base usually was far more varied, bountiful, and dependable, a condition that led to more stable communities, greater diversity of manufactures, and other cultural elaborations. In the east this configuration is best represented in southwest Greenland and probably was much the same for Labrador. To the west, from the Mackenzie delta into Alaska, there were notable departures from the norms and forms described heretofore. Eskimo culture had its deepest roots in Alaska and was far more developed there than anywhere else.

NOTES

ESKIMO OCCUPANCY OF THE CENTRAL LABRADOR COAST AND ADJACENT AREAS. Archaeological excavations by Elmer Harp (1951, 1964, 1976) established that Eskimos identified with Dorset culture once lived in Labrador and Newfoundland on both sides of the Strait of Belle Isle. Radiocarbon dates from a Dorset site along the west coast of Newfoundland range from 157 B.C. to A.D. 463 (Taylor, 1968, 105). The southernmost Dorset site known, and thus the maximum southern range of prehistoric Eskimos, is on Cape Ray at the southwestern tip of Newfoundland (Taylor, 1968, 106). In the Hamilton Inlet sector of Labrador, William W. Fitzhugh (1972) dug sites dating from 3000 B.C. to the early historic era. He found that Dorset Eskimos lived in the vicinity from 800 to 200 B.C., but that Indians later replaced them, only to be replaced by Eskimos from the north after A.D. 1500. The recent Eskimo migrants had European trade goods at the time of their arrival. Farther north in Labrador, in the Hopedale area, Eskimo sites were dug by Junius B. Bird (1945), and the oldest debris included evidence of Eskimo-European contacts. The record seems clear: post-Dorset Eskimo sites from the central coast of Labrador southward were not occupied until historic times.

The most important articles dealing with shifting historic Eskimo and Indian settlements in Labrador and adjacent areas of Quebec are by A. S. Packard (1877, 1885), Frank G. Speck (1931, 1936), and J. Allan Burgesse (1949).

The reproductions (Figures 7-1, 2) of what may represent Eskimos and snowhouses are from the 1550 map by Pierres Desceliers published by H. P. Biggar (1924). The description of the three men taken to England by Sebastian Cabot is from W. G. Gosling (n.d., 38).

IGLULIK SOURCES. The account is based largely on the reports by George F. Lyon (1824) and William E. Parry (1828). John Rae (1866, 147) described the famine of ca. 1850. The information about Iglulik supernaturals is drawn from the account by Rasmussen (1929, 54-91), which is one of the finest descriptions of Eskimo religion. The study of Iglulik material culture by Mathiassen (1928) is an added source. Weyer (1932, 348-64) devoted a chapter to the Sea Goddess and lists or summarizes the most important regional variations of the associated myth.

OTHER CANADIAN ESKIMOS. The *Netsilik* were met by John Ross, who wintered in the region in 1829-33, by George Back in 1834, and John Rae in

1854. None of these men compiled ethnographic data comparable with that recorded previously by Lyon and Parry for the adjacent and culturally similar Iglulik. The Netsilik of this century were described by the Norwegian explorer Roald Amundsen (1908), who wintered with them in 1903-5, and by Rasmussen (1931), who studied the customs in 1921-3. Asen Balikci (1970) studied the Netsilik intermittently between 1959 and 1965 and described their traditional way of life before it was changed by missionaries and traders.

The *Copper Eskimos* were the last major group studied while their traditional culture still was an ongoing system and before epidemics of exotic diseases altered their lives. Explorers had little to say about them, and it was a casual traveler to the region in 1902, David T. Hanbury (1904), who first wrote about them at some length. They were studied by the anthropologist Diamond Jenness in 1914-6; his account is one of the finest ethnographies of aboriginal Eskimos. Apart from the fact that this book centers on descriptions of Eskimos by explorers, the only reason that the Copper Eskimos as reported by Jenness are not described is that they were in many respects similar to the Iglulik. The major works about the Copper Eskimos by Jenness are his general ethnography (1922) and a detailed study of their material culture (1946).

The standard baseline ethnography about the *Caribou Eskimos* is by Birket-Smith (1929), and the best specialized study is an analysis of leadership by Geert Van den Steenhoven (1962). For *South Baffin Island Eskimos* the accounts by Franz Boas (1888a, 1901-7) are accepted as a description of their traditional life. It should be noted, however, that they had hundreds of years of intermittent contact before being studied by Boas in 1883-4. The *Sadlermiut* of Southampton Island were visited briefly by Lyon, but most of what is known about them was recorded in 1922 by Mathiassen (1927, pt. 1, 268-87). The major work about the *Labrador Eskimos* is by E. W. Hawkes (1916) and is based on his fieldwork in 1914, which was about 140 years after the establishment of Moravian missionaries in Labrador and about 400 years after Europeans began fishing intensively off the coast. *Northern Quebec Eskimos* likewise are very poorly known even though they were visited by explorers from the time of Henry Hudson (1610) and the Hudson's Bay Company opened its first trading station in their area in 1749. The only reasonably early accounts we have for these people are by Lucien M. Turner (1888, 1894) and are based on his field study during 1882-4.

POLAR BEAR HUNTING TECHNIQUES.   The account of a polar bear killing a walrus with a block of ice was related by an Iglulik bear hunter (Lyon, 1824, 375-6), and Eskimo accounts of similar instances have been recorded by travelers in the Canadian arctic and Greenland. Some commentators regard the stories as legendary, while others accept them as accurate.

Polar bears at the London Zoo once were seen throwing five-foot chunks of ice about, and they have been known to throw objects in other contexts. Richard Perry (1966, 89-92) reviews the reports without passing judgment. That polar bears hide their noses while hunting has been reported by whites and Eskimos in Canada and Greenland. C. R. Harington (1966) devoted a short article to the subject, and it is mentioned in Perry's book cited above (1966, 76). Milton M. R. Freeman (1973) reports polar-bear predation on adult beluga in the Canadian arctic, while J. D. Heyland and Keith Hay (1976) recorded a polar-bear attack on a juvenile beluga in the same region.

THE FRANKLIN OVERLAND EXPEDITIONS.   The results of the first expedition, 1819-22, were published by Franklin (1823), who drew significant portions of his account from Robert Hood's journal. C. Stuart Houston (1974) edited and published the Hood journal for the first time; it covers the period between the departure from England to mid-September 1820 and thus does not include information about the Copper Eskimos. Members of the expedition built Fort Enterprise, near the headwaters of the Coppermine River, where they wintered in 1820-1 and to which they returned after the laborious trip to and from the arctic coast. On the return from the coast Hood was murdered by the Iroquois voyageur Michel Terohaute, who was in turn killed by Richardson. Fort Enterprise was partially excavated in 1970, and the findings appear in a volume edited by Timothy C. Losey (1973). Houston (1974, 199-200) is the source about the butterfly named after Augustus, one of the Eskimos with Franklin. The background information about Franklin is drawn from his biography by G. F. Lamb (1956).

The results of the second overland expedition, 1825-7, were published by Franklin (1828) and include an account by Richardson about the activities of the eastern party.

MACKENZIE ESKIMOS.   The murder of members of the North West Company party in 1799 is reported by Willard-Ferdinand Wentzel (1822), but Franklin and Richardson effectively introduce these Eskimos to history (Franklin, 1828, 99-107, 179-203). In 1837 when Thomas Simpson and Peter W. Dease descended the Mackenzie to map the area between Franklin's farthest point to the west and Point Barrow, the Eskimos to the west of the delta made half-hearted attempts to waylay them and steal what they could (Simpson, 1843, 109-11, 182-3). In 1848 when Richardson descended the Mackenzie in search of Franklin, he was prepared for Eskimo aggression, but the men in one of the three boats were not sufficiently cautious and nearly were pillaged before being rescued by the others (Richardson, 1854, 146-7). Subsequent Franklin search parties include little meaningful information about these Eskimos. Donat Savoie performed an appreciated service to ethnographers by assembling and translating into English all of the Mackenzie Eskimo information published by the French missionary Father Petitot (1970, v. 1). Vilhjalmur Stefansson (1914, 133-95) provides some useful information for 1906-7, as aboriginal life was breaking down. The best presentation of early historic Mackenzie Eskimo tribal distributions is provided by Peter J. Usher (1971). Finally Robert McGhee (1974) offers the best overview of aboriginal conditions and local variability in his report about archaeological excavations in the area.

Alaskan Inuit

In the earliest accounts, Alaskan Eskimos are characterized as distinct from other Eskimos, even as aberrant, because of "foreign influences." Unlike most Canadian Eskimos, the Alaskans did not base their livelihood on hunting seals at breathing holes or build dome-shaped snowhouses. They did not concentrate on open-water sealing in the manner of the East Greenlanders or emphasize hunting on sea ice as did the Polar Eskimos. Their economies were more diversified, as in West Greenland and Labrador. The Alaskans stood more clearly apart in other respects. Secular leaders often prevailed, social festivities were at times very elaborate, and some groups had a clear sense of common identity, a quality that seldom had been reported elsewhere. Trading relations brought people together at well-established market centers, which were rare in the east. Alaskan supernatural involvements were even more distinctive. The core of Eskimo religion, represented by shamans, inuas, and trances, prevailed, but here significant elaborations existed. Alaskans often held complex annual ceremonies in which all the members of a village participated and great wealth might be redistributed. For the first time masked dancers are reported, and the staging effects for dances sometimes were dramatic. The novel ways of Alaskan Eskimos often were attributed to

Figure 8-1   The earliest illustration of Eskimos at Point Barrow.
The first explorer to visit there was Thomas Elson in 1826. (From
Beechey, 1831)

borrowings from peoples in northeastern Siberia. Eskimo culture
in Alaska was thereby judged enriched but somehow tainted by
exotic influences.

Relationships with the east also are apparent. Cultural ties join-
ing Mackenzie and northern Alaskan Eskimos included men's
houses, driftwood dwellings, fish netting, annual ceremonies, and
secular leaders. They were closely connected not only in ethnological but in historical terms, and together they came to be called
"Western Eskimos."

Some English explorers reached the northern sector of Alaska by
boat from the east, and others arrived by ship from the west.
Franklin explored westward in two boats from the Mackenzie in
1826. Frederick W. Beechey sailed the *Blossom* from England,
around Cape Horn, and cruised north of Bering Strait the same

year. The plan was to make a coordinated survey of the north Alaskan coast. Following the hostile reception by Mackenzie Eskimos, Franklin traveled as rapidly as possible; he did not seek out Alaskan Eskimos and had few contacts with them. Franklin and Beechey were to meet at Kotzebue Sound, but when Franklin did not appear as scheduled the *Blossom* cruised northward beyond Icy Cape. A barge from the *Blossom* commanded by Thomas Elson sailed farther east and Elson was the first European to reach Point Barrow. Franklin boated west as far as the Return Islands, which left an unmapped area of about 250 miles between that locale and Point Barrow.

British national and commercial interests led the Hudson's Bay Company to plan a survey of the void left by Beechey and Franklin. The expedition was led by Thomas Simpson, who had entered the service of the company in 1829, and Peter W. Dease, a former employee of the North West Company and a member of Franklin's second expedition. The small party set out by boat and canoe from the Mackenzie mouth in 1837. For the final leg they walked part of the way and also used Eskimo umiaks. Occasionally they met Eskimos during the trip, but they did not encounter hostility and soon reached Point Barrow without incident. There a hostile reception was expected, based on the experience of the barge party from the *Blossom*. Unpredictably the Barrow people were friendly to Dease and Simpson, but the explorers remained with them little more than a day and thus made few observations. The most notable characteristic reported for the Barrow area people was their craving for tobacco, which was chewed and smoked by young and old, female and male. Tobacco had traveled nearly around the world before it reached Alaskan Eskimos. The smoking of tobacco originated among American Indians and was first introduced into Europe by the Portuguese in 1558. By 1600 tobacco was grown in Europe and widely used there and soon was carried across Siberia by the Russians. The Chukchee and Eskimos of Siberia traded Russian tobacco into Alaska before the arrival of Europeans. At historic contact all Alaskan Eskimos smoked, and the practice had spread as far east as the Mackenzie Eskimos.

A reasonably accurate index to the success of Eskimos on a regional basis is their number. The early historic population for Greenland was about 9000. For all of Canada the figure may have been about 11,500, but in Alaska there were at least 29,000. Even though these figures cannot be precise, they show that Alaskan Eskimos dominated numerically. Likewise, Eskimo culture had its deepest roots and was most diversified in Alaska. A major linguistic boundary delimited two major clusters of Eskimos in Alaska. Those living north of Norton Sound were Inuit, who spoke Inupik. To the south of them lived the Yuit, who were Yupik speakers. The difference between these languages approximates that between English and German and makes them mutually unintelligible. This linguistic diversity in Alaska contrasts with the uniformity of speech among Eskimos elsewhere.

Before 1848 few European ships or boats had sailed along the Alaskan coast north of Bering Strait, but in that year new whaling grounds were discovered in the Arctic Ocean. During the early 1800s American whalers had operated almost entirely in the Atlantic and south Pacific oceans. The north Pacific grounds were found in 1835, and after an unsuccessful season there in 1848, the whaling bark *Superior* of Sag Harbor, New York, passed through Bering Strait into the Arctic Ocean in search of whales. The *Superior* took so many bowhead whales here that during the next year 154 whalers cruised north of Bering Strait, and by 1854 the first whalers sailed east of Point Barrow.

Whalers in the western American arctic, like their counterparts in the east, seldom were interested in Eskimo customs. The first detailed report about northern Alaskan Eskimos was authored by John Simpson, the surgeon aboard the *Plover* throughout its six arctic winterings. This English vessel, commanded by T. E. L. Moore, was one of the ships to search for Franklin along the northern Alaskan and Siberian coasts. The *Plover* wintered at a Siberian harbor and then along western Seward Peninsula, Alaska. In 1852, after the crew of a supply ship had renewed the provisions and repaired the vessel, Rochfort Maguire replaced Moore as commander. The vessel then sailed to Point Barrow, where it wintered in 1852-3 and 1853-4. As the northernmost point on the continent, Barrow was a logical place to focus the northwest search for Franklin. Fortunately for Eskimology, the most important Eskimo settlement facing the Arctic Ocean in Alaska was Point Barrow.

In the following account of Barrow-area Eskimos, their differences from those to the east are emphasized. The sketch by John Simpson for 1852-4 provides the general background and certain details; it is supplemented by two later sources. For United States participation in the First International Polar Year in 1881 the Secretary of War sent a military party to Point Barrow under the command of Lieutenant Patrick H. Ray of the United States Army Eighth Infantry. John Murdoch, a sergeant in the Signal Corps with an A.M. degree from Harvard University, was attached to the expedition. He served as naturalist, and following his studies from 1881 to 1883 he wrote a major monograph about the Barrow Eskimos. In 1952 and 1953 the anthropologist Robert F. Spencer worked with the people at Point Barrow to reconstruct an aboriginal or baseline account of their lives, and this is the third key source.

John Simpson among others was surprised that manufactured goods had come to the Barrow region from eastern Asia along Native trade routes, both before and after European contact. By the early 1850s four or five boats a year carried beads, kettles, knives, tobacco, and other goods from East Cape, Siberia, to the Alaskan mainland. Traders boated to northern Seward Peninsula and on to market centers along northern Kotzebue Sound. Adjacent coastal and riverine Eskimos also arrived there to trade "amid feasting, dancing, and other enjoyments." Some goods were carried along inland drainages and arrived at Point Barrow the following year. The trade network was widespread and well coordinated, with both formal markets and exotic goods imported from afar. Nothing of comparable scope was known among Eskimos to the east.

Eskimo life along the northern coast of Alaska was much the same from near the Colville River mouth on the east to just south of Point Hope on the west. The area from the Colville River mouth to Barter Island, where Mackenzie Eskimos lived, was without a permanent population. The north Alaskan Eskimos of early historic times are called the Tareumiut, which is a label of convenience as much as a "tribal" designation. It recognizes a similarity of dialects spoken, resources exploited, and cultural patterning among the people from the Colville to Point Hope.

In the early 1850s the village at Point Barrow and another one about 10 miles away had a combined winter population of over 500 persons; reportedly the number was considerably greater a few years earlier. More people lived in the vicinity on a relatively permanent basis than had been reported among any Eskimos to the east. The small rectangular houses at Barrow were built in

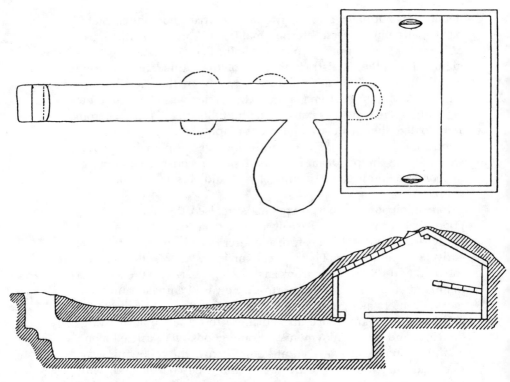

Figure 8-2 A winter house at Point Barrow. (From Murdoch, 1892)

shallow excavations and were framed with planks hewn from driftwood. Each was entered through a long underground tunnel framed with whales' bones, and off to one side of the tunnel was a kitchen. The main room was about 10 by 13 feet, and both it and the kitchen were covered with earth (Figure 8-2). The dominant household furnishing was a low bench along the rear wall of the main room. At each end of the bench were a lamp, its stand, and a drying rack; each of the two families that lived in a house used one set. Behind each house were four or more vertical posts with two levels of platforms built to store kayaks, weapons, and other equipment beyond the reach of dogs. Another platform was built nearby for umiaks, and underground caches were made from whales' bones to store meat and blubber. In the spring the ground thaw caused the house tunnels to flood, and the people moved into conical skin tents for the summer.

The largest buildings were the men's houses, and in each populous village there were at least three, all built above the ground on elevated spots. A men's house or karigi measured about 18 by 14 feet, had plank walls and roof, and was entered through a tunnel. Since only the lower portion of the outer walls was banked with dirt, snow blocks were placed against the outer walls for insulation before a karigi was used in the winter. Each of these named buildings served public functions but technically was owned by the whaling captain or *umelik* who supplied the building materials and maintained the structure. The title of umelik tended to pass down a family line, and a karigi was associated with specific extended families. Ordinarily a man was associated with the karigi of his father and became a member of the same whaling crew, but an individual might change crews and thereby become identified with a different karigi. A low bench extended along each interior wall; the members worked, lounged, and ate meals cooked by their wives at home. This was the place where youthful males learned craft skills and traditional lore, and where they participated in various games. Social festivities, best represented by the Messenger Feast, were centered in the men's houses, as was a great deal of whaling ritual; each karigi had its own set of charms. Women were not permitted in a karigi when they menstruated, but otherwise they were free to visit. Thus a karigi focused the social lives of these people in a manner unprecedented to the east.

Travelers, hunting parties, and temporary residents in a village built snowhouses but not of the dome-shaped form. Instead they made rectangular structures by constructing four straight walls of snow blocks, roofing them with poles placed across the upper row of blocks and topped with skins. Alternatively a snowbank might be excavated as the basic structure, with a wall of snow blocks added at the front if necessary; additional blocks formed the roof.

Men usually wore their hair tonsured at the crown, a hair style with a sporadic distribution farther east. Nearly all men also wore a pair of hat-shaped labrets. The "brim" of a labret or lip plug fitted on the inside of the wearer's lip to prevent the adornment from falling out. The most valuable labrets were made from polished white stone with half a blue bead glued to the flat outer surface. To prepare for wearing such ornaments, a hole was made beneath the

Figure 8-3 Men hunting a walrus, probably in northwestern Alaska. The man at the umiak bow has just harpooned a walrus. The line still wrapped around his left arm will be loosened as the person behind him throws overboard the sealskin float that is attached to the line. The men all are wearing parkas made from sewn intestines. (Reprinted by permission of the Smithsonian Institution Press from *Alaskan Eskimo Life in the 1890s as Sketched by Native Artists*, by George Phebus, Jr. © 1972 by the Smithsonian Institution)

lower lip at each corner of the mouth, and a small labret was fitted in each opening. The operation was performed without ceremony at about the time of puberty, and successively larger labrets were placed in the openings until the holes were about one-half inch in diameter. These ornaments were worn at subzero temperatures with apparently no ill effects. While at Kotzebue Sound, Beechey bought labrets from men willing to sell them. He went on to observe that the sellers did not mind "the inconvenience of the saliva that flowed through the badly cicatriced orifice over the chin; but rather laughed when some of us betrayed disgust at the spectacle, by thrusting their tongues through the holes, and winking their eyes."

Figure 8-4   Men hauling a walrus onto an ice floe. The illustration probably is for northern Alaskan Eskimos. (Reprinted by permission of the Smithsonian Institution Press from *Alaskan Eskimo Life in the 1890s as Sketched by Native Artists*, by George Phebus, Jr. © 1972 by the Smithsonian Institution)

Women parted their hair in the middle and either braided or twisted it into two long bundles that were wound with strips of leather or strings of beads. The ears of most women were pierced to receive copper or ivory hooks, and strings of beads dangled from the hooks. These Eskimo women, like most others to the east, had vertical lines tattooed from the bottom of their lower lips to their chins.

Most of the means used by Barrow Eskimos to obtain food are by now familiar. Swimming caribou were taken with spears from kayaks and with arrows shot from sinew-backed bows on the land. Waterfowl were hunted with multipronged bird darts, and wolves were captured with spring-bait sets. Darts were hurled with throwing-boards at the smaller seals, while toggle-headed harpoons were used against larger seals, walrus, and whales (Figures

8-3, 4). Other forms have not been described previously, and among these were bolas, also used by Mackenzie Eskimos. The bolas at Point Barrow had six oblong weights of ivory with a hole drilled at one end of each. Through each hole one end of a sinew cord about 30 inches long was tied, and the free ends of the cords were bound together. Several bolas, with the strings looped into themselves for carrying, were held in a leather pouch that hung from a hunter's neck. As a flock of ducks flew low, a bola was loosened, whirled about, and then released; its effective range was about 35 yards. The balls cartwheeled through the air with enough force to sometimes stun a bird or break its wing, but more often a cord wrapped around a duck's wing or neck and dropped it to the ground.

However much Eskimo weapons, especially those for capturing sea mammals, may be admired for their complexity, they are in some respects an ineffective use of human energy. The principal disadvantage is that a hunter must be poised at exactly the right moment to bring a weapon such as a toggle-headed harpoon into effective play. Prey-predator and time-place synchronization are absolutely essential. Any hunting device that could operate without this close coordination would have an obvious advantage. The nets used at Barrow for ringed seals are an example. In the fall after the sea water froze and seals began maintaining breathing holes in the ice, one of these openings was located. Two holes, about 35 feet apart, were chipped in the ice nearby. A weighted line was dropped in one hole, and a long pole with a hook at the far end was placed down the second hole to retrieve the line. A rawhide net, some 25 feet long and 14 feet wide, with stone weights at the bottom, was set beneath the ice by drawing it from one hole to the next with the line. This process was repeated until the breathing hole was nearly surrounded by nets as people waited nearby. The mesh of such a net was just large enough to encompass a seal's head, and once an animal was caught, it soon drowned. The net was pulled up, the seal removed, and the net reset. These nets could be used only when it was so dark that seals could not see the netting, and with good conditions as many as 100 seals might be taken at a single breathing hole in a 24-hour period. Nets were set in a like manner a short distance from leads in ice, and as many as 30 seals might be taken by one man in a comparatively brief span of time. Seal nets also were used in the spring after the animals had enlarged their breathing holes to crawl through and bask on the ice. A net was set horizontally beneath the hole, but it operated in the same manner as a net set vertically. Seals were attracted to these nets with different kinds of lures. One form consisted of a handle with seal claws attached at one end. By gently scratching the ice with this lure, a hunter could induce a curious seal to approach the net. Seals also were lured with a rattle, by whistling softly, or by scraping the ice with an ice pick. Vertically hung seal nets were staked out in open water near the shore in the summer. Thus nets were an effective means for taking seals at Point Barrow, but they seldom were used for this purpose to the east.

Additional means for taking fish or game with facilities rather than weapons deserve mention. Deadfalls were set for foxes and baleen snares for waterfowl. Pitfalls were dug in the snow for caribou. Gill nets were set beneath the ice in rivers, primarily to take whitefish. While each of these techniques was employed somewhere farther east, the diversity and intensity of their use at Point Barrow is noteworthy.

Here in northern Alaska we first encounter elaborate rituals, the close coordination of many persons, and well-defined leaders as part of a subsistence routine, that of hunting bowhead whales at Barrow. Comparable complexity for whale hunting may have existed in West Greenland or elsewhere to the east, but it is doubtful that even more information about whaling there will change the picture. We are indebted to Spencer for his detailed reconstruction of whaling at Point Barrow. As he has written, "the activities of the winter—shamanistic seances, karigi games, social events—were marked by the constant emphasis on the coming whaling season in the spring and by the expression of hopes for its success."

At Barrow wealth and authority were concentrated in the role of an umelik, who was not only the owner of an umiak but the captain of a whaling crew. A man identified as an umelik had considerable wealth, commanded great respect, and performed important ceremonial functions, especially with respect to whaling. By caring for his crew members he gained their loyalty. Yet he was not a "chief" because his only followers were relatives and the members of his crew. One prerequisite was that an umelik possess surplus goods. Although he might inherit property, he was expected to accumulate additional wealth through his own skills before launching his career. If he had the ability and the support of relatives, he could acquire enough property to establish his position. Another essential was an ability as a shrewd trader so that he always could expand his wealth but never be considered miserly, openly competitive, or boastful. An umelik might devote years to attaining his position, and yet one unsuccessful whaling season might cause him to be abandoned by his crew and again be considered only an ordinary person.

As the sun began to return in late winter, preliminary preparations for the whaling season began; by early March this was the all-consuming interest of the villagers. The whaling equipment was cleaned with great care, and a new set of clothing was sewn for each member of a whaling crew. The wife of an umelik supervised making a new cover for the boat, and after it was in place, a special meal was prepared for the crew. They then abstained from sexual relations and began sleeping in the karigi identified with their umelik. The leads in the pack ice were carefully watched, and when beluga began to appear, it was a sign that bowhead whales soon would follow. During the four days before they went out on the ice, a crew sat quietly in its karigi and thought of whales. One crew member, often an old shaman, was their spiritual leader. He knew the whaling songs that would ensure the success of a hunt, and he advised youthful crew members, especially novices, about procedures. The restrictions observed by the umelik were more severe than for his crew. He was obligated to give away any whale meat currently in his caches. One instance was remembered when a crew killed 10 whales in a season, and an immense amount of meat remained by the next spring. Yet it was distributed before the new whaling season began. The wife of an umelik had special ceremonial mittens sewn for her, and her husband commissioned the construction of a special wooden container to hold water to be offered to any slain whale. The woman poured fresh water from this vessel on the umiak while she sang her own whaling songs as part of the final preparations. The whaling equipment was assembled in a ritual manner, and as the sun set on the fourth day, the crew loaded the umiak and ran with it to the edge of the ice, usually a distance of a few hundred yards. After reaching the edge of the ice, the crew got into the umiak and pretended to paddle; the umelik sat nearby with his box of whaling charms and sang special whaling songs, while the spiritual leader did the same in the boat. Following this ritual, the boat was hauled to the edge of a lead and all the gear was readied. No fires could be built and no food cooked nor tents erected. The crew ate little and took turns sleeping behind windbreaks and watching for whales.

The whaling season lasted from two to about six weeks, depending on weather and ice conditions. The crew observed food and other taboos, and their families, especially the wife of the umelik, conformed to ritual prohibitions in the village. The success of a whaling season was to a great extent attributed to the power of charms belonging to the umelik and individual charms owned by the crew. These often were kept in wooden boxes whose tops included the figure of a whale in relief; these containers were kept in the umiak. The charms of an umelik might include a beetle, the hair of a famous whaler who had died, a stuffed raven skin, or baleen carvings of seals and whales. Charms such as these might be inherited or obtained either from an independent shaman or the spiritual advisor of a crew. Their purpose was to compel a whale to swim near an umiak, to prevent losing a whale, or to forestall disaster.

The principal weapon for whaling was a large toggle-headed harpoon fitted with a ground slate blade. A heavy rawhide line led from the harpoon head to two inflated sealskin floats. When a whale was sighted, the crew launched its umiak and paddled quietly as the helmsman attempted to predict where the whale would surface. When it appeared beneath the bow, the harpooner thrust his weapon, twisting it slightly so that the toggle would hold, and the floats were thrown overboard immediately. The umelik and the harpooner spat into the water so that their songs would reach the whale as it sounded. When the whale resurfaced, the helmsman attempted to maneuver the umiak so that the next harpoon would strike the whale's side. After a wounded whale tired, a stone-pointed spear was thrust repeatedly into its heart or kidneys to make the most effective kill. Under the best of circumstances a whale was approached by an umiak on each side, each harpooner launching his harpoon and thrusting his lance into one side. In this instance the whale was divided equally between the crews, and each could claim credit for the kill. If one crew assisted another in taking a whale, only the crew making the original strike could claim it, although the meat was divided among any participating crews.

The typical bowhead whale harvested was about 33 feet long, weighed an equal number of tons, and was not regarded as an awesome prey under normal circumstances. The most dangerous situations arose when a whale fouled the lines and surfaced beneath an umiak or when the harpoon head pulled free and the line backlashed into an umiak. After a hunt the carcass was buoyed with floats and towed back by the crew credited with the kill, followed by the other boats that had participated. The whale was hauled to the edge of the ice, and all the villagers turned out to help pull it out of the water. The whale was formally greeted by the wife of the umelik, who wore special clothing and facial paint. She put fresh water in the container made for the occasion and poured it on the snout and then on the blowhole of the whale as she said, "Here is water; you will want to drink. Next spring come back to our boat." Then the wives of the members of the boat crew each thanked the whale for allowing itself to be taken. In this manner the whale became a member of the village.

The umelik and the crew permitted everyone to take as much of the black skin or *muktuk*, a delicacy, as they could haul away. The umelik kept the heart and flippers, which were choice parts, and the remainder was divided among the participating crews. After a bowhead had been killed, everyone kept busy cutting up, hauling, storing, cooking, and eating whale meat. The umelik gave cooked meat to anyone asking for it. By the time he had feasted the villagers and distributed meat to his crew and others who had helped him, very little meat remained. An umelik's wealth increased only after he took a second whale in a season.

As long as good ice and weather conditions prevailed, the whalers returned to wait and hunt again. After the season was over, a series of dances was held in which successful whaling crews were the principal performers and everyone else feasted at their expense. Dances were held in the karigis of the successful crews, who were the performers. They wore parkas with the hoods up and small wooden masks covering their faces (Figure 8-5). Women were not permitted in a karigi when the men put on their masks or during the initial dance held there. The performers later danced through the village from house to house frightening children. This ritual by the members of a voluntary association was a more esoteric performance than has been described previously, and the association has the earmarks of an emerging secret society, a development unknown in the east.

Figure 8-5 Face-sized wooden masks used by Point Barrow Eskimos, probably in ceremonies associated with whaling. (From Murdoch, 1892)

At the end of the whaling season a *nulukatuk* was held as both a victory celebration and "to let the whale know we are happy." The games and feasting were hosted by karigi members at a traditional spot in the open where umiaks were propped up to serve as a windbreak. Competitive games included feats of strength or endurance and wrestling, with the members of one karigi pitted against those of another. On the first evening one karigi umelik after another gave away muktuk as a gesture of generosity. The feasting and games continued the next day and culminated on the third or fourth day; only if many whales had been taken were the festivities extended longer. The close of a nulukatuk was highlighted with a "blanket" toss. Four sets of poles arranged as tripods were set up in a square, and rawhide lines were stretched diagonally between pairs. A walrus hide was centered over the spot where the lines crossed. A whaling crew held the edges of the hide and the lines alternately taut and then slack as their umelik was tossed, and then each of the crew members followed. A person being tossed attempted to stand erect and maintain his balance as the manipulators of the hide and ropes attempted to toss him so high that he would lose control and would fall onto the hide. The wife of the umelik and then anyone else could ask to be tossed as the audience joked about the performances. On this note the festivities ended.

Second only to the nulukatuk, but far more secular in its focus, was the Messenger Feast. It had few religious associations and was held primarily to enhance the social position of umeliks and secondarily the community at large. In essence the umeliks of one village invited their counterparts in another settlement to participate in an ongoing exchange of goods. The Messenger Feast not only integrated the members of a community, but it reinforced their bonds with neighboring villagers. The feast usually was held in January, at the low point of the economic cycle. An umelik who decided to be the principal host spent a number of years accumulating surplus food and property, aided by his relatives and whaling crew. Food was stored, and artifacts such as clothing, kayaks, and sleds were amassed for the event. The principal organizer also enlisted the support of other umeliks as secondary hosts, thus effectively producing village-wide participation. One umelik with great wealth reportedly demanded a given amount from each family, and he or his underlings threatened those who did not comply.

The formal invitation usually was extended to a community with whom trading ties existed. Two respected elders who were not the hosts extended the invitation by carrying messages to guests; this practice gave the feast its name. Each messenger was presented with a paddle-shaped staff with feathers tied at one end and a red mark painted on it to represent each primary guest. The specific host for each guest taught the messenger what he was to say to that particular guest. These were formal invitations involving songs, and each concluded with a list of gifts expected by the host, sometimes also stating what might be given in return. After the messengers learned the texts perfectly a dance was held; then, bearing their staffs, they departed by dog team to the guest village. In the meantime young men of the host village were selected as runners and began training for a foot race against their counterparts among the guests. Members of the host village practiced dances, readied their finest clothing, and often built a special rectangular karigi of snowblocks and skin roofing to hold the many guests.

When the messengers were in sight of the guest village, they stopped their dog teams and waited. The villagers, seeing the staffs, knew their purpose and came out en masse to make them welcome. The messengers went to the karigi of the chief guest, where they recited their messages; the guests in turn told what gifts they expected. As honored persons they could make difficult demands that the host was obligated to meet. When the guests were ready to depart with whatever gifts they could obtain, they left with the messengers. On reaching the host village, the guests camped nearby while the messengers went to the karigi where the feast was centered. They seated themselves behind a low curtain of skins near a pole from which a large box drum was suspended. The messengers alternated in raising their mnemonic staffs to reveal the mark of one guest after another who accepted, and they called out their names but did not indicate how many others might be accompanying that guest. Thus it was essential for the hosts to have an abundance of gifts and food in reserve.

Dances accompanied and followed the announcements by the messengers, who sat in a corner feigning anger after presenting the guest list. They would not speak until coaxed by the primary host and then said that they had been poorly received at the guest village because he had deceived them. They were scorned—which was true and a part of the appropriate behavior—when they told that umiaks and sleds were among the gifts. The chief host and his seconds pretended to be offended and proposed to double the amount they had originally offered. As villagers questioned them, the messengers whispered how many people were coming and what they expected, information that soon was conveyed to the hosts. Included were requests for extremely unusual foods, and in providing such gifts the hosts gained great prestige.

On the second day a foot race was run by young men representing the guests and the hosts. Afterwards the guests broke camp and were received formally in front of the karigi by the hosts, who wore their ceremonial garments. Their parkas were made from carefully matched skins; on their heads were feather headdresses, and bearskin mittens covered their hands. Each host held a bow with an arrow fitted in place and the bowstring taut. The hosts pretended to be angry and to not recognize the guests. After their threats, the hosts shot the arrows above the heads of the guests. At this moment dancers came out of the karigi, danced toward the guests and encircled them; afterwards they returned to the karigi as the guests slowly followed. The hosts named their specific guests and presented each with a small gift and a choice piece of meat. A man then began beating the box drum as a signal for persons with tambourine drums to keep the rhythm for a series of introductory songs. The guests later left the karigi and returned with gifts; they danced in and made the presentations to individual hosts. The guests and hosts then danced together before the guests returned to their sleds. All the hosts followed them to the sleds, and the principal host said in a formal manner, "Not enough is yet given," and offered another small gift as did the other hosts. The guests offered similar gifts in return, and this exchange was repeated four times. At the end the principal host said, "Now that is all," which ended the day's activities. The guests stayed that night in the karigi, and the hosts went to their homes.

The festivities of the third day began with a dance by the guests; then, after dances by special groups such as runners, the primary hosts danced. This was followed by the hosts presenting gifts to the guests and also to fellow villagers who had helped with the arrangements; the presents included beads, labrets, sealskins full of oil, and skins. Afterwards all the visitors who had come with guests also received gifts; the guests then left the karigi and returned to their sleds.

The highlight of the Messenger Feast occurred later on the third day. Piled high in the karigi before the box drum were clothing, kayaks, sleds, weapons, and even umiaks to be presented as major gifts. All the people of the host village probably gathered to see the immense amount of wealth. The primary host then went out to call his honored guest, and they pretended to race back to the karigi, with the guest always running a close second. After entering the karigi, they each kicked an inflated bladder that was suspended above the floor near the door, signaling that the time had come for the most lavish presentations. The major host called out the name of his guest, the drum was beaten four times, and the guest received his presents and the special food he had requested. Thus it was for each guest, who then sat near his pile of gifts and began eating the special food. In the dance that followed, women danced behind men, and they all sang about this aspect of the festivities (Figure 8-6). Thus ended the formal presentations. The guests took their gifts to their sleds and returned to the karigi to sleep. The

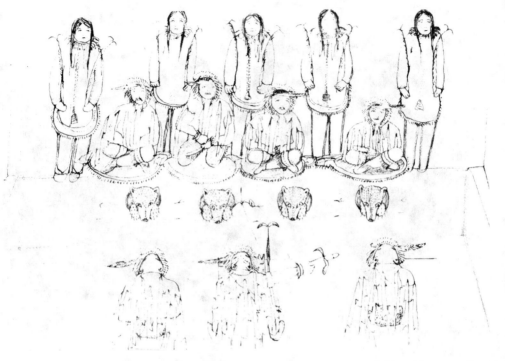

Figure 8-6   Drawing of a ceremony, probably a Messenger Feast ritual in northern Alaska. (Reprinted by permission of the Smithsonian Institution Press from *Alaskan Eskimo Life in the 1890s as Sketched by Native Artists*, by George Phebus, Jr. © 1972 by the Smithsonian Institution)

fourth and final day was dominated by ball games, social dances, and a closing dance, after which guests and hosts left the karigi. Then two men emerged from the karigi wearing loon-bill headpieces and carrying bows with arrows ready to shoot. They danced about and shot the arrows above the heads of the hosts, which signaled the departure of the guests, their sleds laden with gifts.

The ritual overlay of the Messenger Feast thinly masks its purpose as an economic exchange. This was in essence the Barrow Eskimo counterpart of the famous potlatch exchanges held by Northwest Coast Indians. The feast was far more complex than any secular activity reported in earlier chapters of this book; events of a like magnitude were unknown among more easterly Eskimos.

Figure 8-7 Kotzebue Sound Eskimos showing the lateral labrets and hair styles of men as well as the tattoos on the chin of a woman. (From Choris, 1822)

A detailed description of the Messenger Feast as performed at Point Barrow is possible because it was recorded by an anthropologist at a time when people remembered it clearly. Robert F. Spencer published the reconstruction and collected even more information about the Messenger Feast than is conveyed in this summary.

To the southwest of Point Barrow the next major community was Point Hope, and the two groups of villagers are together called the Tareumiut. The Point Hope Eskimos usually held Messenger Feasts with Eskimos to the south because Point Barrow was so far away; thus the Point Hope people were more directly exposed to influences from the south. At Point Hope the karigis were more permanent structures with plank floors and underground passages, and in early historic times there were seven such buildings. At Barrow the charms associated with a particular karigi were simple compared with those at Point Hope, where they also appear to have had a deeper meaning. One Point Hope karigi had as its primary symbol a whale carving made with movable jaws, and another had a wooden mask with ivory eyes and labrets. These and other forms at Point Hope commemorated the great deeds of ancestors, and their use during whaling ceremonies was important. Yet there was no clear idea that the masked performers were impersonating supernaturals. At Point Hope, masks seem to have been used more often and were somewhat better integrated into the ceremonial round. The farther south one goes among coastal Eskimos in Alaska the more developed the ceremonialism.

It may seem that thus far in the presentation of Eskimo life the subject of art has been badly neglected. Yet explorers, and the others whose observations are being reviewed, seldom mentioned Eskimo artistic accomplishments. The most notable exception was the decorative art of Angmagsalik Eskimos in East Greenland described by Holm and reported in Chapter 6. One reason the topic did not command greater attention is that the artistic accomplishments of most Eskimos in Greenland and Canada during the early historic period were not especially notable. However, some of the ivory sculptures made nearly 2000 years ago by Western Eskimos (e.g., Ipiutak, Okvik, and Old Bering Sea cultures) represent rare aesthetic achievements, especially in the portrayal of animal and human figures. In addition, these Eskimos often engraved utilitarian objects, such as harpoon heads, with elaborate designs. Yet by about A.D. 1200, and especially with the approach of historic times, Eskimo sculptures had become less common and were not as pleasing as previously.

Among the coastal Inuit of Alaska in the early historic period, the notable works in wood were associated with shamans or ceremonies, especially those concerned with whaling. The face masks had human features that were sometimes distorted (Figure 8-5). These were primarily dance masks, but they might also be worn by shamans when they communicated with spirit aids. Wooden figures, such as those of whales, were used during karigi rituals that were directly or indirectly associated with whale ceremonialism. Sculptured wooden figures served as individual charms to protect their owners from evil or to perform specific functions, such as attracting game to the owner (Figure 8-8, *a*). Apart from masks and wooden sculptures, the most impressive works are representational engravings in ivory. Strips of ivory made into bow drills and bag handles were engraved on two or three faces. The subject

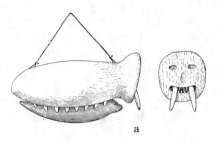

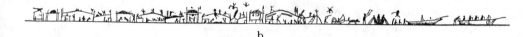

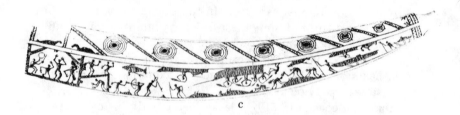

Figure 8-8 Charm and engravings: *a*, Kotzebue Sound hunter's whaling charm (From Nelson, 1899). *b*, Scenes of village life engraved on the ivory handle of a bow drill, southeastern Seward Peninsula (From Hoffman, 1897). *c*, Scenes engraved on an ivory pipestem, Norton Sound area (From Hoffman, 1897).

matter usually included people, scenes from village life, and animals, especially caribou. One bow-drill shaft from southeastern Seward Peninsula is exceptional for the variety of events depicted; one panel is illustrated as Figure 8-8, *b*. The arrival of white whalers, gold seekers, and tourists brought a ready market for souvenir art. Old motifs were readily adapted to new forms; one example is the ivory pipe engraved in a traditional manner. A

pipestem from the Norton Sound region illustrates this development (Figure 8-8, *c*).

*   *   *

Thus far attention has focused entirely on Eskimos who lived
along treeless coasts, but over a fourth of all Alaskan Eskimos had
settled along the banks of rivers. In the northwestern sector two
major rivers, the Noatak and Kobuk, flow into Kotzebue Sound.
The Kobuk attracts attention because in two consecutive years rival
parties of explorers journeyed there, and their combined accounts
effectively introduce Eskimos who were quite different from those
considered previously.

By 1867, when Alaska was purchased from Russia, the coastal
zone was reasonably well surveyed, but some major river systems
were largely unmapped or entirely unknown. In the early years of
control by the United States, traders and whalers rather than
Federal representatives were the most far-flung and visible groups
of outsiders. By about 1880 the commanders of United States Navy
vessels began to represent Federal interests in southeastern Alaska,
and from the Aleutian Islands north the captains of Revenue
Marine (Coast Guard) vessels were the only law. The Revenue
Cutter *Corwin* began plying northern waters in 1880, and the Secretary of the Treasury offered a glowing account of this vessel and its
crew. "To thousands of half-civilized natives she represents the
majesty and power of the nation, and dispenses such justice as
humanity and the needs of the people call for."

Rivalry between Navy and Revenue Marine officers led to Kobuk
explorations; the competition began in a curious manner. In 1879
the *Jeannette*, commanded by United States naval officer George
W. De Long, attempted to reach the North Pole by boldly pushing
into the ice off the northeastern coast of Siberia. The *Jeannette* soon
was trapped and remained ice-locked through two winters. The
vessel finally was crushed by ice off the New Siberian Islands, and
the crew struggled by boat and on foot to the Siberian mainland.
Most of them reached the Lena River delta but died before help
could arrive. The *Rodgers*, sent in search of the *Jeannette*, was
destroyed by fire at winter quarters along the coast of eastern
Siberia. Eskimos in the vicinity clothed and fed the survivors until
they were rescued, and as a gesture of appreciation, the United
States Congress appropriated funds for gifts for them. Delivery of

the gifts was entrusted to a naval officer, George M. Stoney, who took them aboard the *Corwin* when it sailed in 1883. The vessel's captain was Michael A. Healy, whose father was white and whose mother was a Negro, once a slave. After the presents were distributed, the ship sailed to Kotzebue Sound where "Hell Roaring Mike" Healy placed a boat and supplies at the disposal of Stoney and agreed to return for him in about two weeks. Stoney and three others searched for and found the Kobuk, a river mentioned by Beechey. After being confused in the delta, they located the main course and ascended it about 40 miles.

The following year, 1884, Healy again cruised to Kotzebue Sound on the *Corwin*. This time he ordered one of his Revenue Marine officers, Lieutenant John C. Cantwell, to survey the Kobuk River and to prepare a report about its resources, especially a deposit of jade thought to exist there. Cantwell was instructed further, "In dealing with the natives you will be careful to enforce the strictest integrity on the part of each member of your party, and should a collision take place between your people and the natives you will try and make good your retreat without bloodshed. If, however, this be impossible, act with firmness, decision, and moderation." Cantwell and five others, including an interpreter, set off in early July on a steam launch towing two small boats. Soon the marshy lower river delta was behind them, and the first stands of spruce appeared along the banks. The water of the lower river ran fast, but they were able to make about 25 miles a day for the first five days. As the river narrowed and they encountered fast water, their progress was much slower. The Eskimos whom Cantwell met and called Indians were "as usual, impassive and undemonstrative, but not unkind." At one meeting with Eskimos he was told that the jade deposit was farther upstream, but that anyone going there and taking away any of the stone "will be afflicted with some dreadful malady ever afterwards, . . . the stone belongs to the natives and not to the white man." Cantwell countered that the stone did not belong to them individually but was theirs through their great-grandfathers who also were the great-grandfathers of whites. He wrote that "this direct claim to relationship did not meet with a very cordial reception."

In the swift water and shallows of the upper river the launch temporarily was abandoned, and Cantwell, the interpreter, and

Figure 8-9 A Kobuk Eskimo summer camp. The women in the foreground are in a bark-covered canoe; in the background are dome-shaped tents and fish drying on racks. The steam launch of the Cantwell party of 1884 is seen at a distance. (From Healy, 1889)

three other Eskimos went in by umiak. The "Jade Mountain" was seen at a distance as they traveled about 300 miles inland before turning back. On the return trip they tried but failed to reach the mountain, but they did collect pieces of the green stone from a nearby stream. While Cantwell was inland searching for the jade, a Navy party under the command of Stoney passed by, ascending the river. This group was able to push upstream a little farther than Cantwell had traveled.

In the summer of 1885 Cantwell returned to the Kobuk River and reached the river's source. Again as he was traveling downstream Stoney was on his way up. Stoney, however, was accompanied by a comparatively large party: 4 officers, 10 enlisted men, and 2 Eskimos with their families. They had enough provisions for about two years, and in the fall they stopped along the upper river and began building their winter quarters. From there small parties examined portions of the Colville, Noatak, Selawik, and Yukon drainages. The accomplishments of Stoney and his men on this expedition were far more impressive than those of Cantwell. The 1884 report of Cantwell's trip was published in 1889, and his 1885 account appeared in 1887. However, a full report of Stoney's achievements never was published, and the two-part summary did not appear in print until 1900. In the first article Stoney wrote that publication had been ordered by Congress 10 years earlier, but that "in some way the papers have mysteriously disappeared." It seems that rivalry between the Revenue Marine and the United States Navy may have led to the disappearance.

The combined accounts by Cantwell and Stoney effectively introduce a variety of Eskimo culture different from any reported in previous pages. The main difficulty in utilizing their reports is that it sometimes is difficult to determine whether they mean that a particular custom is characteristic of the Kobuk people, since both men were also familiar with surrounding Eskimos. The resulting confusion is not so disconcerting as it might otherwise be thanks to James L. Giddings. He surveyed and excavated archaeological sites along the Kobuk in 1940, 1941, and 1947. Giddings also collected ethnographic information from elderly persons, some of whom recalled the visits of Cantwell and Stoney.

The ancestors of modern Kobuk Eskimos long ago had abandoned sea-mammal hunting along treeless coasts to live along the forested banks of this river. Sites reflecting a continuity of occupation date back to at least A.D. 1250, and most likely to much earlier times. Many cultural forms seen at early historic riverine settlements are by now familiar. The rectangular winter houses built of logs and entered through a tunnel seem ordinary, but the presence of central fireplaces in the houses is unusual. The food-storage facilities also were different. Vertical logs framed and walled a cache built on the ground and covered with a flat roof made of small poles; it was used for storing dried fish. As expected, tents served as summer housing, but along the Kobuk they were dome-shaped and often were covered with slabs of birch or spruce bark and moss rather than with sewn skins. In this area mosquitoes sometimes were very bothersome, and smudge fires were built in front of the tent entrances.

Perhaps the most striking artifactual differences were in the

Kobuk Eskimo modes of transport. For individual water travel, kayaks had been displaced by 10-foot-long canoes that were hip-wide amidships and tapered to a point at each end. A wooden canoe frame was covered with birch bark and the forepart was decked. Sections of bark were sewn together with strips of inner bark from willows, and the seams were sealed with heated spruce gum. In shallow water a canoe was propelled with a pair of short sticks, but otherwise single-bladed paddles served. A canoe weighed about 25 pounds and was therefore highly portable, providing men with great mobility during summer and fall hunting trips. Umiaks were replaced by large canoes covered with spruce or birch bark; these vessels had the same general lines as hunting canoes.

In Canada the dog sleds most often looked like ladders, and teams were hitched in a fan-shaped arrangement. In northern Alaska, however, dogs were staggered on either side of a central trace. This hitching pattern is especially well adapted to localities where there are obstacles such as trees in the trail; the fan-shaped hitch would be a disaster for dogs and sled alike in a wooded area. The sleds in northern Alaska had built-up beds and stanchions topped with rails; sleds used along the Kobuk were of the same style but were lighter. Here a five-dog team could cover about 60 miles a day when trail conditions were relatively good.

In the deep and powdery snow of timbered areas like that along the Kobuk, snowshoes provided valuable winter mobility. The snowshoes were about five feet long and up to eight inches wide. Framed with spruce and turned up slightly at the toe, the shoes were webbed with dehaired rawhide thongs. Among the Eskimos described previously, snowshoes seldom were important because the snow cover over which they hunted usually was not deep or was crusted by the wind.

The relative stability of Kobuk communities is most attributable to the chum (dog) salmon that ascended the river in runs each summer to spawn in tributary streams. Dome-shaped tents were set up in fish camps located along clear sections of beach where the river was relatively narrow and the water comparatively shallow. At this time of year most men were either trading at a coastal market or hunting in the mountains. Women fished intensively for salmon and thus made a major contribution to the welfare of their families. The seines that they used were up to 75 feet long and about 5 feet wide. The netting, made from the inner bark of willows, was buoyed at the top with wooden floats and weighted at the bottom with antler or stone sinkers. As the time for a salmon run approached, women kept their nets folded in large bark canoes resting at the edge of the beach. Children and women watched the downstream waters for ripples produced by a school of salmon. When someone sighted such a rippling, he called out, and pairs of women ran to each canoe. One woman climbed aboard as the other woman shoved the boat off but held onto one end of the net. The woman on shore walked downstream at a brisk pace as the canoeist paid out the net and allowed the boat to drift. As salmon began hitting the seine, the canoe was paddled toward the shore, drawing the seine in an arc. Children helped pull in the net with salmon entrapped, and the larger fish were knocked on the head with wooden clubs. A salmon was processed by cutting off its head, gutting it and removing any roe, and then splitting it down the back. The backbone was removed, but the tail was left intact to keep the body joined. Fish were hung to dry on a pole rack, the heads were buried in pits to decay as headcheese, and the viscera boiled for their oil. The pervasive Eskimo differentiation between edibles from the land and water prevailed. While salmon were being taken, the people did not work the skins of caribou or mountain sheep.

Fish were the staff of life to these Eskimos. Salmon were most important, but other fish, especially whitefish, also were vital as food. Whitefish migrated downstream after the river ice had formed in the fall, and at this time holes were picked in the ice and poles placed to form a weir. At a gap in the weir a net on a frame was inserted. Each time a fish struck the tended net, it was lifted, the fish removed, and the net set again. In the spring cone-shaped fish traps made from spruce splints or willows were set to harvest whitefish as they made their way upstream.

Second to fish among eatables were caribou, taken in already familiar ways. Unlike the Eskimos described previously, the Kobuk people gave vegetable products a significant, yet peripheral, place in the diet. One species of wild root was diligently dug and eaten raw or boiled. A particular kind of grass was boiled, and great quantities of berries, especially blueberries and salmonberries, were collected in birch-bark baskets. Berries most often were mixed with caribou oil or seal oil received in trade from the coast.

This dish, called *agutuk* or "Eskimo ice cream," was a favored food.

The texture of social life understandably had more in common with that of Barrow Eskimos than with any others. Among the Kobuk people "rich men" were analogous to the umeliks at Barrow although they were not nearly as wealthy. Along the Kobuk they appear to have been shrewd traders who organized summer trading trips to coastal markets where pelts and jade blades from the interior were exchanged for products of the sea, especially seal oil and sealskins. The Kobuk Eskimos likewise held Messenger Feasts at karigis built for the occasion. Messengers carried special staffs encircled with strips of skin, each representing an invited family. Runners, a ceremonial greeting of visitors by shooting arrows over their heads, gift exchanges, and the distribution of choice food to guests all were a part of the celebration.

Some aspects of Kobuk Eskimo life seem more Indian than Eskimo. They shared with Northern Athapaskan Indians such forms as finely made snowshoes, bark canoes, birch-bark baskets, and a general emphasis on bark technology. Furthermore, Kobuk Eskimo life was in many ways far more pedestrian than that described for sea-mammal hunters. Thus they seem Indianlike in some respects and atypically Eskimo in other respects. More important than either of these qualities was the adaptive nature of Kobuk Eskimo culture, its tuneful adjustment to a northern riverine setting. As we move farther south in Alaska, the adaptive vitality of Eskimo culture emerges even more as a striking characteristic.

NOTES

EXPLORATIONS IN NORTHERN ALASKA.   The only detailed analysis of Russian and English explorations in the Bering Strait region is by Dorothy J. Ray (1975a). The history of American whaling north of Bering Strait is based on the study by VanStone (1958). Sources consulted for English explorations include Franklin (1828), Beechey (1831), Thomas Simpson (1843), and Rich (1960, v. 3, 485, 647-8), who wrote of the travels of Dease and T. Simpson.

POINT BARROW ESKIMO SOURCES.   These people were studied first by John Simpson in 1852-4, but his chapter in a book about arctic geography and ethnography did not appear until 1875. The 1881-3 study by Murdoch (1892) is best regarding material culture and is supplemented by Patrick H.

Ray (1885) for the same time period. Last and most important is the ethnographic reconstruction by Spencer (1959).

POINT HOPE SOURCES.   Most of the information about whaling and ceremonial activity in early historic times is reported in the 1940 ethnographic reconstruction by Froelich G. Rainey (1947). Nearly all that is known about masks from Point Hope is included in an article by VanStone (1968-9).

KOBUK RIVER EXPLORATIONS AND ETHNOGRAPHY.   The best summary of the Cantwell and Stoney competition is by Morgan B. Sherwood (1965, 119-32). John E. Caswell (1956, 200) suggests that interservice rivalries led to the disappearance of the Stoney manuscript. A brief sketch of Michael A. Healy is authored by Dennis L. Noble (1976).

The ethnographic information by Cantwell was included in the *Corwin* reports for 1884 (Healy, 1889) and 1885 (Healy, 1887), while the summary report by Stoney (1900) appeared much later. These sources are summarized and expanded by Giddings (1961). The recent prehistory of the Kobuk Eskimos was determined by Giddings (1952b).

ADDITIONAL SOURCES FOR THE INUIT OF ALASKA.   The ethnographic reconstruction of Nunamiut life by Nicholas J. Gubser (1965), based on fieldwork in 1959 and 1960-1, is a fine anthropological study of these caribou-hunting Eskimos. Yet this was a remade Eskimo society whose members had abandoned the interior to live along the north coast for about 20 years before they returned inland in 1938. The other comprehensive account of Inupik-speaking Eskimos is the ethnohistory for the Seward Peninsula region by D. J. Ray (1975a). This book contains many details about Eskimo life in the early contact period and also reveals that no comprehensive ethnographic account exists for this time period.

MARKETS.   The Eskimo trade centers along northern Kotzebue Sound are famous but very poorly described. They are mentioned by Beechey (1831, v. 1, 351-2), John Simpson (1875, 236), and Cantwell (in Healy, 1889, 71) among others. VanStone (1962b) published the inventory of trade goods included by Stoney in his manuscript but not in his published account. Weyer (1932, 166-7) summarizes trade relations in West Greenland and concludes that the network was rather well developed.

DETAILS.   The New to Old World spread of smoking tobacco is summarized by Driver and Massey (1957, 260). A statement by Morris Swadesh (1951, 67) characterizes the difference between Inupik and Yupik as approximating the separation between English and German. While the Eskimo use of masks is not confined exclusively to Alaska, masks were very rare elsewhere in the American arctic. Presumably they were aboriginal among the Angmagsalik of East Greenland (Thalbitzer, 1914, 636). The importance of Revenue Marine vessels in representing the interests of the United States along the northern coast of Alaska, as reported by the Secretary of the Treasury, is from a quotation cited by Sherwood (1965, 121).

CHAPTER

9

Alaskan Yuit

More than a third of all Eskimos lived along the coast and adjacent riverine sectors of Alaska from near Bering Strait to the north Pacific rim. These were the Yuit, Eskimos who spoke the Yupik language. Among their northern cousins, the Inuit, a great deal of cultural similarity prevailed, but the Yuit varied widely among themselves. Some Alaskan Yuit never saw a live seal, hunted a polar bear, or sledded with dogs. In one sector the people dressed in sleeveless parkas and went barefoot. Novel social conventions included rigid class distinctions, totemic groups, and friendly relations with Indians. Their religious activities were dominated by elaborate annual ceremonies involving the impersonation of spirits by masked dancers. The customs of these people were tantalizingly varied and contrasted with the relatively uniform ways of the Inuit.

Most Inuit lived in a coastal zone, a region defined as "arctic," where the waters were frozen most of the year. The majority of the Yuit lived in a "subarctic" zone; along the north Pacific area, sea ice did not form, and in much of the remaining region, the winter ice was not as solid as farther north. Most Inuit lived in a tundra zone with sparse vegetation. This was in striking contrast with Yuit environments. The Yuit setting was dominated by dense forests of

233

huge trees along the north Pacific, by tall grasses on Kodiak Island, spruce forests along western Alaska, and tundra elsewhere.

The dramatic differences in habitat led to marked contrasts in economic adaptations among the Yuit. The Siberian and St. Lawrence Island populations, as intensive hunters of sea mammals, were most similar in their life-style to the Inuit. From Norton Sound southward salmon usually played a dominant role in the diet, but for Yuit along the Bering Sea coast beluga and seals also were important foods. The Eskimos living along the lower courses of the three major rivers emptying into the Bering Sea—the Yukon, Kuskokwim, and Nushagak—were salmon fishermen and secondarily caribou hunters. Along the coasts of the Alaska Peninsula fish and seals dominated, and much the same was true for Pacific Ocean drainages, although here great whales also were hunted.

*   *   *

In Russia during the latter part of the 1500s the legendary Cossack Yermak forced a gateway through the Ural Mountains, and the conquest of Siberia was in the offing. Yakutsk was founded along the Lena River in 1632, the Indigirka River was discovered in 1636, and the first settlement on the Kolyma River was established in 1644. A few years later Semen I. Dezhnev, a Cossack, set off with a number of boats on a voyage that would be subject to diverse interpretations. They sailed down the Kolyma to the sea and on to the east. According to some historians the boat bearing Dezhnev was driven south to the mouth of the Anadyr River. Years later some Russians believed that the crew of one boat had landed in Alaska and founded a settlement on Seward Peninsula. Dezhnev apparently discovered Bering Strait 80 years earlier than Bering, but his report was lost until 1736 and was not published until 1742. By the early 1700s information about the "large country," Alaska, was available to the Russians in Siberia, and accounts had begun to filter back to European Russia.

The earliest substantive report about Alaska was prepared by Petr I. Popov, who was sent to collect tribute from the Chukchee in northeastern Siberia and to gather information about the large country across the waters. He wrote in 1711 that the people to the east fought the Chukchee with bows and arrows and that their language as well as their customs differed from Asian ones. Among the Chukchee were some captured Alaskans, whose most unusual characteristic was that they wore labrets. A somewhat later report noted, among other things, that the Alaskan people had tails like dogs, a reference to the Bering Sea Eskimo custom of suspending the tail of a fox, wolf, or wolverine from a man's belt in the back.

Interest in the land-water relationships of eastern Asia led Tsar Peter the Great to organize an expedition to define the separation between Asia and America. In 1728, Vitus Bering, a Dane in the service of the Russian Navy, sailed through the strait named after him and discovered St. Lawrence Island, but he did not see the American continent. Thus geographers still wondered whether a waterway existed between the two landmasses. A second expedition of far greater scope was organized, and eight years were devoted to transporting equipment from European Russia to Kamchatka and building the expeditionary ships. The harbor where the *St. Peter* and *St. Paul* were constructed was named in their honor, Petropavlovsk. Bering commanded the expedition on the *St. Peter*, and Georg W. Steller was aboard as the naturalist. Alexei Chirikov was in command of the *St. Paul*. The ships sailed in 1741 for a region referred to as De Gama Land but soon were separated in the fog. Bering cruised across the region and sighted the American coast in the vicinity of Mt. St. Elias. Shortly thereafter, on July 20, the *St. Peter* anchored off Kayak Island, and Bering reluctantly permitted Steller to go ashore.

Steller soon discovered a native settlement but saw no one, although the remains of a meal indicated that people had been there recently. The Cossack with Steller shot a bird, a jay, that Steller recognized as similar to a species from the Carolinas. He wrote, *"This bird proved to me that we were really in America."* At the abandoned camp Steller saw a fireplace and near it a wooden vessel in which food had been cooked by immersing hot stones. Mollusc-shell dishes, bones, and pieces of dried salmon were scattered about, and nearby trees had been cut with stone or bone tools. Steller also found a fire drill and an underground structure containing cached food and arrows. While the identity of the residents cannot be determined on the basis of these observations alone, the camp appears to have been occupied by Eskimos. Thus the Russians first encountered the Yuit at their northern extreme, in Siberia, and then at their southern extreme, on Kayak Island.

Bering had landed on Kayak Island to take on water, and he was impatient with the delay caused by Steller's frantic search for natural-history specimens. Once the ship was under way again, the men fought contrary winds and storms as they sailed west. In early November they gave up hope of reaching Kamchatka and landed on a small island named after Bering. It was here that Bering and many of his men died. The survivors harvested hundreds of sea otters and built a small boat from the sand-locked *St. Peter*. In this vessel they reached Kamchatka in the fall. Meanwhile Chirikov had reached southeastern Alaska on the *St. Paul*, but the two boats that he sent ashore disappeared. The 15 crew members aboard them no doubt were killed by the Tlingit Indians. Without additional boats Chirikov turned back to Kamchatka, sighting some of the Aleutian Islands on the return voyage.

Bering and Chirikov pioneered the route to Alaska along the Aleutians, and the sea-otter pelts brought back by survivors of the Bering party proved extremely valuable on the fur market. Innumerable fur companies soon were founded to exploit the new-found riches. Enticed by the possibility of fantastic profits, men with little or no experience sailed off in poorly constructed and ill-equipped ships in search of sea otter. By about 1760 these animals were already becoming scarce off the Aleutian Islands, and hunters sailed farther east. By the end of the 1700s, 85 expeditions had been outfitted by 42 companies. The turmoil accompanying this expansion abated somewhat when Grigory I. Shelikhov and other merchants organized the North-Eastern American Company in 1781. They founded a small colony along Three Saints Bay on Kodiak Island in 1784. Eventually, in 1799 the Russian-American Company was formed and was granted a monopoly for the Alaskan fur trade. From its founding until 1818, the company's activities in Alaska were dominated by one man, Alexander A. Baranov. During his tenure nearly all Russian activity was concentrated in the Aleutian Islands and along the north Pacific.

The first major contact between Pacific Eskimos and the Russians occurred during an expedition led by Stepan Glotov in 1762-3. Glotov was an able seaman who previously had voyaged to the Aleutian Islands in search of pelts. In the fall of 1762 he sailed the *Andrean and Natalia* to Copper Island, in the Commander Islands, where they wintered. The next July they pushed steadily eastward, and by early September they reached Kodiak Island and anchored in a tidal stream. Four houses and many people were seen nearby, but the residents fled as the ship approached. The following day some Kodiak Eskimos, or Koniag, appeared in large skin boats. The interpreter aboard the ship, who spoke Aleut, could not satisfactorily understand these islanders. Soon the Koniag returned with an Aleut boy who had been captured and subsequently had learned to speak Eskimo. Glotov attempted to collect tribute from the Koniag, but they refused and paddled back to their settlement. A few days later the Russians requested a hostage, but the Koniag would give up only the Aleut boy. Since the people seemed reasonably friendly when visiting in small numbers, the Russians decided to move the ship farther upstream. Suddenly at daybreak a few weeks later a large number of Koniag attacked the vessel by shooting arrows, but when small arms were fired over their heads, they retreated. A more careful watch was subsequently kept, and a few days later about 200 Koniag approached behind wooden shields. They did not withdraw until the Russians launched an attack. About two weeks later the Koniag appeared at daybreak behind seven large wooden screens, each apparently concealing 30 to 40 men. When arrows were shot at the ship, Glotov gave orders for his crew to fire small arms. The shots did not penetrate the screens, and since the Eskimos kept advancing, the Russians attacked. As they did so, the Eskimos fled to waiting boats. No further hostilities occurred, and after wintering there, the Russians did some trading and sailed off when favorable weather returned. The concerted Koniag effort to dislodge the Russians is unusual in initial Eskimo-European encounters. These Eskimos originally had no idea of the effectiveness of firearms, but they soon attempted different strategies to negate the power of the Russian weapons. The time lapses between attacks were no doubt necessary to make better preparations and to summon more men.

Naval officers often were attached to the Russian-American Company, to serve not only on company vessels but also as administrators and explorers. One such person was Gavriil I. Davydov. In 1798 at the age of 11 he enrolled in the Naval Cadet Corps and soon was serving in the Baltic and North seas. In 1802 he joined the Russian-American Company, crossed Siberia to Okhotsk, and from there sailed to the company station at Kodiak. Davydov wintered at Kodiak in 1802-3 and then returned to Russia via Siberia. He soon traveled the same route back to Kodiak, arriving in 1805, and after a voyage to California in 1806 he returned to

Okhotsk. He was urged to write an account of his travels and had begun recording his 1802-4 experiences before his accidental drowning in 1809. Some of his observations, including ethnographic descriptions, were subsequently assembled from letters he had written and were published. Much of what is known about the Koniag in early historic times we owe to Davydov. His account effectively conveys how much the Koniag contrasted with other Eskimos. Following the pattern in Chapter 8, the Koniag and other Yuit are described largely in terms of how they differed from the Inuit.

The Kodiak Eskimos and those on nearby islands and the adjacent mainland spoke the same dialect of Pacific Eskimo (Suk). If the Koniag numbered about 6500, as reported by some of the reasonably early observers, their population density was far greater than that of any other Eskimos, especially since they seldom utilized the island interiors. In physical appearance a winter settlement, with its semisubterranean houses built from posts and planks, is familiar, but on Kodiak the construction details differed. A small doorway opened directly onto a large rectangular room with a central fireplace, smokehole overhead, and dry grass as flooring. This was the kitchen and workroom for the resident families, who had bedrooms off the main room. A sleeping room, which was entered through a very small hole in a board, had a plank floor and a window of sewn gut. These quarters were lighted with stone lamps, and people from as many as three families slept in one room, which was warmed by bringing in stones heated in a fire. A sleeping compartment or another separate room was used for steam baths; here bathers poured water over heated stones. When women menstruated, they were confined to small structures somewhat removed from a village; here too babies were born. Each settlement also included a kashim, the Yuit counterpart of the Inuit karigi, and as elsewhere festivities were centered in this structure.

The food resources of the Koniag seem to have been far more varied than those reported elsewhere among Eskimos, although dried fish was the primary staple. Four species of salmon ascended the short spawning streams of the island in astounding numbers, judging from runs in later times. Halibut hooked at sea also were important in the diet. In February fur seals were taken along the south coast, and during the summer great whales were hunted with poisoned spears. At this season seals and sea lions were

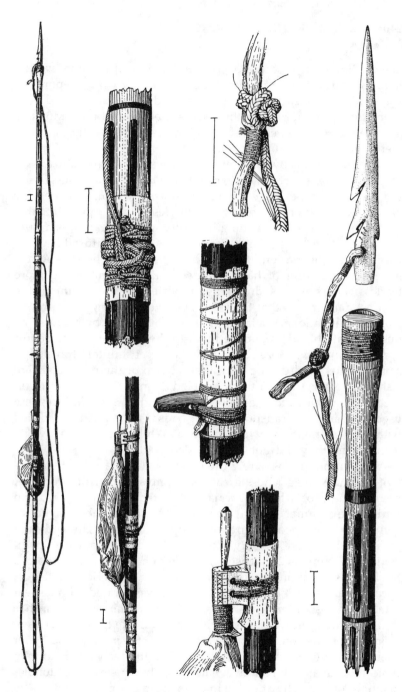

Figure 9-1 A Koniag harpoon bladder dart. The barbed point is attached directly to the shaft, which is decorated with black paint. Pieces of birch bark back the separate lashing, finger rest, and bladder attachments. (From Mason, 1902)

likewise important food resources, and a favored weapon was the harpoon dart (Figure 9-1). Most food cached for winter reportedly was eaten by the end of the festivities held in December, and from then until early spring shellfish were the primary fare. Molluscs also were eaten at other times; Davydov observed that the islanders were "great lovers of shellfish."

Water travel was by kayak and umiak, called *baidarka* and *baidara* respectively by the Russians. The general lines of these vessels are the familiar ones, but in early historic times the Koniag made their kayaks with either one or two manholes. (The form with three manholes, the central opening being for a passenger, was a Russian innovation.) In two-hole kayaks the Koniag ventured far from land and set off on long trips without hesitation, but the Aleuts had the reputation of having superior kayaks and being more fearless sailors. Kayak drownings reportedly were common; the greatest danger was that the skin cover would be ripped during a storm. When a lone Koniag hunter was overtaken by a storm, he might inflate bladders and tie them to the sides of the vessel for greater buoyancy. More commonly, however, hunters traveled in small groups, and during foul weather two or three kayaks were lashed together; this technique enabled them to ride out storms on the open sea for as long as several days and nights. Umiaks were used primarily to transport heavy loads and might be outfitted with sails of matting or thin leather. While the Koniag owned many dogs, they did not use dog sleds.

Whale hunting was surely the most remarkable subsistence activity of the Koniag, and a great deal of mystery surrounded it. A secret society of whalers formally initiated new members, and during the summer whaling season when the members lived together, ordinary people dared not approach them. The bodies of great whalers were preserved in caves, and a sepulcher might contain as many as 20 corpses. The son of a whaler who followed his father's vocation inherited these bodies, esoteric knowledge, special charms, and equipment. A whale was hunted with a spear fitted with a slender, polished slate blade as much as 10 inches long. The weapon was coated with poison made from a species of aconite root; the common name for this plant is monkshood. After special songs were sung, whalers set off in their kayaks. Four men typically searched for large whales together, using two double-manhole kayaks. They hunted in pairs to aid one another in case of

Figure 9-2 Koniag whale hunters. The man in the background is poised to throw a whaling spear. (From Duflot de Mofras, 1844)

an accident. One of the hunters in a forward cockpit launched a spear, attempting to strike deep into the flesh of a great whale so that the point would lodge there. As soon as the blow was struck, the men in the rear cockpits paddled backward to escape the turbulence created by a wounded whale that might be 60 feet long (Figure 9-2). After a whale was struck, the hunters paddled home to wait for it to die, and, if their incantations worked, drift ashore nearby.

The dazzling body adornments of the Koniag are unparalleled among Eskimos elsewhere. Each woman had two to six small holes beneath her lower lip to receive labrets, from which were hung beads, small white bones, or shells. Small holes were pierced around the outer edges of her ears, in her earlobes, and in her nasal septum for suspending beads and other ornaments. Dentalium shells received indirectly in trade from Northwest Coast Indians were the most highly prized adornments. These hollow tusklike mollusc shells were about two inches long. By "sewing themselves beards" Davydov meant that women tattooed designs on their chins, and some also had a line across the chest under their breasts. A Koniag man wore a bone through a hole in his nasal septum, and some men had holes along the outer edges of their ears for ornaments like those of women. Men also wore medial labrets; these were sometimes so large that the empty hole looked like a second mouth. Both sexes tended to wear their hair long, but "children are shorn completely except for a patch on the top of the head," according to Davydov.

These people usually went barefoot, and they preferred to make their long, frock-like parkas from the skins of sea birds such as cormorants and puffins, or from ground squirrels, with the heads and tails intact. Along the seams of birdskin parkas were sewn strips of caribou or mountain-goat hair, ermine fur, or puffin beaks. These garments had either short sleeves or narrow, ornamental sleeves with slits beneath for the wearer's arms to extend. In foul weather and when hunting at sea, men wore parkas sewn from strips of gut, a whale's bladder, or the skin from a great whale's tongue. Fewer seams were required in the manufacture of a rain parka from the skin of a whale's tongue, but it tore easily and was heavy. People often wore brimmed hats woven from spruce roots. Paints of different colors were used to decorate these hats with figures of crabs, seals, or some other animals, and for the design to be more lasting than usual, a man pierced his nose so that he could mix blood with the paint (Figure 9-3).

When describing the personality of the Koniag, Davydov wrote, "Having made a close and careful study of the islanders, under various conditions, I have become convinced of the wit and inventiveness with which, despite poverty of means, they have perfected their artifacts, and with these qualities in mind it is impossible to call them complete savages." He praised their sense of history and ability to recall long-past events. But to him they also were sly, deceitful, and calculating as well as vengeful. A premium was placed on an ability to endure pain and hardship. To develop these qualities children were forced to stand in seawater even in severe weather. As a part of one ritual a young boy might be ordered into a kashim carrying a sharp piece of broken shell. To show his bravery he cut himself from the shoulder to the wrist and danced while boasting of his deed. To instill a fearless attitude toward enemies, a captive might be brought before children, who

Figure 9-3 A Koniag man wearing a hat made from woven spruce roots, a nose pin, and a medial labret. (From Sauer, 1802)

stabbed or shot the victim with arrows. A man might even cut open the stomach of a live enemy and have his children pull out the intestines.

The conventions of adult life surrounding sexual activities and marriage seem especially unusual among Eskimos. Single and married persons alike appear to have had many sexual partners, and while men seldom were jealous, women were jealous of each other. After a girl consented to a marriage proposal, the groom presented gifts to her and to her parents and temporarily moved in with the family. Here he became "virtually a servant of the father-in-law" for an unstated period, and afterwards the couple set up a separate household. The Koniag preferred having daughters rather than sons because of the labor derived from a son-in-law. Important men might have as many as eight wives, and a few women had two husbands. The first or primary husband habitually slept with the woman; the second husband was "a kind of servant" who slept with her only when the first husband was away. Males not infrequently assumed the dress and role of women. A couple might encourage their young son to become a transvestite if he seemed feminine in his behavior. Likewise, if they wanted a daughter and a son was born, they might raise him as a girl. The husband of such a transvestite was considered very fortunate.

The sociopolitical distinctions drawn were far more rigid than those reported among other Eskimos. The generic term "chief" can be used with greater justification for Koniag leaders than for most Eskimos. Each settlement, or localized group of settlements, had a chief, and the title ideally passed along the female line. We know little about the duties of a chief but may reasonably presume that he was an advisor to his constituents and represented them in dealing with other chiefs. Wealthy men formed another distinct social group, and it appears that they gained their status by accumulating property and hosting elaborate give-away feasts. Most residents of a village were ordinary persons, and as such they had a voice in village-wide decisions made at public meetings. Outstanding among them were shamans, men noted for their bravery in warfare, and men who were respected as hunters. Finally there were chattels, persons taken prisoner in war or obtained in trade. Such persons were called "slaves," but slavery defined by its heritability may not have existed. Quite clearly the owners of chattels held life-and-death power over them.

As conveyed in the encounters of Glotov with the Koniag, warfare was an important part of their lives. Conflicts were most frequent among groups living on Kodiak and nearby islands, but the Koniag also were enemies of the Aleuts to the west and of the Tanaina Indians who lived to the northeast along Cook Inlet. During the summer when most men were away hunting, women and children lived at largely inaccessible cliff areas; when an attack was expected, everyone occupied these fortifications. As we have seen, the Koniag carried protective shields into battle, and they fought with slate-pointed spears and arrows. War parties launched attacks only on an unsuspecting enemy and might sometimes wait days for the opportunity to strike. The pattern was to capture women and children and kill all the men except those destined for torturous death or slavery.

Indications are that Koniag ceremonial life was very rich, but few early accounts of particular services are preserved. Thanks to Davydov we have a record of a celebration held in memory of outstanding men who had died. Early one December evening people gathered in the kashim, where a large oil-burning stone lamp was placed at the middle of the room and men with tambourine-like drums of different sizes sat near it. Also near the lamp were two girls who wore gut parkas and had eagle down in their hair. Beside each girl sat a man wearing a headdress of bent twigs from which ferns and feathers hung to obscure his red-painted face. These men held rattles made from the beaks of birds and paddles with animal figures painted on them. The major actors represented men preparing to set off on a hunt. As the girls swayed from side to side, the drums were pounded, and the actors kept time with rattles. A miniature kayak and weapons suspended from the ceiling were made to move by a man off to one side. When the leading actor said "animal," the audience made the sounds of different animals, and boys loudly blew whistles. Later a stone with red dots painted on it, representing a coffin and the persons being honored, was placed near the lamp, and trays of food were brought in. Unfortunately at this point Davydov had a "splitting headache" and left the kashim.

Some Russians thought that a form of sun worship prevailed among the Koniag, just as it had been reported by early European explorers in southwestern Greenland. Davydov wrote that any Koniag who planned a trip at sea got up before the sun and sat on high ground to watch with studied attention the sun's rising. Even when someone did not plan a voyage, he followed the same procedure, apparently to learn to read the weather signs. Davydov was firmly convinced that it was not "a certain kind of religious feeling" being exhibited, but an attempt to acquire the practical knowledge about weather prediction that was so important in the Koniag food quest.

As incomplete as accounts may be for the aboriginal Koniag, they are better than for any other Pacific Eskimo group. The Prince William Sound or Chugach Eskimos were the second major tribe in terms of area occupied and information available. In the late 1700s they were visited by explorers, especially by fur traders from various nations, but substantial reports about them do not exist. We have comments about their appearance, artifacts, and friendly or hostile attitudes but nothing that effectively expands on the regional variations in Eskimo culture. Most of what is known about the Chugach was recorded as an ethnographic reconstruction by Kaj Birket-Smith in 1933, long after the old ways had been abandoned. Yet as the most southerly Alaskan Eskimos the Chugach at least deserve mention.

Surrounded on three sides by high mountains, the mainland and the many islands of Prince William Sound were covered with dense, nearly impenetrable, vegetation. The land was warmed by the Japanese current, and a great deal of rain fell. Among the land animals the mountain goat, ground squirrel, and marmot were most important; caribou did not live in the area. The resources of the sea were rich and varied; both salmon and sea mammals were abundant. Like the Koniag, the Chugach hunted from kayaks and used harpoons as well as bows and arrows. Hunting at sea with bows and arrows is unusual, and the arrows with which they took sea otter were among the most elegant Eskimo weapons. The arrows were actually harpoon darts with small, detachable barbed heads tied to the shafts with cords; the Koniag made similar darts. The Chugach hunted great whales, probably in the manner of the Koniag, but little is known about the complex. Their winter houses, which were built aboveground, had vertical planks for siding and nearly flat roofs covered with bark. A dwelling included sleeping compartments for a number of families and a room for bathing. Men who lived in the same house usually worked and hunted together. Each village, or sometimes small groups of villages, had as a chief a wealthy person whose family commanded respect. A chief presided over meetings and was responsible for guiding subsistence activities above all else. He was succeeded by his son or a brother if he had no sons. Most persons held the status of commoner, but prisoners from raids were kept as slaves. A secret society composed of males existed, but the particulars are confused.

Why the Koniag, and possibly the Chugach if more were known

Figure 9-4 A Chugach man wearing a woven hat, nose pin, ear ornaments, small labrets, and a rain parka made from sewn strips of intestines. (From Cook and King, 1784)

Figure 9-5 A Chugach Eskimo woman wearing nose pins, ear ornaments, and labrets. (From Cook and King, 1784)

about them, were so different from other Eskimos has never been fully understood. Perhaps it was because the Koniag lived at the crossroads of the north Pacific. They were exposed to the complexities of Aleut culture on the west, to mainland Eskimos with whom they had the most in common, and to Athapaskan Indians along Cook Inlet. They also had some intercourse with the Tlingit Indians of southeastern Alaska and were aware of the richness of their cultural developments. Margaret Lantis has pointed out that the Koniag whale cult shared important characteristics with whale hunting among the maritime Indians in the Vancouver Island region of southern British Columbia. Furthermore, Robert F. Heizer drew attention to the similar pattern of whale hunting in Kamchatka and the Kurile Islands; there as among the Koniag weapon points coated with poison were used. Thus Koniag ties spanned the north Pacific. With diverse foods available on Kodiak Island at different times of the year and shellfish a dependable food in times of stress, the Koniag were able to maintain a comparatively large and stable population. They were receptive to innovations and in a position to nurture them more than any other Eskimos.

*   *   *

On his third and final voyage in 1776 the explorer James Cook was instructed to sail around the Cape of Good Hope to the Pacific and on to the Northwest Coast of North America. His purpose in cruising farther north was to search for a waterway to the sea discovered by Hearne at the mouth of the Coppermine River, and to seek a passage to Hudson Bay. The *Resolution*, the famous ship of his second voyage in 1772-5, was overhauled and refitted. Her consort the *Discovery* was commanded by Charles Clerke, who had sailed previously with Cook. The ships called at islands in the south Pacific and discovered the Hawaiian Islands while on the voyage north to Vancouver Island in the spring of 1778. At the entrance to Prince William Sound they met and traded with the Chugach Eskimos. A short time later hopes for finding a passage to the east were high as the ships sailed into the broad entrance to Cook Inlet; disappointment followed as they reached the fresh water of "River Turnagain." They coursed west, sailed between two of the Aleutian Islands to enter the Bering Sea, and met Eskimos along the coast as far north as the vicinity of Bering Strait.

Figure 9-6   The earliest illustration of Norton Sound area Eskimos. (From Cook and King, 1784)

Cook attempted to sail east along northwestern Alaska but was stopped by ice and shallow water at Icy Cape. On the voyage south they anchored at Unalaska to repair the ships before returning to the Hawaiian Islands, where Cook was killed in 1779.

The observations about Eskimos by Cook and those accompanying him are not uninformative, but they are limited primarily to appearances, boats, weapons, and dwellings because the ships never remained very long at their northern anchorages. Since we already know a great deal about these aspects of Eskimo culture, we will concentrate on Cook's report about Prince William Sound, where he more closely observed Eskimos during a stay of nearly a week. He had a copy of *The History of Greenland* by David Crantz aboard, and he wrote the following after seeing the Chugach and other Eskimos in the summer of 1778: "I have frequently had occasion to mention, from the time of our arrival in Prince William's Sound, how remarkably the natives, on this North West side of America, resemble the Greenlanders and Esquimaux, in various particulars of person, dress, weapons, canoes, and the like. However, I was much less struck with this, than with the affinity which we found subsisting between the dialects of the Greenlanders and Esquimaux, and those of Norton's Sound and Oonalaska." Cook went on to offer the opinion "that all these nations are of the same extraction," a clear early statement about the unity of Eskimos east and west. He reasoned further that since Eskimos were similar across the arctic, they must have been in communication with one another by sea; thus the distribution of Eskimos was another piece of evidence to support the existence of a northern waterway.

*   *   *

Initially the Russians on Kodiak Island called the adjacent mainland "Alaska" but meant only the Alaska Peninsula sector. They soon began applying the term to all the mainland region, but before 1818 they knew comparatively little about it. Territory familiar to them included the Aleutian Islands and southeastern Alaska, where they derived a rich harvest of sea-otter pelts. As the number of sea otter diminished, however, company officials began looking north to the mainland as a new source for furs, especially beaver pelts.

Petr Korsakovskii was placed in charge of the first nineteenth-century Russian expedition to explore north of the Alaska Peninsula. The men left Kodiak Island in the spring of 1818 to expand the fur trade and investigate rumors about a lost Russian settlement. One group, led by Eremei Rodionov, portaged from an upper Nushagak River tributary to the Kuskokwim River drainage and descended the Kuskokwim to the point at which it is nearest the Yukon River. They returned with an old Eskimo whose accounts seemed to indicate that he had met Russians from a lost colony farther north, a report later discounted by most persons. During the same year others explored the coast for a short distance. The following year a detachment sent to the mouth of the Nushagak River built the first Russian redoubt or fort north of the Alaska Peninsula. Two other redoubts were built in the north during the Russian era: the northernmost, St. Michael, was established in 1833 near the Yukon River mouth; the other was built along the central Kuskokwim River in 1841.

Between 1819 and 1838 the coastline and to a lesser extent the river systems of western Alaska were surveyed by Russian expeditions. Yet in their haste, and probably because of a lack of interest as well, these men contributed little to our understanding of Eskimos. The situation changed when Lavrentiy A. Zagoskin began his travels in this region.

Zagoskin received his training as a naval cadet from 1822 to 1826 and joined the Russian Navy as a midshipman, serving for eight years in the Caspian Sea. In 1838 he entered the service of the Russian-American Company, and after crossing Siberia to Okhotsk he sailed for Sitka. For two years he cruised from Okhotsk to Sitka as the commander of trading vessels and then voyaged to the Russian outpost at Fort Ross, California. A passenger on the return trip to Sitka, Ilya G. Voznesenskiy, who was an assistant from the Academy of Sciences, succeeded in arousing Zagoskin's interest in natural history. During the spring of 1842 the Commander-in-Chief of the Russian-American Company, Adolf K. Etolin, proposed that Zagoskin undertake a journey into the northern interior. As the plan matured, it was decided that Zagoskin would explore Kotzebue Sound and then the Yukon and Kuskokwim rivers before crossing to a Cook Inlet drainage at the end of his travels. One of his primary purposes was to determine the routes along which the Chukchee in Siberia received furs harvested in Alaska; Chukchee and Eskimo traders were in direct competition with agents of the Russian-American Company. Zagoskin arrived at St. Michael in the summer of 1842 and devoted the next two years to exploring and collecting ethnographic information with special reference to the fur trade. His major trip was to the Yukon River, and he traveled up it for about 600 miles. He also made two trips up the Kuskokwim River after crossing portages from the Yukon. While Zagoskin could not accomplish all that his superiors had anticipated, he did compile and publish an expansive corpus of information about the Eskimos he encountered. He had no great adventures because he was a very well organized traveler and the people he met usually were friendly.

Zagoskin's observations are varied and rewarding, but without the later complementary account by Edward W. Nelson we would know far less about the Yuit of western Alaska. Nelson was interested in natural history as a child, and after attending normal school he taught for a year. Through the efforts of persons at the Smithsonian Institution he then became a weather observer for the

United States Army Signal Corps in Alaska. From 1877 to 1881 he was stationed at St. Michael, and in addition to making meteorologic observations he was charged with obtaining as much information as possible about the surrounding area and its people. In 1878-9 he made an extended trip along the Yukon River, to the central Bering Sea coast, and on to the lower Kuskokwim River before returning to St. Michael. During this journey he not only mapped a partially unknown region but collected a wealth of ethnographic information and artifacts. Nelson traveled widely in western Alaska, and during the summer of 1881 he sailed aboard the *Corwin* to collect information on St. Lawrence Island and the Siberian coast. After this trip he went to Washington, D.C., to work at the Smithsonian Institution on the preparation of his materials for publication. His major ethnographic report, *The Eskimos about Bering Strait*, appeared in 1899. This monograph is primarily a description of the artifacts he had collected, but also includes accounts of Eskimos he met. The major difficulty with the ethnographies by both Nelson and Zagoskin is that they combined information about diverse groups of Eskimos, which makes it difficult to assemble a well-rounded view for any particular tribe. Yet their writings, above all others, reveal previously unknown facets of Eskimo culture.

In many respects the Eskimos of the central Bering Sea coast represent a transition between the northwestern Inuit and the Pacific Eskimos. The emphasis on open-water sea-mammal hunting from kayaks along the Bering Sea, the importance of kashims throughout the year, the popularity of hot baths, and the wearing of an ornament in the nasal septum were among the southern affinities. Yet they were far from carbon copies of a people like the Koniag. Among the central Bering Sea Eskimos transvestites did not exist; they did not hunt great whales with poisoned spearpoints, nor did they have a rigid class system. Conversely, large cooperative hunts by kayakers driving beluga into shallows recall the Mackenzie Eskimo pattern, and an importance placed on netting seals is a reminder of the Barrow Eskimos. What seems to most distinguish the central Bering Sea Eskimos from their northern relatives is their well-developed ceremonial life, and it is best reflected in the Bladder Festival.

The purpose of the Bladder Festival was to insure a continuing supply of sea mammals. The souls of these animals were thought to reside in their bladders, and each year all of the bladders from sea mammals killed were saved until they could be properly honored at the annual ceremony. Early in December the bladders were inflated, painted with designs in different colors, and hung in a kashim. Suspended amidst them, as recorded by Zagoskin, were "fantastic figures of birds, beasts, and fish. These figures, like some animated dolls, can roll their eyes, move their heads, flap their wings, and so on, and demonstrate the cleverness of the natives in mechanical things." During the festivities the images were kept in motion, and between dances they were purified by burning a particular species of grass beneath them. The highlight of the festival was the removal of the bladders from the kashim to a special hole chipped in the ice. Here they were weighted with stones, and as they were placed in the water people watched their movement and listened to the sounds they made to predict the success of sea-mammal hunting in the near future.

The foregoing Bladder Festival summary is taken from Zagoskin, but Nelson recorded many more particulars. He arrived at a village near the Bering Sea coast when a Bladder Festival was in progress. His detailed account better conveys the complexities of the rituals. Hanging from the kashim ceiling was a "fantastic bird-shape image" with a goose-skin covering and wings made from large gull feathers. When a cord was pulled and released, the bird moved up and down. A 10-foot pole painted red and white had been erected at the back of the kashim. Near the middle of the pole hung four strips of caribou skin, and at the top was a bundle of wild celery stalks. On one wall were arranged hundreds of seal and walrus bladders that had been inflated, painted, and attached to spears. Rituals included imitations of birds, a shaman's performance on the roof in the middle of the night, a man throwing water on the bladders in such a manner that it fell back on him and two boys, all of whom were naked. Flaming wild celery stalks were used to purify dancers, and food offerings were made to the inuas of the bladders. Many rites were performed in sets of four: four dances, four directions in which stalks were burned, and four men manipulating paddles at the four corners of the room. Among the accompanying taboos was a restriction against making noise in the kashim. Men avoided physical contact with women, and no females past the age of puberty were permitted near the bladders as they hung in the kashim.

Few if any Eskimo ceremonies matched the drama, pageantry, staging, and community-wide involvement of a Bladder Festival in the central Bering Sea area. As a concerted effort to appease the spirits of animals killed, it represented a common Eskimo goal but one far less developed elsewhere. Here the souls or inuas were lavishly entertained with songs and dances by their Eskimo hosts, were fed, and were accorded great respect. The aim was for the souls to return to their distant home in the sea, enter the bodies of unborn animals, and allow themselves to be killed again by these human hosts who had treated them so well.

*   *   *

Zagoskin and Nelson also traveled among the riverine Yuit, whose most direct counterpart among the Inuit was the Kobuk Eskimo. At least 5000 Yuit lived along the Kuskokwim, Nushagak, and Yukon rivers. These three populations were distinct and yet had a great deal in common. Only the Yukon Eskimos are detailed because they were familiar to both Nelson and Zagoskin.

Alaska's greatest river, the Yukon, was called the *Kwikpuk* or "Big River" by the 1500 or so Eskimos who lived along its banks. They termed themselves the Kwikpagmiut, but they also are referred to as the Ikogmiut. From the river mouth the Yukon Eskimos extended about 175 miles to adjoin the Ingalik, a tribe of Northern Athapaskan Indians. In direct contrast with Eskimo-Indian relations nearly everywhere else, the Ingalik lived in relative peace with the Yukon Eskimos. Ingalik traders traveled to Eskimo villages, and when parties of caribou hunters from the two groups met, the contacts were friendly. While they seldom intermarried, some Ingalik spoke a little Eskimo, and if conflicts did exist, they were most likely to be comparatively minor ones between the members of adjacent communities. The Indians had assimilated many Eskimo artifact types, customs, and even entire ceremonial complexes; by contrast, the Eskimos had borrowed very little from their Indian neighbors.

In appearance the Yukon Eskimos were clearly similar to adjacent ones. The hair of men was tonsured, women had chin tattoos and ornaments suspended from holes in their nasal septums, and both sexes wore labrets. Their parkas were ankle-length, hoodless, and often made from the skins of ground squirrels. Alternatively, shorter, more fitted, hooded parkas sewn from caribou skins also were worn. Footwear was of the typical Eskimo cut, but both the soles and uppers were sewn from chinook (king) salmon skins, an unusual choice of material. Fish-skin boots had the advantage of being lightweight, and when worn with woven grass socks or wadded grass liners, they were warm at subzero temperatures. Their disadvantages were that they tore easily and were ruined if placed near a fire. Parka covers likewise were made from fish skins; they served as rain parkas or were worn as overparkas when it snowed.

A village typically included separate winter and summer houses. A winter dwelling was built from logs, was furnished with high plank platforms on all interior sides, and had a central fireplace. Entry was through an underground tunnel in cold weather, but in warmer weather people used a passage that led from the outside to the bench level. Permanent residents of these homes were women from one to three families, their daughters, and their youthful sons; each adult woman had her own lamp and utensils. Summer houses were built of planks supported by posts and beams; the gabled roofs were covered with planks topped with slabs of bark. If salmon fishing was not good at the winter village locale, the summer houses were built near good fishing spots. At either a winter village or a fish camp, small gable-roofed log caches were constructed above four corner posts for storing fish and other foods.

The most imposing structure in any village was a *kashgee*, commonly called a kashim after the Koniag term adopted by Russians and Anglo-Americans for these men's houses. The lives of Eskimo males were more intensively focused at men's houses along the Yukon and in adjacent sectors than elsewhere. From the age of 10 onward males lived primarily in these buildings. Here the men bathed; older boys learned craft skills, myths, and traditions; ceremonies and social events were held, and male visitors were housed. Kashim residents usually were brought meals by their mothers or wives; unmarried males always slept here, and married men usually did. Each person was assigned a particular place on a kashim bench, but the designation changed with time and circumstances. Old and respected men, the best hunters, and shamans slept at the back of the room. Near the entrance were orphans, the poor, and men considered worthless.

Small villages had one kashim, but populous settlements in-

Figure 9-7   A kashim at St. Michael showing the exterior frame-work of logs. (From Nelson, 1899)

cluded two or more. A single kashim belonged to the entire com-munity; if there were several, each was the property of a given segment of the population. Built of logs and planks with a cribbed roof, a kashim was about 25 feet on a side, and the larger ones could accommodate as many as 500 persons for special occasions. At the center of the roof was a smokehole, and one to three levels of plank benches were built along the inner walls. In the middle of the plank floor was a large fire pit covered with boards when not in use; the interior was lighted with lamps made from clay or stone. A log framework paralleled the outside of a large kashim, and dirt was placed between it and the building (Figure 9-7).

When the activities of a day were over, men began returning to their kashim, usually in the late afternoon. The plank cover was removed from the fire pit and split dry spruce wood was placed in the pit. The men took off their clothing in preparation for bathing; after the fire was lighted, each placed a respirator, made from fine spruce shavings, in his mouth to prevent smoke and hot air from entering his lungs. As the smoke cleared and the fire became a bed of coals, the smokehole cover was fitted in place. The heat quickly intensified, and "a deafening howling and wailing comes out of the kazhim, for as we know the natives are mourning the dead, recalling the great deeds of their ancestors, and the forever vanished days of their youth," as Zagoskin recorded in a somewhat dramatic and possibly overdrawn statement. As the heat began to dissipate, each man bathed with the urine he kept in a container, and when the building cooled, the remaining urine was poured on the coals of the fire. The bathers then went outside to sit naked, regardless of the outdoor temperature.

Fish was the year-round staple here, and the most important species were chinook, chum, and coho (silver) salmon, most often taken in weir and trap sets. A number of posts were driven into the riverbed out from the shore. As many as seven posts might be set in place at about six-foot intervals, and between them on the upstream side were fitted and lashed screens made from spruce splints tied together with spruce roots. Beyond the outer end of a weir additional poles driven into the river bottom held a trap that faced downstream. These cone-shaped traps, as much as 10 feet long, were made from spruce splints bound together with roots. At their open end additional splints formed the funnel-shaped mouth that was about four feet across. As salmon ascended the river in the summer to spawn, some were guided along the weir and into the trap. They could easily enter the funnel but usually could not swim out of it. When a run was heavy, traps were emptied several times a day to prevent them from breaking under the weight or movement of the catch. During a very heavy run a second cone might be added to the rear of a trap to prevent an overload. Literally hundreds of salmon could be harvested in a few hours. Smaller weir-trap sets were made to catch burbot and whitefish in the fall.

Most fish probably were taken in weir-trap facilities, but salmon, whitefish, and lamprey also were harvested in nets. The types included dip nets, seines, and gill nets that either were set in eddies or drifted downstream as they were tended by men in kayaks. Except for the dip nets, all the types were designed to catch many fish at one time. Furthermore, different forms could be used to take the same species, which provided the users with considerable flexibility, depending on water conditions and fish concentrations.

Caribou were killed with arrows, as were beaver and river otter at certain times of the year. Hares were taken with tossing-pole snares, and ptarmigan in simple noose snares. Foxes were lured by bait to an enclosure where they became entangled in a net.

The means of transport included snowshoes used by individuals traveling over powdery snow, especially in timbered areas, and the familiar kayaks and umiaks. Presumably both types of boats most often were covered with sea-mammal skins obtained in trade from the coast. Zagoskin stated that "the art of travel with dogs is in its infancy; they have no lead dogs, no trained teams, and they never sit on the sled." Even more surprising, dogs were harnessed to the stanchions at the *sides* of sleds. A person pushed the sled from behind, and another one or more pulled with lines at the front.

We have come to expect statements such as "Each family is an economically independent unit," and "they recognize no difference of rank among themselves," as Zagoskin wrote about the people of this region. What we do not expect is the identification of family lines with totemic symbols. Nelson was the first to recognize the association, but comparatively little is known about it. Apparently identity with a totem was based on some notable event involving a particular animal and an ancestor. Afterwards the man and his descendants through the male line were identified with that animal. Species with which these associations were drawn included ermines, gerfalcons, ravens, river otters, and wolves. These animals were symbolically represented on diverse artifacts, including masks, and wearing apparel might reflect totemic relationships. Women of the wolf totem braided strips of wolf skin in their hair; a man or boy with the same totem wore a wolf tail at the back of his belt. Furthermore, a hunter habitually carried an object that represented his totem. Contrary to what we expect in the classic form of totemism, these people did not think they were descended from a totemic species, and they did not have taboos against killing their totemic species. Totemism among Bering Sea Eskimos appears to have developed from the common Eskimo practice for individuals to become identified with an animal protector and to carry as a charm a part of the animal's body.

Conflicts between tribes of Bering Sea Eskimos were common and their raids formed part of a warfare complex. Yukon Eskimo practices seem to fit into the regional pattern. They preferred to attack an unsuspecting enemy on a summer night when all the men were sleeping in the kashim. Some attackers guarded the kashim exit to trap the men inside; others shot arrows into the building through the skylight. Overpowered males always were killed; women might be killed or taken captive. After the first enemy was killed, young men on their first raid drank some of his blood and ate a piece of his heart to become brave. The raiders always plundered a defeated village.

The greatest artistic accomplishments of early historic Eskimos were those of the Yuit, especially the ones who lived in the Yukon-Kuskokwim region. Superior wood-carvers, they made elaborate masks and small containers often shaped as animals. We also find productions that might be termed art and yet are very ephemeral; these are best represented by storyknife illustrations. As young girls recounted traditional stories, they used ivory storyknives to draw accompanying sketches of people and places in the mud or snow. An illustrated scene existed for only a few seconds before being obliterated with the knife blade and replaced by other figures as the plot developed. Transient artistry also is represented by paintings on the gut skylight covers used for certain ceremonies. These covers were saved from year to year, but the figures were washed off annually and repainted. Even the masks used in rituals were a temporary art form since they often, perhaps even typically, were burned after use, and new ones were made as required. In the same context, wooden grave monuments and memorial statues (Figure 9-8) were allowed to rot away without being refurbished. Thus diverse artistic forms were made for specific purposes and subsequently were destroyed or else largely ignored. Aesthetic pleasure in permanent works does not seem to have loomed large. The goal of the Eskimo artist most often was to convey a visual image about the deeds of ancestors or the realm of supernaturals. In many instances a mask, carving, or painting meant little to an observer unless he or she knew the "story" behind the imagery, a clear indication that the physical form was largely a vehicle to express a belief, folktale, or story.

The most thorough study of Yuit artistic accomplishments is that of the German ethnographer Hans Himmelheber, whose fieldwork was on Nunivak Island and along the Kuskokwim River in 1936-7. By then much of the old artistic tradition had been abandoned, but the core endured, or at least could be recalled by local Eskimos.

Figure 9-8 Kuskokwim Eskimo (Kuskowagamiut) monuments to the dead, apparently erected when the body of a person was not recovered. (From Hartmann, 1886)

When the observations by Zagoskin and Nelson are added to those of Himmelheber, a reasonably full account emerges, especially of their most notable forms, the wooden masks.

One important group of masks was used during the Bladder Festival and in other services held to insure the continuing harvest of economically desirable species. These Eskimos felt that everything, animate and inanimate alike, had a human essence that could be revealed, and the spirits of various species were invited to a kashim to witness performances by masked dancers designed to please them and thereby make them obtainable in the future. Some masks were animal- or human-like and had appropriate appendages. Others had a human face and an animal one on a single mask. Still another style had an animal represented on the outer surface and a human face concealed beneath a hinged opening, or in the reverse order; in either case the lower face was revealed during the dance. In these masks the human face repre-

Figure 9-9 Masks 2-4 were used by Yukon Eskimos (Kwikpag-miut). Mask number 1, which may be from the same area, apparently represents the inua of a bird; the side panels seem to have been movable. The other masks represent spirits controlled by shamans. (From Nelson, 1899)

sented the inner spirit of the animal portrayed. They were made by accomplished craftsmen or by shamans, and the performers always were men.

The masks of shamans represented either inuas, which are the souls of creatures, or *tunghat*, spirits controllable by shamans (Figure 9-9). Quite often the inspiration for a mask was derived from a shaman's communication with a spirit. The shaman either carved the mask or had someone else make it under his careful supervision. A shaman or a good dancer gave the premier enactment; afterwards the mask and performance became public property.

Other works in wood included humorous masks worn by dancers providing comic relief during ceremonies. When women danced, they often wore finger masks. These were disk-shaped pieces of wood with finger holds attached to the outer rim; they were decorated with feathers and fur and were manipulated in coordination with the drum beat. Other tasteful productions in wood included small containers shaped as animals (Figure 9-10, *b*, *c*, *d*); these may have held weapon points and had magical associations, as was true farther north. Occasionally figures of animals were carved in ivory. These might adorn the wooden hats men wore while hunting, or they might serve as separate charms. Engravings on pieces of ivory were not common, but the examples that do exist are sometimes striking (Figure 9-10, *a*).

After interviewing persons whom he considered artists, Himmelheber concluded that a small number of men found carving wood a pleasurable experience and satisfying to a sense of artistic creativity. Most men, however, found more pleasure in painting scenes on bowls, gut windows, or drumheads and carved wood only to fulfill a request or obligation. Himmelheber further noted that superior mask makers regarded their talent as a craft skill rather than an artistic ability. Although people were interested in the accomplishments of a carver, he was not praised for his work; the opposite was closer to the truth, because greater value was attached to the skills required to produce utilitarian objects. An artist received little or no compensation for what he made, nor were carvings traded from one village to another.

Certain masked dances observed by Zagoskin in a kashim probably were part of a Lesser Feast to the Dead that will be described in the pages to follow. He reported that men sat on the benches while women and children sat on the floor. The stage area began at

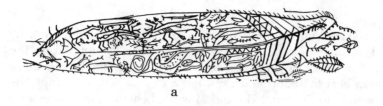

a

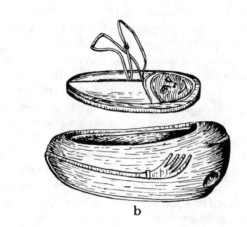

b

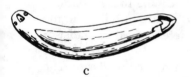

c

d

Figure 9-10 Engraving and wood carvings: *a*, Engraving on a Nunivak Island chisel (From Hoffman, 1897). *b*, Wooden box shaped to represent a seal but with a human face on the lid, Yukon-Kuskokwim region (From Nelson, 1899). *c*, Wooden box carved in the shape of a seal, Nunivak Island (From Nelson, 1899). *d*, Wooden box carved in the shape of a seal, Nelson Island area (From Nelson, 1899).

the tunnel side of the fireplace and was illuminated by two lamps. Curtains made from grass matting were hung before the lower benches near the tunnel to create dressing compartments for performers. As the people gathered, they were entertained by two comedians, old men dressed in tattered parkas who joked with each other and with the audience. Suddenly a man slid down a thong extending through the open skylight. Wearing a fantastic mask in the shape of a raven's head, he quickly jumped on the stage and began cawing like a raven. Two women joined him there as men beat tambourine drums and a chorus began to sing. The masked dancer alternated mimicking the behaviors of a raven and of a person. The plot behind his actions was conveyed in the accompanying song; a shaman at a camp was hungry, but whenever he hunted, a raven frightened the game away by cawing. When he set snares, the raven triggered them until finally the shaman said, "Who are you?" The raven smiled and replied, "Your evil fate." At the end of this enactment the performer, in the memory of dead relatives, presented gifts to the guests. Dramatization of an episode such as this, with original songs, masks, and dialogue, indicates the creativity of theatrical performances among Yukon and Kuskokwim Eskimos.

The hallmark of many cultures is a developed sense of identity with the past. An emphasis on individual genealogies, history, and quasihistory are examples. Links with previous generations also may be reflected in ancestor cults, culture-hero tales, elaborate burials, and memorial ceremonies. Among the Eskimos described thus far, if the dead required recognition it was largely in terms of taboos observed soon after the event, and little attention was devoted even to their physical interment. Unlike these Eskimos, the Yukon people and their neighbors north and south lived in the same villages for generations and had cemeteries in their midst or on nearby hillsides. We know little about the observances at the time of death, but we do know the body was treated with care. The corpse of an adult was flexed and placed in a small plank coffin that was covered with birch bark and raised on four posts. Paintings often adorned the box or were made on a board supported by two posts near the coffin. A caribou might be depicted for an outstanding hunter or a boat for a trader; scenes painted on a coffin or tomb board apparently carried the same implications. Yet these observances were not sufficient; the souls of the dead were not content unless Lesser Feasts to the Dead and a Great Feast to the Dead were held in their honor.

Lesser Feasts to the Dead preceded a Great Feast to the Dead. It was thought that if these memorial services were not held a soul would suffer severely in the land of the dead. As eternal punishment the soul of a disreputable person might purposefully be ignored in these ceremonies. When the day for a Lesser Feast arrived, the nearest male relative went to the grave of the person to be honored and placed a staff in the ground nearby. Attached to it was a small carving of a wooden bowl for a female and a spear for a male; each included the totemic sign of the deceased. The staff summoned the spirit of the individual back to the grave. As a part of the ritual a lamp was lighted in the kashim for each person honored. The ceremonial hosts gathering in the kashim were near relatives of the deceased. As songs of invitation were sung, the souls entered the fire pit and then the bodies of their namesakes. Since the pattern in this region was to name an offspring after a recently deceased person, every soul had a namesake. Food and clothing were presented to the namesake, and this pleased the spirit. Bits of food were thrown on the floor for the souls to partake of the essence, and the audience consumed what was left. At the end of the ritual people stamped on the floor to send the souls away.

Lesser Feasts were held three times a year, whereas a Great Feast to the Dead could not be held until a great deal of food and property was accumulated. Four, six, or even more years might be required to assemble the necessary wealth, and numerous dead were honored at the same feast. The principal mourners and hosts were the nearest blood relatives, either male or female, of deceased persons. A year before a Great Feast was held, special invitation staffs were placed near the coffins of the persons being honored, and songs of invitation were sung at the graves. As the date in January for holding the five-day ceremony approached, special messengers carried invitations to villages as distant as 200 miles, and hundreds of guests might attend.

The audience assembled in the kashim the first evening, and the souls of the commemorated dead were thought to gather in the fire pit. A clay lamp burned day and night in the kashim to light the way for each honored soul to and from the land of the dead. The drummers and singers were men, and their songs welcomed the guests. Those from afar were expected to present the hosts with gifts of considerable value, such as caribou skins. This gift-giving ended the activities of the first day. The next evening, after songs about the difficulties of travel, the primary hosts danced, wearing fine new garments; some had fillets about their heads that included totemic emblems.

Early in the morning of the third day the guests were called to the kashim and seated according to the distance that they had traveled, after which the villagers found seats. Out of respect for the hosts, everyone walked slowly and was quiet on entering and leaving the kashim. The memorial services were coordinated, and participants were prompted by an old man, the village leader, and his brother. The hosts now entered dressed in their oldest and dirtiest garments as a sign of humility, but they changed to new clothing to perform the dance that followed. As the drums beat mournfully, each host in turn sang a song to welcome an honored soul. Afterwards the tempo of the drummers changed to a fast beat as men and women performed pantomimes of daily activities, often to the mirth of the audience. The day was highlighted by food and water offerings to the honored dead, and each namesake ate food provided by his host. At this point, during a feast attended by Nelson at a lower Yukon village, 3000 to 4000 pounds of frozen fish were brought in grass bags and placed in separate piles, one belonging to each host. Each sat beside his fish with a maul and wedges, separating them for guests. Those who had traveled the farthest received the most; Nelson's share weighed about 250 pounds.

Early the next day food was brought to the kashim and was distributed to the audience after the customary offerings to the lamps burning for the dead. The invitational songs to the souls and dances of the previous day were repeated. Next about a ton of dried salmon of superior quality was carried in for presentation to the visitors; Nelson, for example, received about 200 pounds. After additional dances and the distribution of small amounts of food, some persons danced in the kashim, and others danced at the honored graves. It was thought that during these ceremonies any souls not at the land of the dead nor in the kashim were in their coffins. Later in the day more food and small but desirable gifts were exhibited, commented on jokingly, and presented to particular people. Each recipient was called by an apt nickname to receive a gift; Nelson's nickname was "buyer of good-for-nothing things." As this distribution came to a close, there appeared through the smokehole a small stick with a thong tied at the end. A hostess began drawing in the thong as she sang a song of mourning. Attached to the line were many small gifts, and soon each hostess was pulling in a similar thong. Models indicating the sex and activities of the honored dead also were tied to the lines. As they appeared one woman after another held them up and said, "See! I have searched and this is what I have found," meaning that she had sought the dead person but found only things that he or she had used. After all the lines had been drawn in, the women untied the gifts, apologized for their poor quality, and gave them away. Thus the day ended.

About noon on the final day only men and older boys were permitted in the kashim. They were joined by the male hosts, whose bundles of gifts were lowered through the smokehole and placed in piles. Like the women the day before, they sang songs of invitation to the dead; then each disparaged the quality and number of gifts he had assembled. After these were distributed to male guests, the women and children entered, and a large amount of food was brought in, again with each host humbly making his presentations. If the hosts did not assume an attitude of humility, it was thought that the honored souls would be offended and would send disease or disaster to the village. As guests received different foods, small pieces were placed at the lamp of the person honored. Suddenly shouts were heard at the smokehole, and large bags of additional gifts were lowered to each host and hostess. The same distribution pattern was followed as before, to the enjoyment of everyone. At the end each hostess and host called out, "Come to me, my best beloved relative," and the namesake of the deceased came forth. The namesake's clothing was removed and replaced by the host or hostess with a new set of fine garments. The namesake then was presented with additional sets of clothing and other gifts. Afterwards each host or hostess called out for the soul of the honored relative to return to his grave; thus concluded the major activities of the ceremony. The Great Feast to the Dead was called "throwing away" because the hosts gave away everything that they owned. Afterwards their obligations to the persons honored were completed, they had done their duty, and they knew that the souls would be content forever.

*   *   *

This record of death ceremonies among Eskimos along the Yukon completes the narrative about Eskimos at the eve of discovery; the only other group of Eskimos, those living in Siberia, are

discussed in a Note to this chapter. The exposure of explorers to
Eskimos began in the east with the Norse and concludes in the
west with reports by a Russian and an Anglo-American. Between
the two occurrences and during the quest for a waterway across
the American arctic most Eskimo groups were discovered. In the
annals of Eskimo ethnography our debt obviously is greatest to
those naval officers who became arctic explorers. George F. Lyon
and William E. Parry best represent the British. Gustav Holm is
most notable among the Danes, Lavrentiy A. Zagoskin for the
Russians, and Elisha K. Kane for the United States. Missionaries
are best symbolized by Hans P. Egede, and medical doctors by
John Simpson. Men trained in other fields made valuable contributions, and among these, naturalists deserve special recognition.
George Best and Dionyse Settle, both of whom accompanied Martin Frobisher, are early English examples of this genre, while
Edward W. Nelson and John Murdoch are latter-day American
representatives. Without the accounts of these men and some
others, our knowledge of aboriginal Eskimo life would be distress-
ingly bland.

NOTES

RUSSIAN EXPLORATIONS.   For the Bering Strait region the most com-
mendable source is the ethnohistory by Dorothy J. Ray (1975a). In this
book the bits and pieces of early ethnographic information are interpreted
in light of Eskimo culture history and reveal just how little systematic
information was collected by early Russian explorers. Another key source
is the book by Svetlana G. Fedorova (1973), but here the emphasis is on
the Russian colonization of Alaska. Whether or not a "lost" Russian
colony was established on Seward Peninsula is debated by both Fedorova
and Ray.

For the Russian expansion into Alaska the book *Siberia* by Yuri Semyonov (1963, 143-62) and the volume by Ray (1975a) were consulted. The
excellent biography of Georg W. Steller by Leonhard Stejneger (1936, 266-
71) is the source for Steller's brief visit to Kayak Island. The list of artifacts
seen by him and his interpretation of the tribal affinities of the makers is
drawn from the study by Kaj Birket-Smith and Frederica de Laguna (1938,
345-8). Fedorova (1973, 64-70) and VanStone (1973, 7-10) are the sources
about the expeditions led by Petr Korsakovskii in 1818-9.

KONIAG AND CHUGACH ETHNOGRAPHY. Diverse authors made early but usually superficial comments about the Kodiak Island Eskimos. Aleš Hrdlička (1944) surveyed these reports and quoted or summarized many of them. Information about the voyage of Glotov to Kodiak in 1763 is based on the summary published by William Coxe (1804, 185-95). The account by Davydov (1977) is the key source and is based on the translation by Colin Bearne as edited by Richard A. Pierce. Additional details about the Koniag are from the 1790 observations by Martin Sauer (1802) and Gawrila Sarytschew (1806), both members of a 1790-1 Russian expedition commanded by Joseph Billings. The 1804-5 descriptions of Kodiak Eskimos by Urey Lisiansky (1814) likewise are included. Details about Koniag material culture are based on the study of museum collections by Birket-Smith (1941).

A comparative study of the whale cult as found among the Koniag, other Eskimos, and more distant peoples was published by Margaret Lantis (1938). Robert F. Heizer (1943) is the interpretive source about the Koniag use of aconite poison for killing whales.

The major source of Chugach Eskimo ethnography is Birket-Smith (1953). The magnificent biography by J. C. Beaglehole (1974, 596) states that Cook had a copy of *The History of Greenland* by David Crantz aboard the *Resolution* during his third voyage. The comment by Cook about the cultural and linguistic parallels between the Chugach and other Eskimos is in Cook and King (1784, v. 2, 521-2). After the Aleuts and Western Eskimos were encountered by the Russians, impressionistic comparisons were made with Greenlandic artifacts such as boats and isolated words (e.g., Coxe, 1780, 40, 116-7).

LOWER YUKON AND CENTRAL BERING SEA COAST ESKIMO SOURCES. The biographical information about Lavrentiy A. Zagoskin is from the translation of his work edited by Henry N. Michael (Zagoskin, 1967, 11-9); this work is also one source of information about the Eskimos of the Yukon and adjacent area. The second source is the account by Edward W. Nelson (1899); the biographical information about Nelson is from an article by Margaret Lantis (1954). It should be noted that the sketch of the Yukon Eskimos includes some information from both authors as they generalized about the Eskimos in this region.

Ingalik Indian and Yukon Eskimo relations are reported from the Indian perspective by Cornelius Osgood (1958, 62-3), and that Yukon Eskimos borrowed little from the Ingalik was recorded by Edward W. Nelson (1899, 242). Richard K. Nelson (1974) examined ethnographic accounts about Eskimo and Athapaskan Indian borrowings in Alaska. He established that Indians adopted many Eskimo traits but that the reverse was not true. Richard Nelson suggests that the richness of Eskimo material culture compared with that of the Athapaskans was a major reason and that these Indians were more receptive to foreign influences.

Zagoskin (1967, 117) reported that dogs were "harnessed to the stanchions" of a sled and presumably the traces were short, which meant that the dogs were at the sides of a sled. This is a highly unusual means of dog traction, yet it also was reported by Lantis (1946, 167; Fig. 25) as the old practice on Nunivak Island.

OTHER ABORIGINAL YUIT STUDIES. Very few monographic ethnographies exist apart from those by Birket-Smith, Nelson, and Zagoskin that already have been cited. The best additional monograph is a reconstruction of early historic life by Margaret Lantis (1946) about Nunivak Eskimo social, political, and religious life based on her fieldwork in 1939-40. Lantis elaborates on the totemic associations identified by Nelson and demonstrates that in this Eskimo society the male line (patrilineage) was far more important than had been reported previously among Eskimos. For the St. Michael region Eskimos (Unaligmiut) we have the monograph by H. M. W. Edmonds (1966) edited by Dorothy J. Ray. Based on Edmonds' fieldwork in 1890-1 and 1898 when he was a member of the United States Coast and Geodetic Survey parties, this study largely supplements the observations by Nelson and Zagoskin. We also have the general study of Alaskan Eskimos based on fieldwork in 1927 by Edward S. Curtis (1930); his best presentation is about the Nunivak people.

Shorter presentations of importance about Alaskan Yuit include an 1839 report by Ferdinand P. von Wrangell (1970) for the Kuskokwim Eskimos based on the diary Ivan F. Vasilev kept during his 1830 exploration of the Kuskokwim River. The Kuskowagamiut sketch and other less important ones of Alaskan peoples were translated and edited by VanStone (1970b). The best presentation of traditional Kuskokwim Eskimo art is by Hans Himmelheber (1953), and the storyknife tales told by Eskimo girls of this region are reported by Oswalt (1964).

SIBERIAN ESKIMOS. Early explorers do not provide enough information about Siberian Eskimos to write an account comparable to the other sketches that have been presented; thus this note completes the regional diversity among Eskimos. The Siberian or Asiatic Eskimos may have numbered 1200 in early historic times; included are the St. Lawrence Island population estimated at 600. They all spoke a dialect of Yupik, and for convenience I have grouped them with Southwestern Eskimos (*see* Appendix I). The great ethnographer of the Chukchee, Waldemar G. Bogoras, generalized that Asiatic Eskimo and Chukchee material cultures were alike, and many forms were similar to those reported among American Eskimos. Included were dog sleds, kayaks, umiaks, bolas, harpoons, sinew-backed bows, spring bait, and so on. Reports about Siberian Eskimos are not only comparatively recent but partially inadequate because the information about their early history is often confused with data about the Chukchee, who were in the process of assimilating them. Siberian Eskimos contrast most with the others in social terms. The Asiatic and St.

Lawrence Island populations traced their kinship ties through males (patrilineal descent), which contrasts with the Eskimo norm of tracing relatives on both sides of the family (bilateral descent). The Siberian people had named patriclans that probably were exogamous, meaning that a spouse was obtained from a different clan. Furthermore, a marriage was not valid until the groom had lived with and worked for his father-in-law for an extended period (temporary matrilocal residence with bride service). After a groom's obligations to his father-in-law were fulfilled, the couple lived with the husband's family (permanent patrilocal residence). Families related through males occupied a common semisubterranean community house that also formed a village.

Siberian Eskimos were distinct among Eskimos in other ways as well. Women were tattooed with complicated patterns on their cheeks and arms. We also have the novel report of an incubator for premature babies. It consisted of a birdskin, with the feathers intact, turned inside out. The neonate was placed in it, and the incubator was suspended over a lamp with a small flame burning day and night. The baby was kept there for one to four weeks and fed oil in addition to milk from the mother's breasts.

Every male aspired to be a "strong man," skilled in running, wrestling, and feats of strength. Each man had a series of cylindrical "lifting stones" with which he practiced, and rock-lifting contests were especially popular as competitive demonstrations of strength. Strong men were not expected to die natural deaths, and if one became fatally ill, he asked to be strangled or stabbed to death. Shamans appear to have been more influential here than among other Eskimos, and some women were powerful shamans. The apparel of shamans was different from that of ordinary persons since pendants and other adornments were suspended from their garments. Men who were shamans wore their hair long, while all others followed a tonsured styling.

In aboriginal times all Asiatic Eskimos appear to have been coastal-dwelling sea-mammal hunters, but by about 1870 some people began herding reindeer in the manner of the Chukchee. The coastal dwellers organized into umiak crews, whose core members were closely related through males. The most important sea mammals harvested were great whales and walrus. One distinctive walrus-hunting technique was for men in boats to strike the surface of the water with clappers when walrus were nearby. The walrus apparently thought that the sound was made by their deadly predators, killer whales, and they hauled up on beaches, where they were easily killed with spears. Wild reindeer were the most important land mammals hunted; while they were swimming, the reindeer were speared from kayaks.

The core of their belief system focused on good and evil spirits in the manner of other Eskimos, yet the religion of Asiatic Eskimos was distinct in some respects. Animal cults loomed large, with people forbidden to kill killer whales, ravens, and wolves. In their thinking, during the winter killer whales changed into wolves to plague the owners of reindeer. Rituals were performed to appease and to perpetuate the animals killed, but these have a cast somewhat different from those reported among other Eskimos. When umiaks first were launched in the spring, a special ceremony was held to insure hunting success in open water for the coming season. In a fall ritual the owner of an umiak killed a dog, and its blood and food were thrown into the sea to "feed" the spirits of the sea. At this time too whale spirits were fed in a special manner. The human dead likewise were honored in a fall ceremony, Feeding the Dead. Prepared food was taken to the graves, which usually were stone covered and had a large headstone. This headstone was removed, a fire built at the spot, and pieces of meat thrown into the fire as the spirit of the dead was summoned. Later the oldest surviving relative of a person being honored took dead coals from the fire, daubed each person present, and said, "Now all sickness will leave here." The headstones were then replaced, and after further rituals the participants left.

The best English synopsis of aboriginal and historic Siberian Eskimo life is by G. A. Menovshchikov (Levin and Potapov, 1964, 836-50). Scattered through the classic study of the Chukchee by Bogoras is information about the Asiatic Eskimos, but it is not systematic. Charles C. Hughes (1959) has translated the brief study of Siberian Eskimo ceremonies by I. K. Voblov, and the best summary of Asiatic Eskimos on St. Lawrence Island was compiled in 1912 by Riley D. Moore (1923).

CHAPTER

10

Before and After Explorers

Eskimo culture had originated, spread, and diversified long before its bearers met the Norse and other Europeans. Studies about Eskimo origins matured slowly, but in recent years archaeologists have been able to identify the region in which their culture coalesced and dispersed. As contacts with Westerners expanded, Eskimos eventually were drawn into the web of colonialism and lost their autonomy. Yet the Eskimo cultural tradition persists, although in a form unimaginable by European explorers. This chapter begins with a brief review of the theories of Eskimo cultural origins. Next, highlights in their history are presented, and finally the recent past and near future are considered. Thus this chapter serves as both a preface and a postscript to the preceding chapters.

PREHISTORY

As worldwide cultures became reasonably well known, the uniqueness of Eskimo culture became apparent. As a consequence, Westerners focused considerable attention on Eskimo origins and dispersal. Most early scholarly efforts to locate the Eskimo homeland were based on cross-cultural ethnographic information, but they proved unrewarding. One reason for this cross-cultural approach was that widespread archaeological excavations in the Eskimo region did not begin until the 1930s. As more sites were dug in northern North America, archaeologists could identify one particular sector for Eskimo cultural genesis. While early theories have been discredited, David Crantz's proposal deserves note because it provided a backdrop for the first pertinent archaeological theory.

In a book about Greenland that appeared in 1767, Crantz compared the cultures of northern peoples around the world and concluded that the Eskimos were most closely tied with peoples of eastern Siberia. He suggested that these peoples were Eskimo ancestors who eventually entered the New World and arrived in Greenland during the fourteenth century A.D. This theory eventually failed, as sites in northeastern Siberia with key Eskimo cultural traits proved to be more recent than those in Alaska.

For about sixty years archaeologists firmly believed that Eskimo culture arose in western Europe. The foremost early advocate of this view was W. Boyd Dawkins. In an 1866 book review, Dawkins stressed the similarity between Eskimo artifacts and those from Magdalenian culture in western Europe that dates from 14,000 to 10,000 B.P. Dawkins elaborated his thesis in books that appeared in 1874 and 1880. In 1888, supportive evidence appeared to be provided by the Chancelade skeleton, identified as possessing Eskimo morphological characteristics; it was associated with Magdalenian artifacts. With his 1878 edition of *Pre-historic Times*, a highly influential book, John Lubbock accepted the conclusions of Dawkins, as did William J. Sollas in the 1911 through 1924 editions of his popular book, *Ancient Hunters*. Further support, based on ethnographic evidence, was offered by Gutorm Gjessing in 1944. He sought to demonstrate the continuous distribution of select artifact types around the top of the world as a means of linking Stone Age Europeans with Eskimos.

Doubt began to be cast on these studies by Ferderica de Laguna in 1932-3. She examined the widely prevailing idea that Upper Paleolithic European and Eskimo art were related. De Laguna concluded that the parallels were overdrawn and were probably invalid. Finally, in 1930, G. M. Morant determined that the Chancelade skeleton fit into the morphological range of Upper Paleolithic European populations and was not Eskimo; this interpretation remains accepted.

Gjessing and his archaeologically oriented predecessors oversimplified circumpolar continuities in material culture. Neither did they adequately recognize the possibility that among unrelated populations similar artifacts associated with northern hunters may have originated at more than one place. Summarily, no acceptable evidence suggests that late Paleolithic hunters in Europe wandered north to the arctic coasts of Eurasia, became sea-mammal hunters, and emerged as Eskimos.

Early New World and Eskimo prehistory each center in the Bering Strait region. It was here that a land bridge, the central portion of a land mass stretching from what is now the Chuckchee Peninsula into western Alaska, and known as Beringia, periodically existed in comparatively recent geological times to provide a gateway to the New World for the earliest Native Americans. The first migrants from eastern Siberia may have made the crossing about 14,000 years ago. Much more recently, and on the Alaskan side, Eskimo culture emerged. Books by Don E. Dumond (1977, 1987) and an article by Dumond and Richard L. Bland (1995) provide a thoughtful synthesis of Eskimo sociocultural evolution.

In the Bering Strait region some 10,000 years ago a late Siberian Paleolithic technology appeared. This technology is best associated with wedge-shaped microcores from which small blades were struck. Some of these artifact makers filtered southward to the Alaska Peninsula and adjacent areas, such as the Kodiak Island sector, at least 6000 years ago and developed a maritime economy. Some 3000 years later their descendants, direct or indirect, occupied the Aleutian Islands. (The exploitation of northern aquatic resources also evolved in the Okhotsk Sea region of eastern Siberia but more recently than did broadly similar developments in southwestern Alaska.) About 3000 years ago, people derived from the originators of the maritime adaptations along the Alaskan North Pacific region spread to northern Alaska and beyond.

This outline encapsulates the origins and spread of Eskimo culture. Notably, early populations from Siberia appear to have been primarily caribou hunters when they began to settle in Alaska; they were not sea-mammal hunters. The technological heirs of some of these people eventually developed a maritime economy adjacent to the *ice-free* waters of the Alaska Peninsula region. They provided the general economic and technological background for the genesis of Eskimo culture. North of them, some of the earliest sites are identified with the Arctic Small Tool tradition (Paleo-Eskimo culture) that spread north, across Canada and to northern and western Greenland. Around 3000 years ago some of the southern, more maritime people in turn migrated northward in Alaska and emerged as intensive sea-mammal hunters along icebound coasts, where they amalgamated with the predecessor folk of the Arctic Small Tool tradition. Thus the culture identified as Old Whaling was followed by Choris, and then, as the coastal knowledge of the immigrants was combined with the ability of the Small Tool people to exploit the hinterlands, the historic Eskimo emerged.

LANGUAGES

Linguists have determined that Eskimos and Aleuts are members of a single language family whose distinct branches possibly separated in the southern Bering Sea region of Alaska some 3000 years ago. Aleut is represented by two dialects. Eskimo is divided into two language branches, Yupik and Inuit. Yupik is represented by six languages. Three are, or were until recently, spoken on the Chukchee Peninsula of Siberia, and two others are spoken in Alaska. By contrast, Inuit is a single language with about sixteen dialects, spoken from the Bering Strait region to east Greenland and identified with Thule or Neo-Thule culture. The rapid spread of Inuit across northern North America makes these Eskimos the most adaptable people in the circumpolar region, if not in the world.

Within the Eskimo-Aleut language family the linguistic diversity among Yupik speakers is especially striking. They had access to an aquatic resource base that was richer and more varied than in the Inuit region, which appears to have fostered localized cultural specializations and language diversity. Likewise, the cluster of Yupik speakers in the Bering Strait region was in a good position to receive new ideas from Siberia to enrich their material culture and contribute to economic adaptations. In combination, these factors may help to explain why there were more different ethnic groups ("tribes" or "nations") among the Yuit than among the Inuit.

AFTER DISCOVERY

Eskimos are not only the most widely dispersed aboriginal people in the world, but they have also adapted to more varied ecological settings than any other indigenous population. Their north-south and east-west distribution is in itself astounding. Additionally, their homeland eventually came under the political domination of four Western nations whose colonial policies varied at any particular time and over time, leading to critical administrative differences. This factor alone impedes any relatively brief presentation of historical developments. Therefore, my goal is to provide select highlights of what history has done to and for Eskimos. Russian Eskimo life contrasts in numerous ways with what has happened from Alaska to Greenland. Thus Russian Eskimos are considered separately in the last part of this chapter. The notes at the end of the chapter provide the interested reader with a publication guide to the historical background of modern Eskimo life.

Material Culture. Technological knowledge was the undisputed cornerstone of Eskimo cultural vitality. Life in the far north cannot be sustained without cold-resistant garments and protective structures. Likewise, the technological means to obtain local edibles must be both varied and effective, considering the seasonal changes.

Eskimo material culture was complex. Comparative technological complexity among aboriginal peoples is not a prominent anthropological interest. Nonetheless, with Eskimos the topic begs for attention. Technological complexity may be measured by the number of different artifact types used by a population combined with the different kinds of parts that make up each type. In these terms, the early historic Polar Eskimos of northwestern Greenland had 157 artifact types with 559 parts; the average number of parts per type was 3.6. The Tareumiut at Point Barrow, Alaska, had 266 artifact types with 1178 parts; the average was 4.4. These differences suggest that far greater technological variability prevailed among the approximately 35 additional Eskimo groups. One also would suspect that the complexity of Eskimo artifacts ranked high among aboriginal foragers.

As Polar Eskimo and Tareumiut artifact types are compared by subsets (e.g., tools, containers, domestic equipment), we find that clothing and structures were far more complex than any other subsets, including food-getting forms. Thus harpoons and bows and arrows were less complex than were garments and shelters. Artifacts that provided protection from the cold appear to represent the apex of Eskimo technological complexity, at least for these two populations.

Paradoxically, as opportunities arose Eskimos appear to have abandoned most of their traditional artifacts with disarming ease. They relished direct interaction with Europeans, who provided local trading contacts. As conveyed in earlier chapters, Eskimos were especially eager to obtain iron. Iron was far superior to stone for processing hard materials such as bone and ivory, and iron-bladed tools were valuable for making the small parts of essential artifacts such as harpoons. By the early centuries of the Christian era, terrestrial iron was obtained by Alaskan Eskimos from Siberian sources, and by A.D. 1200 some Greenlandic and Canadian Inuit were using meteoritic iron, as well as terrestrial iron from Norse sources. Thus Eskimos, east and west, had centuries of familiarity with iron but limited access to it before the arrival of Europeans. In the central area, where iron had not been available, explorers encountered the Inuit, who seemed most anxious to obtain it.

Other Western products sought in the early trade were steel needles, copper and iron utensils, tobacco, and beads. As firearms and ammunition became increasingly available, they emerged as desirable items. The eventual shift from harpoons and spears to rifles changed not only hunting methods but also seasonal subsistence patterns. This was especially true among the people drawn tightly into the fur trade. The availability of spring steel jaw (leg-hold) traps seems to have been an important step in advancing the fur trade, especially as these traps began to be made by machines in the 1850s.

As trade opportunities intensified, some traditional forms made with new materials continued to serve their original purpose. Some of these artifacts were skin scrapers produced from bottle glass, semilunar knife blades cut from old handsaws, and blunt arrowpoints made from spent cartridges. Some harpoon heads were cut from brass. Harpoons continued to be used for taking sea mammals, because although guns might wound or kill prey, harpooning it assured more successful retrieval.

An interesting category of imported forms consisted of those put to novel uses. A good example is the conversion of empty containers in western Alaska. Upright oil drums served as posts for caches; buried in the ground they provided storage for fish in the fall, or, reworked, they became stoves and doghouses. Oil drums also were cut with chisels, flattened, and used as roofing or siding for structures. Empty five-gallon cans served as end floats for gill nets, and small plastic containers became net floats. The range of adaptations is broad, but a few more instances deserve note. Thermos bottles carry water for icing sled shoes. Dental floss sometimes replaces sinew as thread. Under certain conditions, foxes can be run down with snowmobiles, and mosquito repellent, having a high alcohol content, is ideal for starting a fire.

Physical mobility is a prerequisite for hunters and trappers in the north, where seasonal changes are often dramatic. Aboriginal kayaks and umiaks were elegant vessels, but the tendency of wet covers to expand and the relatively delicate nature of the skins were disadvantageous. Before long in some sectors imported whaleboats replaced umiaks; kayaks of aboriginal design were often covered with canvas. Homemade plank boats, imported canoes, aluminum boats, and large imported vessels eventually came into use. A second dramatic change in water transport followed the introduction of relatively reliable inboard and outboard motors.

Where dog teams existed, early historic Eskimos usually had few dogs, because they were difficult to feed. Human effort could be as important as dog power in pulling sleds. Historically, teams with large numbers of dogs became popular in times of affluence, only to decline in number with economic stress. Physical mobility during the winter expanded dramatically in the 1960s as snowmobiles became increasingly popular. Before long in many areas the speed and effective range of the "iron dog" displaced dog sled travel. The economic advantages of snowmobiles are many. For instance, a caribou hunter can drive rapidly into a herd and shoot numerous animals before they scatter. Nonetheless, the cost of a snow machine, along with maintenance and fuel expenses, began to give some people pause. Then, too, the dangers in operating a snowmobile at high speeds, as well as breakdowns, could prove deadly. In a storm, when the person managing a dog team became lost or intoxicated, the dogs usually could find their way home; but with a snow machine the experience might be fatal. Then, too, a lost and hungry hunter could eat his dogs to survive. In recent years, especially in difficult economic times, dog team travel has had a revival, not only for working teams but also for racing and recreational purposes.

All-terrain vehicles also became popular and are widely used. Trucks and automobiles added another dimension to local travel, even in remote communities where roads extended for only a few miles. Finally, improvised airfields have been replaced with permanent ones, and scheduled air service has become the norm.

At present, and especially since the 1970s, most artifacts are imported. In addition to items cited previously, household furnishings, stoves, refrigerators, freezers, washing machines, radios, television sets, and so forth are in common use. The westernization of Eskimo material culture is pervasive—and appreciated by its users.

*   *   *

Explorers, as is apparent from previous chapters, often traded for Eskimo artifacts, and it became obvious that Europeans provided a market for select manufactures. Consequently, Eskimos made some traditional forms for themselves and also for outsiders; garments and footwear are examples. Among Eskimos themselves the last complete sets of skin clothing probably were made to outfit hunters. At present garment types of old, and their substitutes sewn imported furs or cloth, have become largely special-occasion wear. In some Eskimo communities efforts have been made to reintroduce old skin-working methods. Continuity in skin working may best be reflected in the clothing for dolls made by women for sale to outsiders.

A cultural boundary was crossed when Eskimos began to produce particular artifact types for foreigners. When gold seekers began to arrive in the Nome area of Alaska in 1898, representational scenes etched on walrus ivory soon became popular for sale to miners and others. Before long, local Eskimos were producing a wide variety of novelties with appeal to Euro-Americans.

A widely known craft item produced for outsiders at Kulusuk in east Greenland has been the tupilak. Originally a tupilak was made by a sorcerer to cast a spell on someone. These small figures are sculptured from wood or ivory with an often bizarre and fearful combination of animal and human motifs. They were bought by Danes and other Europeans in the 1930s. When a U.S. air base was built nearby in the late 1950s, the market began to expand.

In Canada a major development dates from 1948 to 1953. It was then that the Canadian artist James Houston encouraged soapstone carving, a traditional pursuit, for the arts and craft market at Port Harrison and elsewhere. Westerners soon came to appreciate the style and subject matter of these "primitive" carvings, and the demand increased rather abruptly. As a result, men and women in numerous Inuit communities produced soapstone sculptures. The subject matter and execution soon became far more developed and varied. Prints, wall hangings, tapestries, and other nontraditional forms of artistic products came into the market. Many Inuit depended heavily on the resulting income. Around 1975, however, the demand began to peak. Although the market has endured and the variety of items has continued to expand, the number of full-time artists has declined, along with the profits realized by most of the persons involved.

It is ironic that the Eskimo craft tradition survives largely in the production of arts and crafts for foreigners. Yet the technical skills and originality these artists and craftpersons bring to their work have been widely praised. In this context, Eskimos again demonstrate that they are technological empiricists. This goes a long way toward explaining why arts and crafts for outsiders best represent continuity with Eskimo material culture of old. Catering to the tourist market is an eminently practical manifestation of Eskimos' ongoing adaptation to modern life.

Socioeconomic Developments. Historically, trading relations with the great monopolistic companies had a profound impact on the course of Eskimo life. The companies were the Hudson's Bay Company, the Royal Greenland Trade Department, and the Russian-American Company, which became the Alaska Commercial Company. Not only did the fur trade dominate throughout most of Eskimo history, but the agents of these companies, as well as independent traders, differed widely in their operations. Traders have been criticized for price fixing, usury, and excessive profits. Yet their risks were great, and the goods and services that they provided had positive as well as negative aspects. In time of local food stress, traders usually fed people even though there was little hope of repayment, and it was common for traders eventually to write off bad debts. In addition, it often was the trader's medical chest to which people could turn in times of illness.

In the early trade with Westerners, the people were pulled in two directions. Tradition and habit encouraged them to continue to exploit resources as they had in the past. Yet to obtain imports they were forced to make concessions to Western markets. Initially these foci could be relatively balanced and compatible. To trade polar bear skins or beaver pelts and consume that meat locally was acceptable in traditional trading contexts. But that did not satisfy traders. They upset the balance by encouraging people to systematically harvest relatively useless food animals, such as white fox. To comply required major departures from the old food-getting cycle. Eskimos reluctant to become intensive trappers might be pressured by traders who offered credit, free traps, and other inducements. Typically, hunting and fishing for traditional foods were partially displaced by trapping and increased Eskimo dependence on imported edibles. This arrangement became acceptable to Eskimos and traders, but circumstances could and did upset the new balance. Not only did fur prices fluctuate, but also a man's harvest varied from year to year. Illness, bad luck, and the presence or absence of fur animals were unpredictable. If a man was unable to obtain enough meat and fish to feed his family, hunger could give way to starvation and death. There are reports of men starving to death at trapping camps even while surrounded by valuable white fox pelts.

Trappers were understandably encouraged by traders to harvest the pelts of species that commanded the highest prices. Sooner or later, however, a particular market was likely to decline and lead Eskimos from prosperity to hardship. In southwestern Alaska, the Russsian-American Company agents strongly urged Eskimos to harvest beaver pelts that were desirable in Europe for the manufacture of hats. The market began to diminish in the 1830s as silk hats became fashionable, and Eskimos suffered accordingly. The use of long-hair furs for women's coats, jackets, and accessories provides another example. Fox pelts brought high prices at times, but when a "slim look" gained, or regained, popularity, pelt prices responded accordingly. In recent years, the efforts by animal-rights advocates to reject the use of *all* animal fur in any context has had its own impact on trappers and hunters. The European Economic Community ban on the import of sealskins in the early 1980s was a crushing economic blow. Furthermore, campaigns by Westerners to prohibit the use of jaw traps because of the suffering of captured animals have had their own negative consequences. Fluctuations in the market for pelts and skins over which Eskimos have no control exposed them to economic vulnerability in the world market. In this general context, antiwhaling campaigns have also negatively affected some Eskimos in terms of traditional hunting.

Although trapping fur animals was probably the greatest single source of Eskimo income until shortly after World War II, during this war, wage labor opportunities expanded. These opportunities intensified during the Cold War era; military installations were built from east Greenland to western Alaska. In the 1950s the governments of Canada, Denmark, and the United States began to express serious concerns about the quality of Eskimo life and provided funds to launch major programs of culture change. Substantial houses were constructed in permanent settlements to concentrate families that had previously been scattered, a major and far-reaching change. Local schools were built, and year-round airfields constructed. Community wells were developed along with household electrical service, and fuel delivery to homes might be provided. Unprecedented health care became available as nursing stations were built, and ready access to hospital treatment became standard. Administrative centers were constructed, and a village might have laundry facilities and a community hall. These construction projects provided far greater local wage labor opportunities then ever before. Equally important, permanent local jobs maintaining the infrastructure became available. In addition, standard welfare benefits, old age assistance, and special relief funds were provided. Thus Eskimos were drawn into a combined subsistence, wage labor, and welfare economy. Living off regional resources understandably declined. Most people could not, and no longer desired to, return to the life-style of their parents or grandparents.

The outward appearance of a modern Eskimo settlement might suggest to an outsider that Eskimos "lived like people to the south." Yet in many, possibly most, villages, this was not the case, especially with respect to the nutritional and social importance of traditional foods. A study at Kwethluk in southwestern Alaska is especially noteworthy. In 1986-7 the vast majority of the 540 residents were Eskimo, and nearly half of the population was younger than 20 years old. The median wage employment income from the 112 households was about $17 thousand; most earnings were from government-funded jobs. The cost of living at Kwethluk was more than twice the average in the United States. Members of every household obtained wildlife as food, especially salmon and other fish. The annual wildlife harvest for food was 800 pounds of edible weight per capita. In 1994 at Sanikiluaq, on the Belcher Islands in southeastern Hudson Bay, there were 112 Inuit households, but again imported food costs were high and jobs were limited. In a sample of 102 households, traditional foods were consumed 3.2 times per day per household. The local edibles consumed most often included ringed seal, blue mussels, eider ducks, and arctic char. In this study, the people felt that traditional edibles, especially seals, were desirable for good health and general well-being. Studies in other Eskimo communities have produced broadly similar results, although in some instances store-bought imported foods have been of greater importance.

As the social implications of comparatively recent economic changes are reviewed, any number of observations appear to be self-evident, at least in this overview. Hunters and trappers customarily obtained pelts and skins to exchange for imports at trading stations. Throughout most of the year, however, small families lived in isolated and largely self-sufficient camps where cooperative hunting or fishing could be important. Broader kinship bonds with extended family members were critical not only in social terms but also and especially in times of economic stress. Children were enculturated primarily by parents and older relatives, and adolescence was a time of ever-increasing adult responsibilities. A year was highlighted by one or more trips to a trading post to obtain supplies and to socialize with friends and relatives. Eventually a trading station, mission center, or a combination of the two often became the site for a government-sponsored settlement in which the people were strongly encouraged to live. If a relatively stable village already existed, other Eskimos moved there, and government programs had a head start. In either instance, interactions with friends, neighbors, relatives, and others became far more intense than ever before, and cooperative subsistence activities were likely to decline. In this new settlement pattern, family ties were crucial, and one or a few large families tended to dominate social and emerging political life. Trapping, hunting, and fishing camps in the area became less rewarding because so many people were clustered. Some people literally gave up and depended most on welfare aid. Then came the snow machine. A man with a snowmobile could travel far and fast, returning home the same day. Extended trips away from a settlement for subsistence purposes became less common or desirable. Then came the animal-rights advocates, and the sale of pelts and skins plummeted.

Most Eskimos today represent the "snowmobile generations," in whose lives the trials of dog team travel, isolated camp life, dangerous cold, and other privations have had little or no place. A study of Inuit at Holman is worth noting. Located on Victoria Island in northwestern Canada, the village emerged in the 1960s under government sponsorship. By the early 1990s, declining numbers of youth had become interested in traditional subsistence pursuits. Why? They lacked the necessary skills and possibly the ability to purchase the essential equipment, and the rewards were not especially appealing. Furthermore, wage labor jobs were important to them, and thus hunting and fishing opportunities were restricted. For some youth, store-bought food was more desirable than traditional edibles. Finally, sports such as baseball, basketball, and hockey had become compelling interests.

There is reason to believe that situations like that at Holman are widespread. In this context, a study of the aspirations of Eskimo high school students in the early 1990s attracts attention. In northwestern Alaska and the Bristol Bay region, most of the students in towns and nearly half of the students in villages expected to leave their homes *permanently*. Out-migration was attractive because of the greater opportunities, and more young women than young men expected to leave. A shortage of women in some Greenland villages through out-migration has also been reported. Furthermore, an analysis of the 1990 census for Alaska demonstrated that in the 20- to 39-year-old age group about 1000 more Native Alaskan men lived in villages than did women. About 1000 more Native women were in towns and cities, and an additional but unknown number had left the state.

Why youthful Eskimos have been turning away from their cultural heritage is without doubt a complex issue. To seek a primary cause is probably unwise. Nevertheless, it is not far-fetched to fault the formal systems of education to which Eskimos have been exposed. The negative aspects are many. Some youths, like their parents before them, were sent to boarding (residential) schools as small children and were obligated to return there year after year. One result was that they had a difficult time learning to be Eskimo. Typically, they were punished for speaking Eskimo, and many aspects of their school lives were rigidly controlled in a Western model with little or no consideration of the heritage of these children. Physical punishment was commonplace.

In village schools, little or no allowance was made for the subsistence routine of parents, especially once a school was well established. Even in a home village, it could be difficult for a child to learn Eskimo subsistence methods. Again, speaking Eskimo in school was widely forbidden. Most teachers were Westerners with little or no appreciation of Eskimo culture, and many disparaged Eskimo ways. The teacher turnover rate was and remains high in many areas. Efforts in village schools to teach Eskimo ways have gained popularity, especially as villagers have obtained at least some control over the curriculum, but most of these endeavors have been superficial. As if all of this were not sufficient, the formal education received by students has typically been poor to bad. Finally, there was often a link between formal education and the efforts by Christian missionaries. Mission schools had the reputation of being more concerned with saving souls than broadly educating minds.

How many Eskimos currently live in their homeland? The answer provides a useful measure of the cultural vitality of any indigenous population, irrespective of how little or how much their lifestyle has changed in the course of history. By the mid-1990s, about 127,000 Eskimos were still on their lands of old. No one knows how many others had moved elsewhere. One estimate suggests that about 5000 lived in European Denmark, 10,000 in the Anchorage area of Alaska, and possibly another 7000 in southern Canada; the number living in the contiguous states of the United States appears to be unavailable. Nonetheless, the vast majority continue to be residents of the far north.

How many Eskimos continue to speak their aboriginal language? Again, the answer is a good indicator of a people's sense of cultural identity. Of the 127,000 Eskimos living in their homeland by the mid-1990s, about 85,000, or 66 percent, spoke an Eskimoan language. In the Thule area of Greenland, the 800 people spoke Inuit. On St. Lawrence Island, Alaska, nearly all of the 1100 people spoke Yupik. Of the 30,000 Inuit in Canada, about 24,000 spoke their native language, whereas in western Alaska, of a regional population of about 21,000, some 10,000 individuals spoke Yupik. Much smaller numbers of Eskimo-language speakers lived in Siberia and elsewhere in Alaska. In broad context, a higher percentage of Eskimos spoke their languages than is reported for other Native Americans north of Mexico, with one exception. The percentage of Navajo speakers virtually was the same as that found among Eskimos.

Missionaries. Beginning in 1721, with the first Lutheran mission in Greenland, missionaries emerged as the most powerful early intellectual influence on Eskimo life. In historical perspective, one might disparage the doctrinaire attitudes of many mission workers, but they usually served as the most effective and visible buffer between Eskimos and the harsher representatives of Western cultures. They learned to speak Eskimo languages to win converts, and this knowledge enabled them to help villagers in their contacts with other outsiders. They fought the liquor trade and attempted to lessen exploitation by traders. They routinely cared for the sick and buried the dead and did their best to nurse people back to health during epidemics. Although modern missionaries, who are themselves often Eskimos, remain very much involved with the spiritual well-being of their converts, they are often equally concerned with providing social services.

As Christian missionaries attempted to destroy the aboriginal religion, their most intense attack was on shamanism. There was little or no cooperation among individual shamans in their activities, and it was only in the west that a yearly round of religious ceremonies was well established. As part-time religious specialists, shamans had a difficult time competing with missionaries. Although shamans and missionaries alike attempted to cure the ill, shamans were at a disadvantage, especially as epidemics of exotic diseases such as smallpox struck. Shamans were unsuccessful in their attempts to cure patients of these new diseases, and they lost the confidence of the people as curers, especially when shamans themselves died in epidemics. Furthermore, and equally important, the magic and innumerable taboos surrounding the food quest diminished as firearms replaced harpoons and spears; hunting shifted from a sacred to a secular activity.

The goal of missionaries was to replace Eskimo religion, and it was quickly realized that the future of Christianity among Eskimos depended on changing the lives of children through education. The pattern was for missionaries to learn to speak the local language, to translate religious texts, and to open schools. In Greenland the first mission school was established in 1740, and the program expanded slowly to far-flung settlements along the west coast. Reading and writing were stressed, and with rare exception instruction was in Eskimo. In 1861 a monthly newspaper began publication in Greenland.

In Labrador, mission schools were funded and controlled by the Moravians until a small government subsidy in 1939 provided for the maintenance of a boarding school that had been founded in 1929. Inuit education was controlled primarily by missionaries until 1947, when the government began to establish secular schools. The educational system was not radically revised until the 1950s, when it had become clear that the schools were not preparing students adequately.

In Alaska the pattern of religious influences on education differed somewhat. Missionaries of Episcopalian, Moravian, Roman
Catholic, Russian Orthodox, and other denominations competed
with one another. Religious texts were translated and published in
Eskimo, but these efforts were out of step with federal policies in
the United States. In 1884 Congress began to exert realistic political
control over Alaska. It had the goal of providing schools to assimi-
late Eskimos into the general population; to achieve this end, all
instructional materials were in English. The number of mission
schools partially funded by the federal government expanded rapidly, but in 1895 it became U.S. policy for the Bureau of Education to
hire teachers who were not missionaries.

The biggest failing of mission schools was that the education provided was rudimentary or inadequate. Since the 1950s there has
been a trend toward doing away with boarding schools, although
they still exist. Another trend has been toward greater Eskimo control over various school systems and toward making the curriculum more responsive to local needs. Furthermore, the teaching of
Eskimo languages in schools represents another major policy change.

In sum, the long-term efforts by missionaries have been more
successful than those of any other agents of Western culture. As a
result, the core of old religious life is gone; what remains exists largely
in the minds of some older Eskimos.

Colonialism. Effective political control by colonial governments
obviously was realized at very different times in various regions. In
southwestern Greenland, meaningful political influence began in
1721; in the Angmagsalik area of Greenland, it began in 1894; and in
the Thule area, it was 1933. Political domination began in Labrador
in 1935, in northern Canada between 1903 and 1921, and in Alaska
from 1880 to 1900.

Once Denmark gained control of West Greenland, the government effectively closed the country except to its own administrators, traders, and missionaries. Greenlanders were to retain their
purity and innocence and be protected from corrupting influences.
Included were prohibitions against intoxicants and tea. Whites from
whaling ships and trading-post employees could visit Eskimos only
by special permission. In 1857 limited self-government was introduced, and in 1908 the scope of local government was expanded to
include provincial councils. Efforts to keep Eskimo and Danish so-
cieties separate were doomed as the number of intermarriages in-

creased and as more people became bilingual. During World War II local presence of the United States military became a dominant influence on Greenlanders, and their age-old isolation was destroyed. In 1953, Greenland was made a part of Denmark and sent representatives to the Danish parliament.

In the area of Canada occupied by Inuit, political domination began only after the federal government became fearful that other nations might claim the region. In 1903 the ship *Neptune* was sent to establish a police station near Cape Fullerton, where whalers wintered. The same year North West Mounted Police posts were established at Fort McPherson and on Herschel Island, and by the 1920s a few more far-flung police stations were founded to represent Canadian authority. The Inuit were encouraged to abide by Canadian law but to maintain their own life-style and not assume white ways. In effect, the government prior to 1939 had not formally acknowledge obligations to the Inuit population. In the late 1950s the Canadian government began stationing Northern Service officers in scattered communities to coordinate federal activities. One of their obligations was to foster the development of local village councils, which would lead to a certain degree of political autonomy.

In Labrador, for the region north of Hamilton Inlet, Moravian missionaries dominated politically throughout most of history, but without any formal authority. From the time the first permanent mission was established at Nain in 1771, these devoted missionaries had no rivals among other denominations. They enlisted for life, were selected with care, and were trained to be self-sufficient. They learned to speak fluent Eskimo, had their own trading posts, and provided medical care. As late as 1909 there were "no prison, no police, no magistrate" in the region, and neither was there crime. In 1934 the government of Newfoundland, which included Labrador, was forced by economic conditions to give up its Dominion status, and a Commission of Government ruled until Labrador and Newfoundland joined the Confederation of Canada in 1949. The most radical change in northern Labrador was the stationing of "Rangers" in 1935 as the first local representatives of the law. Their primary purpose was to distribute governmental relief, of which there was comparatively little despite the adverse conditions. Over the years intermarriages with white settlers have caused the people to lose much of their identity, and federal responsibilities toward them were not effectively recognized until 1949.

Under the terms of purchase of Alaska in 1867, Eskimos were "uncivilized tribes" subject to the laws and regulations that the United States government might adopt toward them. The Organic Act of 1884 led to the opening of many schools in remote villages, and some teachers encouraged the formation of village councils to help manage local affairs. By and large these efforts failed, and traders, missionaries, or teachers, singly or in combination, guided and often dominated community life. In 1936, when the Indian Reorganization Act was extended to Alaska, the thrust was a "New Deal" for Eskimos along with Indians and other Americans. The Act's provisions were designed to revive waning Eskimo traditions, stimulate the economy, and encourage local political control through village corporations; by 1949 only 32 such bodies were functioning. It should be stressed that only a few small reservations were established among Alaskan Eskimos and no formal treaties were negotiated. The innovative plans formulated in the mid-1930s generally were abandoned during World War II.

In 1959 Alaska became a state, an extremely important event for Alaskan Eskimos. One reason was that the state was required by the courts to settle aboriginal claims before it could gain clear title to the land for which it qualified under terms of the statehood act. A second reason was the oil industry's realization that a pipeline to carry oil from the North Slope could not be built over land with a clouded title. These factors, plus vigorous pressure from Eskimo and Indian groups, eventually resulted in the Alaska Native Claims Settlement Act of 1971. The act granted aboriginal Alaskans, considered to be those with one-quarter or more native ancestry, title to 40 million acres of land and the scheduled payment of $962.5 million as compensation for lands they relinquished. Twelve regional business corporations were established and funded on a per capita basis. Seven of these corporations were made up exclusively or primarily of Eskimos; with 38,435 members in 1976 they controlled funds totalling $479 million. (A thirteenth regional corporation was established with $50 million for the 4000 Native Alaskans no longer living in Alaska.) Under the terms of the settlement act, Native Alaskans had all the rights of other citizens.

World War II and the Cold War had a direct influence on the lives of many Eskimos and an indirect impact on all Eskimos, as was mentioned previously. The direct impact of World War II was greatest in Alaska, where a "tundra army" was created in 1941 as the

Alaska Territorial Guard. Its purpose was to repel any Japanese attack on the unprotected western and northern coasts. The volunteer guard members were trained primarily in guerrilla warfare. Units were organized in about 60 communities where the residents usually were Eskimo. In 1948 the units were reorganized as the Alaska National Guard, which was especially active during the Cold War. Eskimo members of both organizations typically joined for economic gain. A study of the continuing impact of the guard on village life has not been made. My impression is that the military hierarchy of the guard and its rigidity represent a negative influence on the essentially egalitarian structure of village life. At the same time the guard appears to have been an important institution in the acculturation process.

The Cold War likewise influenced Eskimos everywhere. This influence can be seen at Thule in northwestern Greenland, where the United States Air Force built a huge base in the early 1950s at which as many as 6000 airmen were stationed. By 1975 airmen and Danish civilians at the base numbered 3000. The Danish government relocated the 700 Polar Eskimos farther north. The Cold War also led to the creation, beginning in 1953, of the Distant Early Warning radar network (DEW line) in northern North America. This produced close contacts of unprecedented scope and intensity between Eskimos and outsiders. These and other intrusions by the military during and after World War II enabled Eskimos to interact locally with outsiders who were quite different from traders, missionaries, and administrators.

The increasing scope of government funds received by Eskimos in their homeland constitutes a long-term trend. These allocations may be identified as administrative costs, grants, subsidies, income supplements, welfare payments, and so on. Irrespective of the label, it is money provided by non-Eskimos for Eskimo benefit. The present-day infrastructure of Eskimo settlements could not have conceivably emerged without the support of Canada, Denmark, and the United States. Eskimo dependency on government money began as a trickle in the 1950s, emerged as a stream by the 1970s, and then became a river. Examples suggest the extent of financial assistance. The Alaska Native Claims Settlement Act in Alaska, already discussed, awarded funds to corporations, *not* to individuals. In anticipation of the establishment in 1999 of Nunavut ("our land"), a new territory in north central Canada, the government has allocated

$1.15 billion. The Nunavut population will be about 85 percent Inuit. In 1998 the 8000 Inuit and 800 non-Inuit in northern Quebec were negotiating the creation of another new territory in Canada, Nunavik. The people involved are to have limited control over education, health, housing, and the justice system. It is anticipated that each year millions of dollars in block funding will be provided by the federal and provincial governments.

The negative aspects of life resulting from Western contacts cannot be ignored. Prominent among these is the knowledge that "the government will provide." This dependency attitude is realistic considering the market for local products, limited job opportunities, and the restrictions on the harvest of fish and game in some sectors. Personal pride and aspirations often have diminished and led to feelings of aimlessness. As indicated earlier, many Alaskan high school students plan to leave their village homes. For them village life is "boring." It is little wonder that among youthful individuals in particular the excessive consumption of alcoholic beverages and the use of illegal drugs are commonplace, and suicide rates are often alarming. Likewise, some persons who move to urban areas have a difficult time making a living, in part because they are poorly educated.

The Pan-Eskimo Movement. Since the 1950s Eskimo success in gaining substantial control over their homeland has been phenomenal. In retrospect, their accomplishments are understandable. The worldwide reaction against colonialism following World War II provided a positive backdrop for major changes. Then too American Indian advocates of "self-determination" and "sovereignty" have had an impact. One thing is clear: in Danish and Euro-American relationships, the "north" is beginning to win over the "south." If there is a collective Eskimo dream, it is to establish their own nation.

The first dramatic change in Eskimo political status originated in Denmark. In 1953 the colonial status of Greenland was abandoned, and the island became a part of the Kingdom of Denmark. Because of this change the Danish presence in Greenland increased. It was not until 1979 that the Greenland Home Rule Act became law, a major step toward local control. Inuit became the "principle language," but Danish was taught in schools as a co-official language. Relations with foreign governments, defense, and the fiscal system remained in Danish hands. Yet the act permitted eventual control by the people over local government, taxes, religion, businesses, education, and other key aspects of Greenlandic life. Greenlanders are justifiably proud of their new status, but inequities between the rich and poor and towns as opposed to villages persist. Despite local developments, Danish power and influence remain intrusive.

The most significant formal assembly of Eskimos from Canada, Greenland, and the United States was inspired by Eben Hopson of Barrow, Alaska. His efforts led to the first Inuit Circumpolar Conference in 1977, the charter for which was approved in 1980. Sustaining the identity of arctic peoples in cooperation with national governments became a primary goal. Over the years this organization has worked with units of the United Nations to foster the rights of indigenous peoples throughout the world and to aid them in developing self-government.

With respect to the future of Eskimos, I can do no better than quote Marc G. Stevenson (1997, 336) regarding the new territory of Nunavut in Canada. "Today, Inuit face a challenge different than that confronted by previous generations. No longer are cultural and physical survival one and the same. Once again, in order to remain Inuit, they must change. And, once again, they must do it by someone else's rules. How to preserve Inuit cultural values, customs, and traditions under such circumstances is one of the greatest challenges that Nunavut faces." And so it is with Eskimos elsewhere.

Even if an Eskimo nation is politically feasible, finances will be a critical concern. An obvious solution would be for the nations that have Eskimo populations to provide substantial and ongoing funds. A seductive alternative may also exist, that is, to tap mineral resources in the region. With some major exceptions, especially in Alaska, the geological potential of the arctic is not well known. Despite high costs in the far north for mineral exploration, development, and transportation, prospects have been encouraging. For example, in the emerging Canadian territory of Nunavut systematic geological studies are few. In 1998 about 50 mineral exploration projects were being pursued in Nunavut for gold, silver, base metals, and diamonds; diamond mines were beginning to be developed in a nearby sector of the new Western Arctic Territory. The greatest hope for long-range Eskimo self-sufficiency could be what is beneath the tundra and ice fields.

Siberian Eskimos. These people were largely ignored by the Tsarist government, a situation that led to their partial domination by resident and intinerant traders from Alaska. In the 1920s the Soviets proposed that small nationalities such as these Eskimos be self-governing, but this goal went astray. In one negative development, a small number of Eskimos were relocated to Wrangell Island in 1926 by the Soviets to support government claim to the island. Soviet collectivization of the Eskimos and Chukchee occurred between 1928 and 1952. The Eskimo-Chukchee collective nearest St. Lawrence Island, Alaska, began in 1930, with sea-mammal hunting and white-fox trapping as an economic base. By 1948 the collective owned about 900 reindeer; about 600 others were privately owned. By 1954 walrus- and seal-hunting brigades made the greatest contribution to the economy of the collective. Major resistance to collectivism arose because of economic ties with Alaska that were not severed until the 1940s.

With *perestroika*, introduced by Mikhail S. Gorbachev, and the end of censorship in 1988, the problems of Eskimos and other eastern Siberian peoples began to be exposed in the press. Resettlement programs were revealed as disasters, the economy was a shambles, and health conditions were deplorable, all of which had been known but not publicized previously. One result was that sovereignty was advocated among the peoples involved. In 1990 the Society of Eskimos of Chukotka was formed to preserve their ethnic identity. By then the Siberian Eskimo population was about 2000, of whom 1300 appear to have been Yupik speakers. The unsettled conditions in Russia during the 1990s have been shared by these Eskimos, among whom life expectancy was short, an exceedingly high rate of tuberculosis prevailed, and pervasive government neglect continued. The goals of the Society of Eskimos include language preservation, self-government, and full participation in a market economy as hunters and trappers. Finally they anticipated full membership in the Inuit Circumpolar Conference to further the social, economic, and political goals of Eskimos everywhere.

NOTES

This section expands on select topics, references the sources consulted, and provides a guide to anthropological studies about Eskimos, especially books and monographs.

ORIGINS.   The most coherent group of theories based primarily on ethnographic evidence proposed a New World center for the development of

Eskimo culture. The essence of the thesis was the gradual movement of subarctic hunters from the interior of North America to the coast by adapting riverine- or lake-fishing techniques to sea-mammal hunting. These theories had differing inland points of origin for the migrants. Henry Rink (1875, 70-2) thought that Eskimo culture probably emerged as inland hunters followed Alaskan rivers to the sea, where they developed a maritime economy. John Murdoch (1888, 129) suggested that Eskimos originated in the area to the south of Hudson Bay and spread from there. From a detailed analysis of ethnographic data H. P. Steensby (1917, 169-71, 185-6, 206, 211) thought he recognized a "layering" of traits. He felt that Eskimo genesis was in the culture of northern Indians who had reached the coast in the area from Coronation Gulf to Melville Peninsula; here they learned to hunt on the sea ice and to build snowhouses. These people, Paleo-Eskimos, pushed east and west along the coast. Steensby reasoned that Neo-Eskimo culture emerged as influences from peoples in eastern Asia reached the coastal dwellers. The most recent inland-to-the-sea theory was advanced by Birket-Smith (1929, pt. 2, 229-33). He saw evidence for people moving from an inland lake-ice fishing stage in the Mackenzie region to the arctic coast. Here they adapted fishing techniques to hunting seals at their breathing holes and at man-made holes in the ice. The Caribou Eskimos at the time of historic contact represented to Birket-Smith a survival of the old inland fishing tradition. Contemporary advocates of this thesis do not exist. The reason is that no archaeological evidence supports a transition from inland fishing to maritime hunting in the far north. The Caribou Eskimos, the cornerstone of the reconstruction by Birket-Smith, apparently did not begin living on the Barren Grounds until recent prehistoric times.

An east Asian point of origin, based on ethnographic comparisons, first was advanced by Crantz (1767, v. 1, 258-60), but his thesis gained comparatively few advocates outside Russia. S. I. Rudenko (1961, 7-19) summarized the case for Asian origins proposed by Russian archaeologists and ethnologists. On the basis of Eskimo legends about their origins, John Rae (1866, 151-2) reasoned that they once lived in Asia. After analyzing a substantial body of myths, Franz Boas (1888b, 39) concluded that they originated in "the lake region west of Hudson Bay."

Linguists most consistently have pointed to Alaska as the area of Eskimo dispersal. On the basis of language differences Rink (1891, 3-23) continued to favor the Alaskan-river-to-the-sea thesis that he had earlier based on ethnographic data. After studying Eskimo dialects Thalbitzer (1904, 266) pointed out that words in Alaska were more heterogeneous than those in Greenland, and that while comparatively few data were available about Alaskan Eskimos, they seemed to represent "an earlier stage of development." Anthony C. Woodbury (1984) presents a comprehensive analysis of Eskimo linguistic relationships. Michael Krauss (1997) offers a slightly different classification; he includes population statistics for the early 1990s as well as estimates of how many people spoke particular Eskimoan languages.

The following-the-reindeer theory of Dawkins is best presented in historical perspective by de Laguna (1932, 477-87) in the introduction to her comparative study of Upper Paleolithic and Eskimo art (de Laguna, 1932, 1933). Dawkins (1866, 712-3) began formulating the idea in a book review titled "Esquimaux in the South of Gaul," and he later elaborated the theme in two books (Dawkins, 1874, 353-9; 1880, 233-42). The suggestion of racial affinities between the Chancelade skeleton and Eskimos was reviewed and rejected by G. M. Morant (1930, 158). Gjessing (1944) most recently advocated a "circumpolar stone age," but as Carl-Axel Moberg (1960) has noted, the thesis seems invalid because the traits cited are comparatively recent and of diverse origins in Scandinavia. In addition, as Chester S. Chard (1959, 81-2) stressed, the evidence of Eskimo culture along the northern coast of Siberia is oldest in the east, and it extends westward only to the Bear Islands, off the mouth of the Kolyma River, where the sites date from the period of historic contact.

William N. Irving began to isolate the Arctic Small Tool tradition in 1957 (p. 47) and later (1962) designated it with precision in a broader range of sites. I have followed the discussion of Eskimo cultural origins and development in a book by Don E. Dumond (1977, revised 1987) and the article by Dumond and Richard L. Bland (1995). The most recent survey of Eskimo prehistory is by Robert McGhee (1996). The best single source for articles about ongoing research in Eskimo prehistory is the journal *Arctic Anthropology*.

ETHNOHISTORY. An article by McGhee (1984) about Norse-Eskimo contacts is superior and a welcome supplement to my discussion of the subject in the opening chapter. The early book about Greenland by Henry Rink (1877) is an invaluable source. For Labrador the monographs by Helge Kleivan (1966) and David W. Zimmerly (1975) are essential works to consult. For the Bering Strait region the book by Ray (1975a) is excellent. The Nushagak Eskimos (Kiatagmuit) are presented by VanStone (1967), and the Kuskokwim Eskimos (Kuskowagamiut) are described by Oswalt (1963a). VanStone*(1988) published the journals of early Russian explorers in southwestern Alaska and discusses the ethnographic content of the accounts. W. Gillies Ross (1975) authored a fine study concerning the impact of commercial whaling on Eskimos along northern Hudson Bay. Eskimo life in northwestern Greenland is presented with historical and cultural insight by Richard Vaughan (1991). John C. Kennedy (1995) provides a comprehensive analysis of settlements in southeastern Labrador, a badly neglected but important area. The most detailed historical presentation about Eskimo culture-carrying units or "nations" is by Ernest S. Burch Jr. (1998), and deals with northwestern Alaska.

ETHNOARCHAEOLOGY. To expand on the information about Eskimos near the time of historic contact, especially to fill in major gaps in ethnographic accounts, archaeologists have dug historic Eskimo sites. The most important contributions have been made by VanStone (1968, 1970a, 1972a), who worked along the Nushagak River drainage in Alaska. In addition are the study by Oswalt and VanStone (1967) for Crow Village along the Kuskokwim River and the excavations by Dumond and VanStone (1995) at Paugvik along Bristol Bay in Alaska. For Canada Robert McGhee (1972) wrote a major work about the Copper Eskimos. His focus is on the broader cultural background from which this tribe emerged. The earliest, if not the classic, excavation was that of Mathiassen (1931) at the Inugsuk Island site in West Greenland.

ETHNOLOGICAL OVERVIEWS. The following references provide a brief topically arranged guide to important sources. Aboriginal baseline accounts are not included because they are referenced by area in the notes for chapters 4 through 9. Major pre-1979 sources are cited in the notes to chapter 1.

The most outstanding comparative study about the variability in Eskimo culture, as also cited in the chapter 1 notes, was written by Edward M. Weyer (1932). Researchers with topical interests can do no better than to begin with Weyer and then turn to Harold E. Driver (1961) for comparisons with other Native Americans. Another key source is the 1984 *Arctic* volume (5) of the *Handbook of North American Indians*, edited by David Damas. This 829-page work, published by the Smithsonian Institution, deals with *all* aspects of prehistoric and historic North American Eskimo culture. It is widely available and might be the first source consulted under most circumstances. (For the sake of economy, with rare exception, I do not list specific *Arctic* volume chapters in the following citations, nor in the references to this book.)

Popular and authoritative books about Eskimos in general have been written by Kaj Birket-Smith (1936, 1959, 1971 editions) and by Ernest S. Burch Jr. (1988). An overview of peoples in areas of eastern Russia and Alaska adjacent to the Bering Sea area was edited by William W. Fitzhugh and Aron Crowell (1988); included are chapters devoted to aspects of Eskimo life.

The best ethnographic bibliographic source for publications about Eskimos is the work by George P. Murdock and Timothy J. O'Leary (1975), along with its supplement by M. Marlene Martin and O'Leary (1990).

MATERIAL CULTURE. The importance of iron to Eskimos in early historic times was documented in previous chapters. The information about iron uses in central Canada comes from an article by A. P. McCartney and D. J. Mack (1973). The best detailed discussions of early firearm usage are by Dorothy J. Ray (1975b), covering the Bering Strait area, and W. G. Ross (1975, 97-110), dealing with northwestern Hudson Bay. The early impact of snowmobiles in Canada is discussed by Lorne Smith (1972), on Banks Island by Peter J. Usher (1972), and in northern Alaska by Edwin S. Hall (1971).

Trading relations are summarized in the monographs about Eskimo administration by Diamond Jenness (1962, 1964, 1965, 1967). Particulars concerning Russian-American Company policies are taken from the report by Gavrill I. Davydov, edited by Richard A. Pierce (1977). Ross (1975) examines the activities of whalers in Hudson Bay. Hudson's Bay Company and Canadian government relations in the north are discussed by Damas (1993), and William Barr (1994) considers eighteenth-century trade with the Inuit by Hudson's Bay Company ship crews. A recent book by Betty Kobayashi Issenman (1997) examines Eskimo clothing past and present, in rewarding detail.

Comparatively little systematic attention has been paid to the details of changes in Eskimo material culture. At the same time, however, summaries are provided in books and monographs about modern communities; see the citations in the "Socioeconomic Developments" section. A superior inventory for Alaskan villages in 1930-1 is provided by H. Dewey Anderson and Walter C. Eells (1935, 123-37). Robert E. Ackerman (1970, 28-9) presents an inventory for an Eskimo fish camp in 1966 along the Goodnews River, Alaska. In an article (Oswalt, 1972), I examine continuity and change in material culture in four Eskimo villages in western Alaska. I also describe early historic Tareumiut and Polar Eskimo artifact types in terms of their comparative complexity (Oswalt, 1987). Some particulars about material culture changes in this chapter are based on my observations in Alaska and Canada.

ART. A comprehensive but dated study of Eskimo graphic art is by Walter J. Hoffman (1897). Ray (1967) and Ann Fienup-Riordan (1996a, b) have written the best books about Eskimo masks. A notable book about prehistoric, aboriginal, and comparatively recent art is introduced by Alma Houston (1988). Bodil Kaalund (1983) provides an excellent discussion of Greenlandic arts and crafts into the 1970s. Ray (1977) wrote possibly the most comprehensive overview of Eskimo art. A classic 1936-7 field study about artists and art along the Kuskokwim River and Nunivak Island, Alaska, was done by Hans Himmelheber; it appears in German (1938, 1953) and English editions (1987, 1993). Eskimo sculpture is examined by Jørgen Melgaard (1960), and volumes by George Swinton (1965, 1972) are devoted primarily to modern soapstone carvings. The *Inuit Art Quarterly* is a source about the topic. H. Goetz (1977) presents Inuit print making during the early years, and Kyra Vladykov Fisher (1997) discusses a recent revival of print making at Baker Lake, Canada.

SOCIOECONOMIC DEVELOPMENTS. For information prior to the mid-1980s, the best initial source may be the *Arctic* volume (5, 1984) of the *Handbook of*

North American Indians. Broad-scale surveys are rare. The best early review of conditions in Alaska is the 1930-1 study by Anderson and Eells (1935). The next intensive Alaskan study was prepared by the Federal Field Committee for Development Planning in Alaska (1968). A somewhat comparable but superior report on Canada is the three-volume study prepared by Milton Freeman Research Limited (1976). For a general survey of conditions in Greenland to the mid-1920s, a long article by Birket-Smith (1928) is informative, and a more recent monograph by Poul P. Sveistrup (1967) provides a comprehensive review of economic conditions. The latter half of the volume edited by Victor F. Valentine and Frank G. Vallee (1968) contains articles about changing Inuit life; the first half is devoted to traditional culture.

The following books and monographs are devoted to life at one or more of the communities studied since the 1950s: Gambell, Alaska, by Charles C. Hughes (1960); Wainwright, Alaska, by Fred Milan (1964) and by Richard K. Nelson (1969); Barrow, Kaktovik, and Wainwright, Alaska, by Norman A. Chance (1966); Point Hope, Alaska, by VanStone (1962), and his study on the Bristol Bay area of Alaska (1967); Napaskiak, Alaska, by Oswalt (1963a); Barrow and Kotzebue, Alaska, by Arthur E. Hippler (1969) and his study of Nome, Alaska (1970); a Netsilik group in northern Canada by Jean L. Briggs (1970); Holman in northwestern Canada by Richard G. Condon (1983, 1987); Sugluk, Quebec, by Nelson H. H. Graburn (1969); Nelson Island, Alaska, by Fienup-Riordan (1983); East Greenland by Joëlle Robert-Lamblin (1986); Gambell, Wainwright, and Unalakleet, Alaska, by Joseph G. Jorgensen (1990); northwestern Greenland by Mark Nuttall (1992); and Quaqtaq in Canada by Louis-Jacques Dorais (1997).

The town of Frobisher Bay, Canada, was studied by John J. Honigmann and Irma Honigmann (1965). John Honigmann (1975) authored a monograph about five northern towns, of which four (Churchill, Frobisher Bay, Great Whale River, and Inuvik) included Inuit populations.

Modern whaling by Eskimos and other peoples is a contentious issue addressed in articles published by the journal *Arctic* (v. 46, no. 2: 1993).

The forced relocations of Inuit in Canada from Quebec and the Keewatin areas in the 1950s have recently been examined in books by Frank J. Tester and Peter Kulchyski (1994) and by Alan Rudolph Marcus (1995).

FORMAL EDUCATION. The best general survey that includes Eskimos in Alaska, Canada, and Greenland is by Frank Darnell and Anton Hoëm (1996). For Alaskan Eskimos, the pioneering study is by Anderson and Eells (1935). John Collier (1973) focused his work in the Bethel area of Alaska and examined the impact of education on modern life. Judith Smilg Kleinfeld (1979) studied bicultural education at a Roman Catholic boarding school in western Alaska and convincingly conveys the positive results of a carefully conceived program. A. Oscar Kawagley (1995), a

Kuskokwim Yupik, focused to a great extent on the formal education of children at the village of Akiak, Alaska, in the recent past.

RELIGION AND MISSIONARIES. A broad view of tradition Eskimo religious life is presented by Daniel Merkur (1991), while I. Kleivan and B. Sonne (1985) address the same topic relating to Canada and Greenland. The best overview of traditional religion in Alaska is by Margaret Lantis (1947). A book edited by Takashi Irimoto and Takako Yamada (1994) includes chapters about religion and ecology among Alaskan and Canadian Eskimos. Fienup-Riordan (1990, 1994, 1996a, 1996b) presents Yukon-Kuskokwim-area Eskimo masks and rituals, as well as a world-view of the past and links with the present in an insightful and thought-provoking combination.

A comprehensive and comparative book-length study about Christian missionaries apparently has not appeared. The monographs by Jenness (1962, 1964, 1965, 1967, 1968) about Eskimo administration are possibly the best sources for an overview of missions from Alaska to Greenland. The second and third volumes of the Greenland history by Finn Gad (1973, 1982) include discussions about missions.

Book-length ethnohistories and regional and community studies include discussions of varied missionary efforts. Books centering on particular denominations have also appeared. A work on Moravians in western Alaska by Oswalt (1963b) is now dated and surpassed by a book about Moravians in the same area by Fienup-Riordan (1991).

BIOLOGY AND HEALTH. The best brief discussion of Eskimo and northern Indian biology is by Emöke J. E. Szathmary (1984). Aldur W. Eriksson et al. (1970) and Roy J. Shephard and S. Itoh (1976) have edited somewhat dated but worthwhile surveys of circumpolar peoples and health issues. The best coverage of Alaskan Eskimo health during the critical 1950s was compiled by Thomas Parran (1954). Community and regional studies typically include information about health and related concerns.

In an earlier chapter (p. 134, p. 138), "arctic hysteria" was discussed, but its cause had not been established. Lyle Dick (1995) analyzed the primary accounts and determined that it was not a specific disorder. He concluded that the behavior associated with arctic hysteria was an Inuit stress response to contacts with Euro-Americans between 1890 and 1920.

THE PERSISTENCE OF SUBSISTENCE EFFORTS. Michael W. Coffing (1991) has written the most thoroughly documented study for an Eskimo community of the continuing importance of local edibles, focusing on the Alaskan village of Kwethluk. The attitudes of youthful Inuit at Holman, Canada, regarding local foods are explored by Richard G. Condon, Peter Collings, and George Wenzel (1995). The general topic also is examined by Ole Marquardt and Richard Caulfield (1996) for West Greenland. A Belcher Island study is presented by Eleanor E. Wein, Milton M. R. Freeman, and Janette C. Makus (1996).

SOCIAL ORGANIZATION.The best literature review is by Marc G. Stevenson (1997); it is highly recommended.

ADMINISTRATION.   The major studies are monographs by Jenness; included are volumes about Alaska (1962), Canada (1964), Labrador (1965), and Greenland (1967). A fifth volume (1968) provides an overview with recommendations. In addition, the three volumes about Greenland by Finn Gad (1971, 1973, 1982) are exceptional down to 1808, the end date for volume three. For Alaska, the book by Robert D. Arnold et al. (1976) provides a review of relatively recent developments. For central Canada, a book by Hugh Brody (1975) also concentrates on the comparatively recent past. The recent publications listed in the "Socioeconomic Developments" section of the notes for this chapter usually consider administrative matters.

OUT-MIGRATION.   Fred Milan and Stella Pawson (1975) wrote a pioneering article about urban Eskimos in Fairbanks, Alaska, and a notable monograph by Susan Ruddy and Irene Rowan (1975) examined the problems of urban Native Alaskans. More recent articles by Lawrence C. Hamilton and Carole L. Seyfrit (1993, 1994) concern the aspirations of youth in Alaskan villages and the gender balance to provide a new dimension in the interpretation of Eskimo life.

ANIMAL RIGHTS.   The campaigns by animal-rights advocates and the historical background to their efforts in the Canadian arctic are presented in an excellent book by Wenzel (1991).

SOCIAL ILLS.   General studies about Eskimos since World War II typically include discussion of the impact of alcoholic beverage consumption. A recent comprehensive study of contemporary problems for the Baffin Island region of Canada is by Willem C. E. Rasing (1994).

THE PAN-ESKIMO MOVEMENT.   Papers published in *Études/Inuit/Studies* (v. 16, nos. 1-2; 1992) are a key source about recent efforts of Eskimos to gain greater political freedom.

SIBERIAN ESKIMOS.   The best recent sources are books by James Forsyth (1992) and by Yuri Slezkine (1994).

APPENDIX

I

Aboriginal Population and Distribution of Tribes

The standard maps for the early historic distribution of Eskimo groups were published by Weyer (1932, end maps), Birket-Smith (1936, endpapers), and Kroeber (1939, Map 1). Only the map by Kroeber and Weyer's map for Alaska include precise tribal boundaries. Tribes were identified and labeled largely on the basis of geographical factors, food-getting adaptations, and expressions of local differences by the Eskimos involved. When the word "tribe" is applied to Eskimos, it does not mean a distinct, named, and integrated political entity with clearly defined boundaries. To Eskimos the term means those people living in adjacent bands or villages who share a common social identity, similar economic patterns, and a dialect slightly different from those of their neighbors.

Since the appearance of these maps in the 1930s, more has been learned about the distribution of Eskimos early in their history. On Map 1 of this book are tribal designations that have proven useful for denoting differences among Eskimos. Canadian tribes have not been differentiated to the same extent as Alaskan tribes because localized differences among the latter presumably were of greater magnitude. Some authorities might, however, divide the Mackenzie Eskimos into five tribes. Be that as it may, certain boundaries still are based as much on conjecture as on ethnohistorical information. Population estimates by tribe for the era of the first intense contacts also are included. When attached to a tribal name, the suffix "miut" means "the people of" a particular place. The sources for the population data and boundaries on the map follow.

Eastern Eskimos.   On the east coast of Greenland the Angmagsalik, with 413 people (Thalbitzer, 1914, 348), had the greatest population concentration; their boundaries were defined by Holm and Thalbitzer (1914, 108, 109, 343-7). To the south were another 500 people (Graah, 1837, 115) at small scattered villages. To the north of Angmagsalik 12 people were seen at Clavering Island (Clavering, 1830, 24), and it arbitrarily is assumed that the total population there was 50 persons.

The West Greenland Eskimos extended from the vicinity of Cape Farewell north to the vicinity of Upernivik, and their aboriginal population was estimated at 8000 (Birket-Smith, 1928, 13, 19). For the Polar Eskimos the population estimate by Kane (1856, v. 2, 108, 211) of 140 is accepted, and their geographic distribution is based on the determinations by Kroeber (1900, 266).

Central Eskimos.   The map prepared by David Damas (1968, 117) for the core tribes, the Copper, Iglulik, and Netsilik Eskimos, is followed, but two changes have been made. The northern boundary of the Iglulik is extended farther north on the basis of compilations by Ross (1976, Map 75), and the Back River Eskimos are included with the Netsilik on the basis of their genealogical ties (Cheryl Kabloona, verbal communication). The Caribou Eskimo boundaries are based on Birket-Smith (1929, v. 1, 29-30).

In 1914 Jenness (1922, 42) estimated the number of Copper Eskimos as being from 700 to 800, but Peter J. Usher (1971, 169, 182 fn. 3) thought their aboriginal population to be 1000, with a decrease prior to the arrival of Jenness. Usher's figure is accepted. In 1922 Mathiassen (1928, 15) counted 504 Iglulik and thought that the population had been somewhat reduced by that time. From diverse accounts their number was estimated at 550 by T. H. Manning (1943, 103), and this is accepted. No one really knows how many Netsilik there were in early historic times, but 500 probably is a reasonable estimate, with an additional 200 added to include the Back River Eskimos. For the early historic Caribou Eskimo population an estimate of 700 seems acceptable, based in part on Birket-Smith (1929, v. 1, 66).

The Baffin Island Eskimo population estimate of 6000 by James Mooney (1928, 26) seems unreasonably high. We have no idea of the number of persons living there in early historic times. Boas (1888a, 426) estimated that the total population was between 1000 and 1100 in 1883; 2000 is offered as a reasonable interim estimate for the Eskimos living on the southern part of the island. Their distribution is based on Boas (1888a) and Ross (1976).

For Labrador and northern Quebec the distribution of groups provided by Nelson H. H. Graburn (1969, 34) is followed except that the Uqumiut and Sirqinirmiut boundary is modified to conform with the settlement pattern presented by J. Garth Taylor (1975). The population estimate of 700 for the Uqumiut by Taylor is accepted, but to his total of 1630 for the Sirqinirmiut (Taylor, 1975, 274) are added another 200 persons, the presumed population of the Hamilton Inlet area that he did not consider.

The Itivimiut population along the eastern shore of Hudson Bay was estimated at about 450 in 1895 (Hawkes, 1916, 22); 700 may approximate the aboriginal number. There were 152 Kigiktagmiut on the Belcher Islands in 1949 (Honigmann, 1962, 4), and perhaps 200 lived there during the early era of contact. The Sadlermiut concentrated on southern Southampton Island numbered 70 in 1902 (Mathiassen, 1927, pt. 1, 285); the population may have been 300 shortly before contact. The Mackenzie Eskimo boundaries and population estimate of 2500 are based on studies by Peter J. Usher (1971, 171).

Northwestern Eskimos. The boundaries for Alaskan Eskimos by Oswalt (1967, 4-9, Map 2) form the base from which revisions were made as a result of more recent studies. In the northwestern sector the boundaries were modified on the basis of work by Ernest S. Burch (1975, 10-3), and his population estimates for the region have been accepted. The Nunamiut boundaries represent a compromise between the maps of Burch (1975, 11) and John M. Campbell (1968, 2).

Southwestern Eskimos. The geographical areas, names, and population estimates provided by Oswalt (1967, 4-9, Map 2) for most southwestern tribes are accepted in lieu of more up-to-date findings. The Yukon Eskimo designation as Ikogmiut by William H. Dall (1877, 17) has been changed to Kwikpagmiut because the latter term has precedence in the 1842-4 report by Zagoskin (1967, 209) and because it is the name by which the people call themselves; Ikogmiut refers more correctly to a single village. Part of the interior region occupied by the Kuskowagamiut includes Ingalik settlements; at least one village was occupied jointly by these Indians and Eskimos (Zagoskin, 1967, 306-7). The Kiatagmiut boundaries were modified somewhat on the basis of statements by V. S. Khromchenko, who explored in the early 1820s and whose writings have been interpreted by VanStone (1973, 31; personal communication). This in turn required modification of the Aglegmiut boundaries. The western Peninsular Eskimo boundary is changed to conform with conclusions reached by Don E. Dumond (1973, 3). Dumond (1973, 3, 5) also would exclude the mainland adjacent to Kodiak Island from the Koniag domain and consider the Koniag population as between 3000 and 4000. Some early reports include the mainland sector adjacent to Kodiak Island as Koniag and others do not; my inclination is to include it until further reasons emerge to the contrary. I prefer to accept the Koniag population figure as 6500 based on the 1792 report of 6510 persons living there and on the adjacent mainland (Petroff, 1884, 33), and the 1803 estimate of "not much less than seven thousand" for Kodiak by Davydov (1977, 147). The Chugach population might be estimated more correctly at 600 rather than the 1600 proposed earlier (Oswalt, 1967, 5). It has been established by Osahito Miyaoka (1974) that the easternmost group of Chugach, the Cilqarmiut of Controller Bay and Kayak Island, did not speak a Pacific Eskimo dialect. Instead their language seems more closely related to those languages of the Aglegmiut and Nunivagamiut.

The distribution of Siberian Eskimos during the 1600s is based on the map reproduced by M. G. Levin (1963, 209). Bogoras (1904-9, 31) is the source for the Asiatic Eskimo population figure of 1200 for the year 1900; an aboriginal estimate of 1800 seems reasonable when St. Lawrence Island Eskimos, who had their closest affinities with Siberia, are included.

II

The Eskimo Culture Area

Thousands of aboriginal tribes once lived around the world, and the culture-area concept was developed by anthropologists to consolidate them into a comparatively small number of culturally meaningful groups. A culture area embraces a geographical region whose occupants shared a similar way of life in contrast to peoples in surrounding areas. Eskimos always have been considered as representing one or more such areas; if any other people are grouped with them, it is the Aleuts. If Eskimos are judged to occupy a single culture area, the variability among them can best be appreciated by listing *all* the notable characteristics that they probably shared in the era of discovery.

All Eskimos spoke languages of the Eskimo linguistic stock. They all lived by killing wild animals for food, and in times of stress edibles were widely shared. A man, his wife or wives, and their children formed the basic social unit, and small children were treated with great kindness. Marriages were brittle, especially before an offspring was born, divorce was informal, and the tranquility of life was disrupted by family feuds. When a boy made his first significant contribution to the economic welfare of his family, such as killing his first seal, he was accorded ritual recognition by friends and relatives. Whenever secular leadership emerged, it was most likely concentrated in a highly successful hunter. Shamans communicated with supernaturals through personally controlled spirits. The concept of Sila as a supernatural force in the air probably existed everywhere, as did the idea of an inua, the soul or spirit of things animate and inanimate. While Eskimo culture often is identified on the basis of material culture, comparatively few distinctive manufactures were used everywhere. Included among them are the semilunar knife, skin scrapers, hunting knives, needles, bags made from the split feet of birds, and wooden trays.

A list of major traits shared by *most* Eskimos is longer and far more specific. Material items include lamps and cooking pots made from stone or clay, ivory needlecases, kayaks and umiaks, sleds and dog traction, harpoon darts, and toggle-headed harpoons used with floats and hurled with the aid of throwing-boards. Tailored skin garments include winter parkas, trousers, mittens, boots, and waterproof parkas made from intestines. Eskimos lived in skin tents during the summer and in semisubterranean winter houses built of stone and turf with long attached tunnels. In their kinship designations "Iroquois," not "Eskimo," cousin terms predominated. This means that cross-cousins were distinguished from parallel cousins, and certain parallel cousins were equated with siblings. Social life was organized around nuclear and extended families with descent traced on both sides of the family (bilateral descent and kindred). With respect to the individual life cycle, a pregnant woman was subject to behavioral restrictions, and the names for babies were not sex-linked. Males were integrated into the subsistence round as youths; girls married young. Age and sex formed the basis for a division of labor, and the rights of women were essentially equal to those of men. A rigid dichotomy separated the use of resources from the land and sea, and it was supported by taboos. Marriage and divorce were without ceremony, and at the time of death there was comparatively little ritual. Hereditary leaders did not exist; instead the greatest authority was vested in men who were able hunters and also had reputations as extraordinary shamans.

References

Ackerman, Robert E. "Archaeoethnology, Ethnoarchaeology, and the Problems of Past Cultural Patterning." In: *Ethnohistory in Southwestern Alaska and the Southern Yukon*, Margaret Lantis, ed., pp. 11-47. Lexington: University Press of Kentucky. 1970.

Amdrup, G. *See:* Thalbitzer, 1914.

Amundsen, Roald. *The North West Passage*. 2 v. New York: E. P. Dutton. 1908.

Anderson, H. Dewey, and Walter C. Eells. *Alaska Natives*. Stanford: Stanford University Press. 1935.

Arnold, Robert D., et al. *Alaska Native Land Claims*. Anchorage: Alaska Native Foundation. 1976.

Asher, G. M. *Henry Hudson the Navigator*. London: Hakluyt Society. 1860.

Balikci, Asen. *The Netsilik Eskimo*. Garden City, New York: Natural History Press. 1970.

Barr, William. "The Eighteenth Century Trade between the Ships of the Hudson's Bay Company and the Hudson Strait Inuit." *Arctic*, v. 47, 236-46. 1994.

Barrow, John. *Voyages of Discovery and Research within the Arctic Regions*. New York: Harper & Brothers, n.d.

———. *An Auto-biographical Memoir of Sir John Barrow*. London: J. Murray. 1847.

Beaglehole, J. C. *The Life of Captain James Cook*. Stanford: Stanford University Press. 1974.

Beechey, Frederick W. *Narrative of a Voyage to the Pacific*. 2 v. London: Henry Colburn and Richard Bentley. 1831.

Bessels, Emil. "The Northernmost Inhabitants of the Earth." *The American Naturalist*, v. 18, 861-82. 1884.

Biggar, H. P. "The Voyages of Jacques Cartier." *Publications of the Public Archives of Canada*, no. 11. 1924.

Bird, Junius B. "Archaeology of the Hopedale Area, Labrador." *Anthropological Papers of the American Museum of Natural History*, v. 39, pt. 2. 1945.

Birket-Smith, Kaj. "Ethnography of the Egedesminde District." *Meddelelser om Grønland*, v. 66. 1924.

———. "The Greenlanders of the Present Day." In: *Greenland*, M. Vahl, ed., v. 2, 1-207. Copenhagen: C. A. Reitzel. 1928.

———. "The Caribou Eskimos." *Report of the Fifth Thule Expedition*, v. 5, pts. 1, 2. 1929.

———. "Early Collections from the Pacific Eskimo." *Nationalmuseets Skrifter, Etnografisk Raekke*, v. 1, 122-63, 1941.

———. "The Chugach Eskimo." *Nationalmuseets Skrifter, Etnografisk Raekke*, v. 6. 1953.

———. "The Earliest Eskimo Portraits." *Folk*, v. 1, 5-14. 1959a.

———. *The Eskimos*. London: Methuen. 1959b (also 1936 and 1971 editions).

———, and Frederica de Laguna. *The Eyak Indians of the Copper River Delta, Alaska*. Copenhagen: Levin & Munksgaard. 1938.

Boas, Franz. "The Central Eskimo." *Sixth Annual Report of the Bureau of Ethnology*, 399-669. 1888a (1964 reprint).

———. "The Eskimo." *Proceedings and Transactions of the Royal Society of Canada*, v. 5, 35-9. 1888b.

———. "The Eskimo of Baffin Island and Hudson Bay." *Bulletin of the American Museum of Natural History*, v. 15. 1901-7.

Bobé, Louis. "Early Exploration of Greenland." In: *Greenland*, M. Vahl, ed., v. 1, 1-35. Copenhagen: C. A. Reitzel. 1928.

———. *Hans Egede*. Copenhagen: Rosenkilde and Bagger. 1952.

Bogoras, Waldemar G. "The Chukchee." *Jesup North Pacific Expedition*, v. 7. New York: American Museum of Natural History. 1904-9.

Briggs, Jean L. *Never in Anger*. Cambridge, Mass.: Harvard University Press. 1970.

Brody, Hugh. *The People's Land*. London: Penguin. 1975.

Bruemmer, Fred. "Narwhal the Sea Unicorn." *The Beaver*, Spring, 30-7. 1966.

Burch, Ernest S., Jr. *Eskimo Kinsmen*. St. Paul: West. 1975.

———. *The Eskimos*. Norman: University of Oklahoma Press. 1988.

———. *The Iñupiaq Eskimo nations of northwest Alaska*. Fairbanks: University of Alaska Press. 1998.

Burgesse, J. Allan. "Esquimaux in the Saguenay." *Primitive Man*, v. 22, nos. 1-2, 23-32. 1949.

Campbell, John M. "Territoriality Among Ancient Hunters." In: *Anthropological Archeology in the Americas*, Betty J. Meggers, ed., pp. 1-21. Washington, D.C.: The Anthropological Society of Washington. 1968.

Cantwell, John C. *See:* Healy, Michael A.

Caswell, John E. *Arctic Frontiers*. Norman: University of Oklahoma Press. 1956.

Chance, Norman A. *The Eskimo of North Alaska*. New York: Holt, Rinehart and Winston. 1966.

Chard, Chester S. "The Western Roots of Eskimo Culture." *Proceedings of the Thirty-third International Congress of Americanists*, v. 2, 81-7. 1959.

Chiappelli, Fredi, ed. *First Images of America*. 2 v. Berkeley: University of California Press. 1976.

Choris, Louis. *Voyage Pittoresque autour du Monde*. Paris: Firmin Didot. 1822.

Christy, Miller. *The Voyages of Captain Luke Foxe and Captain Thomas James*. 2 v. London: Hakluyt Society. 1894.

Clavering, Douglas C. "Journal of a Voyage to Spitzbergen and the East Coast of Greenland in His Majesty's Ship Griper." *The Edinburgh New Philosophical Journal*, April-June, 1-30. 1830.

Coffing, Michael W. "Kwethluk Subsistence." *Alaska Department of Fish & Game, Division of Subsistence, Technical Paper* 157. 1991.

Collier, John. *Alaskan Eskimo Education*. New York: Holt, Rinehart and Winston. 1973.

Condon, Richard G. *Inuit Behavior and Seasonal Change in the Canadian Arctic*. Ann Arbor: UMI Research Press. 1983.

———. *Inuit Youth*. New Brunswick: Rutgers University Press. 1987.

———, Peter Collings, and George Wenzel. "The Best Part of Life." *Arctic*, v. 48, no. 1, 31-46. 1995.

Cook, James, and James King. *A Voyage to the Pacific Ocean*. 3 v. and atlas. London: G. Nicol and T. Cadell. 1784.

Corner, George W. *Doctor Kane of the Arctic Seas*. Philadelphia: Temple University Press. 1972.

Coxe, William. *Account of the Russian Discoveries Between Asia and America*. London: T. Cadell. 1780 (fourth edition, 1804).

Crantz, David. *The History of Greenland*. 2 v. London: Brethren's Society. 1767.

Curtis, Edward S. *The North American Indian*. 20 v. Cambridge, Mass.: Harvard University Press. 1930 (1970 reprint).

Cyriax, Richard J. *Sir John Franklin's Last Arctic Expedition*. London: Methuen. 1939.

Dall, William H. "On the Distribution and Nomenclature of the Native Tribes of Alaska and the Adjacent Territory." *Contributions to North American Ethnology*, v. 1, pt. 1, article 1. 1877.

Damas, David, ed. *Arctic*, v. 5. *Handbook of North American Indians*. Washington, D.C.: Smithsonian Institution. 1984.

———. "Shifting relations in the administration of Inuit." In: *Études/Inuit/Studies*, v. 17, no. 2, 5-28. 1993.

Darnell, Frank and Anton Hoëm. *Taken to Extremes*. Oslo: Scandinavian University Press. 1996.

Davis, C. H. *Narrative of the North Polar Expedition*. Washington, D.C.: Government Printing Office. 1876.

Davydov, Gavriil I. *Two Voyages to Russian America, 1802-1807*, Richard A. Pierce, ed. Kingston, Ontario: Limestone. 1977.

Dawkins, W. Boyd. "Esquimaux in the South of Gaul." *The Saturday Review*, v. 22, no. 580, 712-13. 1866.

———. *Cave Hunting*. London: Macmillan. 1874.

———. *Early Man in Britain*. London: Macmillan. 1880.

Dick, Lyle. "'Piblotoq' (Arctic Hysteria)," *Arctic Anthropology*, v. 32, no. 2, 1-42. 1995.

Diebitsch-Peary, Josephine. *My Arctic Journal*. London: Longmans, Green. 1894.

Dorais, Louis-Jacques. *Quaqtaq*. Toronto: University of Toronto Press. 1997.

Drage, Theodorus Swaine. *See:* Swaine, Charles.

Driver, Harold E. *Indians of North America*. Chicago: University of Chicago Press. 1961.

———, and William C. Massey. "Comparative Studies of North American Indians." *Transactions of the American Philosophical Society*, n.s., v. 47, pt. 2. 1957.

Duflot de Mofras, Eugène. *Exploration du Territoire de l'Oregon, des Californies, et de la Mer Vermeille*. 2 v. Paris: Librairie de la Société de Géographie. 1844.

Dumond, Don E. *The Eskimos and Aleuts*. New York: Thames and Hudson. 1977 (revised 1987).

———, and Richard L. Bland. "Holocene Prehistory of the Northernmost North Pacific," *Journal of World Prehistory*, v. 9, 401-51. 1995.

———, and James W. VanStone. "Paugvik: A nineteenth-century Native village on Bristol Bay, Alaska," *Fieldiana Anthropology*, n.s., no. 24. 1995.

Edmonds, H. M. W. "H. M. W. Edmonds' Report on the Eskimos of St. Michael and Vicinity," Dorothy J. Ray, ed. *Anthropological Papers of the University of Alaska*, v. 13, no. 2. 1966.

Egede, Hans P. *A Description of Greenland*. London: C. Hitch, S. Austen, J. Jackson. 1745 (also 1818 edition).

Ehrström, M. Ch. "Medical Investigations in North Greenland 1948-1949." *Acta Medica Scandinavica*, v. 140, 254-64. 1951.

Elder, William. *Biography of Elisha Kent Kane*. Philadelphia: Childs and Peterson. 1858.

Ellis, Henry. *A Voyage to Hudson's-Bay, by the Dobbs Galley and California*. London: H. Whitridge. 1748 (1967 reprint).

Eriksson, Aldur W., et al., eds. "Health and Biology of Circumpolar Human Populations." *Arctic Anthropology*, v. 7, no. 1. 1970.

Federal Field Committee for Development Planning in Alaska. *Alaska Natives & The Land*. Washington, D.C.: Government Printing Office. 1968.

Fedorova, Svetlana G. *The Russian Population in Alaska and California*, ed. and trans. by Richard A. Pierce and Alton S. Donnelly. Kingston, Ontario: Limestone. 1973.

Fienup-Riordan, Ann. *The Nelson Island Eskimo*. Anchorage: Alaska Pacific University Press. 1983.

———. *Eskimo Essays*. New Brunswick: Rutgers University Press. 1990.

———. *The Real People and the Children of Thunder*. Norman: University of Oklahoma Press. 1991.

———. *Boundaries and Passages*. Norman: University of Oklahoma Press. 1994.

———. *The Living Tradition of Yup'ik Masks*. Seattle: University of Washington Press. 1996a.

———. *Our Way of Making Prayer*. Seattle: Anchorage Museum of History and Art. 1996b.

Fisher, Alexander. *A Journal of a Voyage of Discovery*. London: Longman, Hurst, Rees, Orme, and Brown. 1821.

Fisher, Kyra Vladykov. "The Baker Lake Printmaking Revival," *Arctic*, v. 50, no. 2, 1926. 1997.

Fitzhugh, William W. "Environmental Archeology and Cultural Systems in Hamilton Inlet, Labrador." *Smithsonian Contributions to Anthropology*, no. 16. 1972.

———, and Aron Crowell. *Crossroads of Continents*. Washington, D.C.: Smithsonian Institution. 1988.

Forsyth, James. *A History of the Peoples of Siberia*. Cambridge: Cambridge University Press. 1992.

Foulks, Edward F. "The Arctic Hysterias of the North Alaskan Eskimo." American Anthropological Association, *Anthropological Studies*, no. 10, 1972.

Foxe, Luke. *See:* Christy, Miller.

Franklin, John. *Narrative of a Journey to the Shores of the Polar Sea*. London: John Murray. 1823.

———. *Narrative of a Second Expedition to the Shores of the Polar Sea*. London: John Murray. 1828 (1969 reprint).

Freeman, Milton M. R. "Polar Bear Predation on Beluga in the Canadian Arctic." *Arctic*, v. 26, 162-3. 1973.

Freuchen, Peter. *Arctic Adventure*. New York: Farrar & Rinehart. 1935.

Gad, Finn. *The History of Greenland*. Montreal: McGill-Queen's University Press. v. 1, 1971; v. 2, 1973; v. 3, 1982.

Garn, Stanley M. "A Comment on Wilber's 'Origin of Human Types.'" *Human Biology*, v. 30, 337-9. 1958.

Gathorne-Hardy, G. M. *The Norse Discoverers of America*. Oxford: Clarendon Press. 1921.

Giddings, James L. "The Arctic Woodland Culture of the Kobuk River." *Museum Monographs*, The University Museum, University of Pennsylvania. 1952.

———. "Kobuk River People." *Studies of Northern Peoples*, no. 1. 1961.

Gjessing, Gutorm. "Circumpolar Stone Age." *Acta Arctica*, v. 2, 1944.

Goetz, H. *The Inuit Print*. Ottawa: National Museum of Man, National Museum of Canada. 1977.

Gosch, C. C. A. *Danish Arctic Expeditions, 1605 to 1620*. 2 v. London: Hakluyt Society. 1897.

Gosling, W. G. *Labrador*. Toronto: Musson. n.d.

Graah, Wilhelm A. *Narrative of an Expedition to the East Coast of Greenland*. London: John W. Parker, 1837 (1832 and 1932 editions).

Graburn, Nelson H. H. *Eskimos Without Igloos*. Boston: Little, Brown. 1969.

Gubser, Nicholas J. *The Nunamiut Eskimos*. New Haven: Yale University Press. 1965.

Gussow, Zachary. "*Pibloktoq* (Hysteria) Among the Polar Eskimos." In: *The Psychoanalytic Study of Society*, W. Muensterberger and Sidney Axelrad, eds., v. 1, pp. 218-36. New York: International Universities Press. 1960.

———. "A Preliminary Report of Kayak-Angst Among the Eskimo of West Greenland." *The International Journal of Social Psychiatry*, v. 9, 18-26. 1963.

Hakluyt, Richard. "Discourse on Western Planting." Charles Deane, ed., *Documentary History of the State of Maine*, v. 2, 1877.

Hall, Charles F. *Arctic Researches and Life Among the Esquimaux*. New York: Harper & Brothers. 1865.

Hall Edwin S. "The 'Iron Dog' in Northern Alaska." *Anthropologica*, n.s., v. 13, nos. 1-2, 237-54. 1971.

Hamilton, John T. *A History of the Church Known as the Moravian Church*. Bethlehem, Pa.: Times. 1900.

Hamilton, Lawrence C., and Carole L. Seyfrit. "Town-Village Contrasts in Alaskan Youth Aspirations." *Arctic*, v. 46, no. 3, 255-63. 1993.

———. "Coming Out of the Country." *Arctic Anthropology*, v. 31, no. 1, 16-25. 1994.

Hanbury, David T. *Sport and Travel in the Northland of Canada*. London: Edward Arnold. 1904.

Harington, C. R. "The Bear behind the Paw." *The Beaver*, Autumn, 14-5. 1966.

Harp, Elmer. "An Archaeological Survey in the Strait of Belle Isle Area." *American Antiquity*, v. 16, 203-20. 1951.

———. "The Cultural Affinities of the Newfoundland Dorset Eskimo." *National Museum of Canada, Bull.* 200. 1964.

———. "Dorset Settlement Patterns in Newfoundland and Southeastern Hudson Bay." In: *Eastern Arctic Prehistory*, Moreau S. Maxwell, ed., pp. 119-38. *Memoirs of the Society for American Archaeology*, no. 31. 1976.

Harris, Donald A. "Canada, Newfoundland." *The Society for Historical Archaeology Newsletter*, v. 7, no. 4, 32-3. 1974.

Hartmann, J. A. H. "Exploration in Western Alaska by the Moravians, Rev. J. A. H. Hartmann and W. H. Weinland, 1884." In: *Report on Education in Alaska*, Sheldon Jackson, ed., Appendix I, 55-75. Washington, D.C.: Government Printing Office. 1886.

Hawkes, E. W. "The Labrador Eskimo." *Canada Department of Mines Geological Survey, Memoir 91.* 1916.

Hayes, Isaac Israel. *The Open Polar Sea.* New York: Hurd and Houghton. 1867.

Healy, Michael A. *Report of the Cruise of the Revenue Marine Steamer Corwin in the Arctic Ocean in the Year 1885.* Washington, D. C.: Government Printing Office. 1887.

———. *Report of the Cruise of the Revenue Marine Steamer Corwin in the Arctic Ocean in the Year 1884.* Washington, D.C.: Government Printing Office. 1889.

Hearne, Samuel. *A Journey from Prince of Wales's Fort in Hudson's Bay to the Northern Ocean*, Richard Glover, ed. Toronto: Macmillan. 1958.

Heizer, Robert F. "Aconite Poison Whaling in Asia and America." *Bureau of American Ethnology, Bull.* 133, 415-68. 1943.

Hendrik, Hans C. *Memoirs of Hans Hendrik.* London: Trübner. 1878.

Heyland, J. D., and Keith Hay. "An Attack by a Polar Bear on a Juvenile Beluga." *Arctic*, v. 29, 56-7. 1976.

Himmelheber, Hans. *Eskimo Artists.* German editions, Eisenach/Kassel: Roth-Verlag, 1938; Eisenach: Roth-Verlag, 1953. English translations, Zürich: Museum Rietberg Zürich, 1987; Fairbanks: University of Alaska Press, 1993.

Hippler, Arthur E. *Barrow and Kotzebue.* Training Center for Community Programs. Minneapolis: University of Minnesota. 1969.

———. *From Village to Town.* Training Center for Community Programs. Minneapolis: University of Minnesota. 1970.

Hodge, Frederick W., ed. "Eskimo." Handbook of American Indians, pt. 1, 433-7, *Bureau of American Ethnology, Bull.* 30. 1907.

Hodgen, Margaret T. *Early Anthropology in the Sixteenth and Seventeenth Centuries.* Philadelphia: University of Pennsylvania Press. 1964.

Hoffman, Walter J. "The Graphic Art of the Eskimos." *Annual Report of the . . . Smithsonian Institution . . . for the Year Ending June 30, 1895*, 749-968. 1897.

Holm, Gustav. *See:* Thalbitzer, 1914.

Holtved, Erik. "Tôrnârssuk, an Eskimo Deity." *Folk*, v. 5, 157-72. 1963.

———. "Contributions to Polar Eskimo Ethnography." *Meddelelser om Grønland*, v. 182, no. 2. 1967.

Honigmann, John J. "Social Networks in Great Whale River." *National Museum of Canada Bull.* 178. 1962.

———. "Five Northern Towns." *Anthropological Papers of the University of Alaska*, v. 17, no. 1. 1975.

———, and Irma Honigmann. *Eskimo Townsmen.* Ottawa: Canadian Research Centre for Anthropology. 1965.

Houston, Alma, et al. *Inuit Art.* Winnipeg: Watson & Dwyer. 1988.

Houston, C. Stuart. *To the Arctic by Canoe 1819-1821.* Montreal: McGill-Queen's University Press. 1974.

Hrdlička, Aleš. *The Anthropology of Kodiak Island*. Philadelphia: Wistar Institute of Anatomy and Biology. 1944.

Hughes, Charles C. "Translation of I. K. Voblov's 'Eskimo Ceremonies'." *Anthropological Papers of the University of Alaska*, v. 7, 71-90. 1959.

———. *An Eskimo Village in the Modern World*. Ithaca: Cornell University Press. 1960.

Hulton, Paul H. "John White's Drawings of Eskimos." *The Beaver*, Summer, 16-20. 1961.

———, and David B. Quinn. *The American Drawings of John White, 1577-1590*. London: British Museum. 1964.

Ingstad, Helge. *Land under the Polar Star*. New York: St. Martin's Press. 1966.

———. *Westward to Vinland*. New York: St. Martin's Press. 1969.

Irimoto, Takashi, and Takako Yamada. *Circumpolar Religion and Ecology*. Tokyo, Japan: University of Tokyo Press. 1994.

Irving, William N. "An Archaeological Survey of the Susitna Valley." *Anthropological Papers of the University of Alaska*, v. 6, 37-52. 1957.

———. "A Provisional Comparison of some Alaskan and Asian Stone Industries." In: Prehistoric Cultural Relations Between the Arctic and Temperate Zones of North America, John M. Campbell, ed. *Arctic Institute of North America Technical Paper*, no. 11, pp. 55-68. 1962.

Issenman, Betty Kobayashi. *Sinews of Survival*. Vancouver: University of British Columbia Press. 1997.

Jansen, Henrik M. "A Critical Account of the Written and Archaeological Sources' Evidence Concerning the Norse Settlements in Greenland." *Meddelelser om Grønland*, v. 182, no. 4. 1972.

Jennes, Diamond. "The Life of the Copper Eskimos." *Report of the Canadian Arctic Expedition*, v. 12. 1922.

———. "Material Culture of the Copper Eskimo." *Report of the Canadian Arctic Expedition*, v. 16. 1946.

———. "Eskimo Administration: I. Alaska." *Arctic Institute of North America, Technical Paper*, no. 10. 1962.

———. "Eskimo Administration: II. Canada." *Arctic Institute of North America, Technical Paper*, no. 14. 1964.

———. "Eskimo Administration: III. Labrador." *Arctic Institute of North America, Technical Paper*, no. 16. 1965.

———. "Eskimo Administration: IV. Greenland." *Arctic Institute of North America, Technical Paper*, no. 19. 1967.

———. "Eskimo Administration: V. Analysis and Reflections." *Arctic Institute of North America, Technical Paper*, no. 21. 1968.

Jones, Gwyn. *The Norse Atlantic Saga*. London: Oxford University Press. 1964.

Jonsson, Finnur. "On the Icelandic Colonization of Greenland." In: *Greenland*, M. Vahl, ed., v. 2, 231-61. Copenhagen: C. A. Reitzel. 1928.

Jorgensen, Joseph G. *Oil Age Eskimos*. Berkeley: University of California Press. 1990.

Kaalund, Bodil. *The Art of Greenland*. Berkeley: University of California Press. 1983.

Kane, Elisha K. *The U.S. Grinnell Expedition in Search of Sir John Franklin*. New York: Harper & Brothers. 1854.

———. *Arctic Explorations*. 2 v. Philadelphia: Childs and Peterson. 1856.

Kawagley, A. Oscar. *A Yupiaq Worldview*. Prospect Heights: Waveland Press. 1995.

Kennedy, John C. *People of the Bays and Headlands*. Toronto: University of Toronto Press. 1995.

Kleinfeld, Judith Smilg. *Eskimo School on the Andreafsky*. New York: Praeger Publishers. 1979.

Kleivan, Helge. "The Eskimos of Northeast Labrador." *Norsk Polarinstitutt Skrifter*, no. 139. 1966.

Kleivan, I., and B. Sonne. *Eskimos Greenland and Canada*. Leiden: E. J. Brill. 1985.

Krauss, Michael. "The Indigenous Languages of the North," In: *Northern Minority Languages*. Hiroshi Shoji and Juna Junhunen, eds., pp. 1-34. Senri Ethnological Studies 44. Osaka, Japan: National Museum of Ethnology. 1997.

Kroeber, Alfred L. "The Eskimo of Smith Sound." *Bulletin of the American Museum of Nautral History*, v. 12, 265-327. 1900.

———. *Cultural and Natural Areas of Native North America*. Berkeley: University of California Press. 1963 (1939 reprint).

Labaree, Leonard W., ed., *The Papers of Benjamin Franklin*, 4 v. New Haven: Yale University Press. 1961.

Laguna, Frederica de. "A Comparison of Eskimo and Paleolithic Art." *American Journal of Archaeology*, v. 36, no. 4, 477-511, 1932; v. 37, no. 1, 77-107. 1933.

Lamb, G. F. *Franklin*. London: Ernest Benn. 1956.

Lantis, Margaret. "The Alaskan Whale Cult and Its Affinities." *American Anthropologist*, n.s., v. 40, 438-64. 1938.

———. "The Social Culture of the Nunivak Eskimo." *Transactions of the American Philosophical Society*, n.s., v. 35, pt. 3. 1946.

———. *Alaskan Eskimo Ceremonialism*. New York: J. J. Augustin. 1947.

———. "Edward William Nelson." *Anthropological Papers of the University of Alaska*, v. 3, no. 1, 5-16. 1954.

Larsen, Helge, and Froelich G. Rainey. "Ipiutak and the Arctic Whale Hunting Culture." *Anthropological Papers of the American Museum of Natural History*, v. 42. 1948.

LeBlanc, Jacques. *Man in the Cold*. Springfield: Charles C. Thomas. 1975.

Lee, Sidney. "The American Indian in Elizabethan England." In: *Elizabethan and Other Essays*. Frederick S. Boas, ed., pp. 263-301. Oxford: Clarendon Press. 1929.

Levin, M. G. "Ethnic Origins of the Peoples of Northeastern Asia." Henry

N. Michael, ed. *Arctic Institute of North America, Anthropology of the North: Translations from Russian Sources*, no. 3. 1963.

———, and L. P. Potapov, eds. *The Peoples of Siberia*. Chicago: University of Chicago Press. 1964.

Lisiansky, Urey. *A Voyage Round the World*. London: John Booth. 1814.

Lloyd, Christopher. *Mr. Barrow of the Admiralty*. London: Collins. 1970.

Loomis, Chauncey C. *Weird and Tragic Shores*. New York: Alfred A. Knopf. 1971.

Losey, Timothy C., ed. "Fort Enterprise." *The Boreal Institute for Northern Studies, Occasional Publication*, no. 9. 1973.

Lubbock, John. *Pre-historic Times*. London: Williams and Norgate. 1865. (7th and final edition in 1913).

Lynam, Edward. *The Carta marina of Olaus Magnus, Venice 1539 & Rome 1572*. Jenkintown, Pa.: Tall Tree Library. 1949.

Lyon, George F. *The Private Journal of Captain G. F. Lyon*. London: John Murray. 1824.

———. *A Brief Narrative of an Unsuccessful Attempt to Reach Repulse Bay*. London: John Murray. 1825.

McCartney, A. P., and D. J. Mack. "Iron Utilization by Thule Eskimos of Central Canada." *American Antiquity*, v. 38, 328-39. 1973.

McFee, William. *The Life of Sir Martin Frobisher*. New York: Harper & Brothers. 1928.

McGhee, Robert. "Copper Eskimo Prehistory." *National Museum of Man, Publications in Archaeology*, no. 2. 1972.

———. "Beluga Hunters." *Newfoundland Social and Economic Studies*, no. 13. 1974.

———. "Contact between Native North Americans and the Medieval Norse." *American Antiquity*, v. 49, no. 1, 4-26. 1984.

———. *Ancient People of the Arctic*. Vancouver: University of British Columbia Press. 1996.

Mackenzie, Alexander. *Voyages from Montreal*. New York: Evert Duyckinck. 1803.

Manning, T. H. "Notes on the Coastal District of the Eastern Barren Grounds and Melville Peninsula from Igloolik to Cape Fullerton." *Canadian Geographical Journal*, v. 26, 84-105. 1943.

Marcus, Alan Rudolph. *Relocating Eden*. Hanover, NH: University Press of New England. 1995.

Markham, Albert H. *The Voyages and Works of John Davis*. London: Hakluyt Society. 1880.

Markham, Clements R. "On the Origin and Migrations of the Greenland Esquimaux." *The Journal of the Royal Geographical Society*, v. 35, 87-99. 1865.

———. "The Arctic Highlanders." *Transactions of the Ethnological Society of London*, n.s., v. 4, 125-37. 1866.

———. *The Voyages of William Baffin*. London: Hakluyt Society. 1881.

———. *A Life of John Davis.* New York: Dodd, Mead. n.d.

Marquardt, Ole, and Richard A. Caulfield. "Development of West Greenlandic Markets for Country Foods Since the 18th Century." *Arctic,* v. 49, no. 2, 107-19. 1996.

Martin, M. Marlene, and Timothy J. O'Leary. *Ethnographic Bibliography of North America,* 4th edition supplement. New Haven: Human Relations Area Files Press. 1990.

Mason, Otis T. "Aboriginal American Harpoons." *Annual Report of the Smithsonian Institution for the Year Ending June 30, 1900,* 189-304. 1902.

Mathiassen, Therkel. "Archaeology of the Central Eskimos." *Report of the Fifth Thule Expedition,* v. 4, pts. 1, 2. 1927.

———. "Material Culture of the Iglulik Eskimos." *Report of the Fifth Thule Expedition,* v. 6, no. 1. 1928.

———. "Inugsuk, A Mediaeval Eskimo Settlement in Upernivik District, West Greenland." *Meddelelser om Grønland,* v. 77, 145-340. 1931.

Meldgaard Jørgen. *Eskimo Sculpture.* New York: Clarkson N. Potter. 1960.

Merkur, Daniel. *Powers which We Do Not Know: The Gods and Spirits of the Inuit.* Moscow: University of Idaho Press. 1991.

Milan, Frederick A. "The Acculturation of the Contemporary Eskimo of Wainwright, Alaska." *Anthropological Papers of the University of Alaska,* v. 11, no. 2, 1-95. 1964.

———, and Stella Pawson. "The Demography of the Native Population of an Alaskan City." *Arctic,* v. 28, 275-83. 1975.

Milton Freeman Research Limited. *Inuit Land Use and Occupancy Project.* 3 v. Ottawa: Department of Indian and Northern Affairs. 1976.

Mirsky, Jeannette. *Elisha Kent Kane and the Seafaring Frontier.* Boston: Little Brown. 1954.

———. *To the Arctic!* Chicago: University of Chicago Press. 1970 (original edition titled *To the North,* 1934).

Miyaoka, Osahito. "An Eskimo Tribe near 'Mount Saint Elias (Alaska)'." *Arctic Anthropology,* v. 11, no. 1, 73-80. 1974.

Moberg, Carl-Axel. "On Some Circumpolar and Arctic Problems in Northern European Archeology." In: The Circumpolar Conference in Copenhagen, 1958, Helge Larsen, ed. *Acta Arctica,* v. 12, 67-74. 1960.

Mooney, James. "The Aboriginal Population of America North of Mexico." *Smithsonian Miscellaneous Collections,* v. 80, no. 7. 1928.

Moore, Riley D. "Social Life of the Eskimo of St. Lawrence Island." *American Anthropologist,* n.s., v. 25, 330-75. 1923.

Morant, G. M. "Studies of Palaeolithic Man, Part IV." *Annals of Eugenics,* v. 4, 109-214. 1930.

Morison, Samuel E. *The European Discovery of America, The Northern Voyages A.D. 500-1600.* New York: Oxford University Press. 1971.

Murdoch, John. Review of *The Eskimo Tribes* by Henry Rink. *American Anthropologist,* v. 1, 125-33. 1888.

————. "Ethnological Results of the Point Barrow Expedition." *Ninth Annual Report of the Bureau of Ethnology*, 3-441. 1892.

Murdock, George P., and Timothy J. O'Leary. *Ethnographic Bibliography of North America*, 5 v. New Haven: Human Relations Area Files. 1975.

Nansen, Fridtjof. *In Northern Mists*. 2 v. New York: Frederick A. Stokes. 1911.

Neatby, Leslie H. *The Search for Franklin*. Edmonton: M. G. Hurtig. 1970.

Nellemann, George. "Caribou Hunting in West Greenland." *Folk*, v. 11-2, 133-53. 1969-70.

Nelson, Edward W. "The Eskimo About Bering Strait." *Eighteenth Annual Report of the Bureau of American Ethnology*, pt. 1. 1899.

Nelson, Richard K. *Hunters of the Northern Ice*. Chicago: University of Chicago Press. 1969.

————. "Relationships Between Eskimo and Athapaskan Cultures in Alaska." *Arctic Anthropology*, v. 11, supplement, 48-53. 1974.

Noble, Dennis L. "Hell Roaring Mike." *The Chief*, March, 11-3. 1976.

Nuligak. *I, Nuligak*. Edited and translated from Eskimo to French by Maurice Metayer, translated into English by Olive Koyama. New York: Pocket Books. 1971 (also 1966 edition).

Nuttall, Mark. *Arctic Homeland*. Toronto: University of Toronto Press. 1992.

Olearius, Adam. *Enlarged Muscovite and Persian Travel Description* (translated title). Schleswig: Johan Holwein. 1656 (1971 reprint).

Oleson, Tryggvi J. *Early Voyages and Northern Approaches, 1000-1632*. Toronto: McClelland and Stewart. 1963.

Osgood, Cornelius. "Ingalik Social Culture." *Yale University Publications in Anthropology*, no. 53. 1958.

Ostermann, H. "The History of the Mission." In: *Greenland*, M. Vahl, ed. v. 3, 269-349. Copenhagen: C. A. Reitzel. 1929.

Oswalt, Wendell H. *Mission of Change in Alaska*. San Marino, Cal.: Huntington Library. 1963a.

————. *Napaskiak*. Tucson: University of Arizona Press. 1963b.

————. "Traditional Storyknife Tales of Yuk Girls." *Proceedings of the American Philosophical Society*, v. 108, 310-36. 1964.

————. *Alaskan Eskimos*. San Francisco: Chandler. 1967.

————. "The Eskimos (Yuk) of Western Alaska." In: *Modern Alaskan Native Material Culture*, Wendell H. Oswalt, ed., pp. 73-95. University of Alaska. 1972.

————. "Technological Complexity." *Arctic Anthropology*, v. 24, no. 2, 82-98. 1987.

————, and James W. VanStone. "The Ethnoarcheology of Crow Village, Alaska." *Smithsonian Institution, Bureau of American Ethnology, Bull.* 199. 1967.

Packard, A. S. "The Esquimaux of Labrador." In: *The Indian Miscellany*, W. W. Beach, ed., pp. 66-72. Albany: J. Munsell. 1877.

————. "Notes on the Labrador Eskimos and Their Former Range Southward." *The American Naturalist*, v. 19, 471-560. 1885.

Parran, Thomas. *Alaska's Health*. Pittsburgh: University of Pittsburgh, Graduate School of Public Health. 1954.

Parry, William E. *Journal of a Voyage for the Discovery of a North-West Passage*. London: John Murray. 1821.

————. *Journal of a Second Voyage for the Discovery of a North-West Passage*. London: John Murray. 1824.

————. *Journals of the First, Second and Third Voyages for the Discovery of a North-West Passage*. 5 v. London: John Murray. 1828.

Pearce, Roy H. *The Savages of America*. Baltimore: Johns Hopkins Press. 1953.

Peary, Robert E. *Nearest the Pole*. New York: Doubleday, Page. 1907.

————. *The North Pole*. New York: Frederick A. Stokes. 1910.

————. *Northward over the 'Great Ice.'* 2 v. New York: Frederick A. Stokes. 1914.

Perry, Richard. *The World of the Polar Bear*. Seattle: University of Washington Press. 1966.

Persson, Ib. "The Fate of the Icelandic Vikings in Greenland." *Man*, n.s., v. 4, 620-8. 1969.

Petersen, Robert. "The Last Eskimo Immigration into Greenland." *Folk*, v. 4, 95-110. 1962.

Petitot, Émile. *Monographie des Esquimaux Tchiglit*. Paris: Librairie de la Société Asiatique. 1876.

————. *Les Grands-Esquimaux*. Paris: E. Plon, Nourrit. 1887.

————. *The Amerindians of the Canadian Northwest in the 19th Century, as seen by Émile Petitot*. v. 1. "The Tchiglit Eskimos." v. 2. "The Loucheux Indians." Donat Savoie, ed. Department of Indian Affairs and Northern Development. 1970.

Petroff, Ivan. "Report on the Population, Industries, and Resources of Alaska." Washington, D.C.: *Department of the Interior, Census Office*. 1884.

Phebus, George, Jr. *Alaska Eskimo Life in the 1890s as Sketched by Native Artists*. Washington, D.C.: Smithsonian Institution Press. 1972.

Poincy, Louis de. *Histoire Naturelle et Morale des Iles Antilles*, revised by Charles de Rochefort. Lyon: Chez Christofle Fourmy. 1667.

Potter, Guy R. L. "Peary and the North Pole." *Polar Notes*, no. 10, 15-24. 1970.

Purchas, Samuel. *Hakluytus Posthumus: or, Purchas His Pilgrimes*. Glasgow: James MacLehose and Sons. 1906 (1965 reprint).

Rae, John. "On the Esquimaux." *Transactions of the Ethnological Society of London*. v. 4, n.s., 138-53. 1866.

Rainey, Froelich G. "The Whale Hunters of Tigara." *Anthropological Papers of the American Museum of Natural History*, v. 41, pt. 2. 1947.

Rasing, Willem C. E. *'Too Many People.'* Nijmegen: Katholieke Universiteit. 1994.

Rasmussen, Knud. *The People of the Polar North*. London: Kegan Paul, Trench, Trübner. 1908.

———. *Greenland by the Polar Sea*. New York: Frederick A. Stokes. n.d.

———. "Intellectual Culture of the Iglulik Eskimos." *Report of the Fifth Thule Expedition*. v. 7, no. 1. 1929.

———. "The Netsilik Eskimos." *Report of the Fifth Thule Expedition*, v. 8, no. 1-2. 1931.

Rawlins, Dennis. "A Retrospective Critique of Peary's North Pole Claim." *Polar Notes*, no. 10, 24-54. 1970.

Ray, Dorothy J. *Eskimo Masks*. Seattle: University of Washington Press. 1967.

———. *The Eskimos of Bering Strait, 1650-1898*. Seattle: University of Washington Press. 1975a.

———. "Early Maritime Trade with the Eskimo of Bering Strait and the Introduction of Firearms." *Arctic Anthropology*, v. 12, no. 1, 1-9. 1975b.

———. *Eskimo Art*. Seattle: University of Washington Press. 1977.

Ray, Patrick H. "Ethnographic Sketch of the Natives of Point Barrow." In: *Report of the International Polar Expedition to Point Barrow, Alaska*, 35-88. Washington, D.C.: Government Printing Office. 1885.

Rich, E. E. *Hudson's Bay Company*. 3 v. Toronto: McClelland and Stewart. 1960.

Richardson, John. *Arctic Searching Expedition*. New York: Harper & Brothers. 1854 (also 1851 edition).

Rink, Henry (Henrik). *Tales and Traditions of the Eskimo*. London: William Blackwood and Sons. 1875.

———. *Danish Greenland*. London: Henry S. King. 1877 (1974 reprint).

———. "The Eskimo Tribes." *Meddelelser om Grønland*, v. 11 supplement. 1891.

Robert-Lamblin, Joëlle. "Ammassalik, East Greenland—end or persistance of an isolate?" *Meddelelser om Grønland, Man & Society 10*. 1986.

Rosing, Jens. "Two Ethnological Survivals in Greenland." *Folk*, v. 3, 13-22. 1961.

Ross, John. *A Voyage of Discovery*. London: John Murray. 1819.

Ross, W. Gillies. "Whaling and Eskimos." *National Museum of Man Publications in Ethnology*, no. 10. 1975.

———. "Inuit and the Land in the Nineteenth Century." In: *Inuit Land Use and Occupancy Project*, Milton Freeman Research Limited, v. 2, 123-40. Ottawa: Department of Indian and Northern Affairs. 1976.

Ruddy, Susan, and Irene Rowan. *The Problems of Alaska's Urban Native Peoples*. Anchorage: Kish Tu, Inc. 1975.

Rudenko, S. I. "The Ancient Culture of the Bering Sea and the Eskimo Problem." *Arctic Institute of North America, Anthropology of the North: Translations from Russian Sources*, no. 1. 1961.

Rundall, Thomas. *Narratives of Voyages towards the North-West*. London: Hakluyt Society. 1849.

Sarytschew, Gawrila. *Account of a Voyage of Discovery*. London: Richard Phillips. 1806.

Sauer, Carl O. *Northern Mists.* San Francisco: Turtle Island Foundation. 1968.

Sauer, Martin. *An Account of a Geographical and Astronomical Expedition.* London: T. Cadell, Jun, and W. Davies. 1802.

Sawatzky, H. L., and W. H. Lehn. "The Arctic Mirage and the Early North Atlantic." *Science,* v. 192, 1300-5. 1976.

Semyonov, Yuri. *Siberia.* Montreal: International Publishers' Representatives. 1963.

Shephard, Roy J., and S. Itoh, eds. "Circumpolar Health." *Proceedings of the 3rd International Symposium.* Toronto: University of Toronto Press. 1976.

Sherwood, Morgan B. *Exploration of Alaska, 1865-1900.* New Haven: Yale University Press. 1965.

Simpson, John. "The Western Eskimo." In: *A Selection of Papers on Arctic Geography and Ethnology,* 233-75. London: John Murray. 1875.

Simpson, Thomas. *Narrative of the Discoveries on the North Coast of America.* London: Richard Bentley. 1843.

Sixel, Friedrich Wilhelm. "Die deutsche Vorstellung vom Indianer in der ersten Hälfte des 16. Jahrhunderts." *Annali del Pontificio Museo Missionario Etnologico già Lateranensi,* v. 30, 9-230. 1967.

Slezkine, Yuri. *Arctic Mirrors.* Ithaca: Cornell University Press. 1994.

Smith, Lorne. "The Mechanical Dog Team." *Arctic Anthropology,* v. 9, no. 1, 1-9. 1972.

Sollas, William J. *Ancient Hunters.* New York: Macmillan. 1911 (also 1915 and 1924 editions).

Speck, Frank G. "Montagnais-Naskapi Bands and Early Eskimo Distribution in the Labrador Peninsula." *American Anthropologist,* n.s., v. 33, 557-600. 1931.

———. "Inland Eskimo Bands of Labrador." In: *Essays in Anthropology,* Robert H. Lowie, ed., pp. 313-30. Berkeley: University of California Press. 1936 (1968 reprint).

Spencer, Robert F. "The North Alaskan Eskimo." *Smithsonian Institution Bureau of American Ethnology, Bull.* 171. 1959.

Steenhoven, Geert van den. *Leadership and Law Among the Eskimos of the Keewatin District, Northwest Territories.* Rijswijk: Uitgeverij Excelsior [1962].

Steensby, H. P. "An Anthropogeographical Study of the Origin of the Eskimo Culture." *Meddelelser om Grønland,* v. 53, 39-228. 1917.

Stefansson, Vilhjalmur. "Preliminary Ethnological Report." *American Museum of Natural History, Anthropological Papers,* v. 14, pt. 1. 1914.

———. *The Friendly Arctic.* New York: Macmillan. 1922.

———. *The Three Voyages of Martin Frobisher.* 2 v. London: Argonaut. 1938.

———. *Greenland.* Garden City, New York: Doubleday, Doran. 1943.

Stejneger, Leonhard. *Georg Wilhelm Steller.* Cambridge: Harvard University. 1936.

Stevenson, Marc G. *Inuit, Whalers, and Cultural Persistence.* Don Mills, Ontario: Oxford University Press. 1997.

Stoney, George M. "Explorations in Alaska." *Proceedings of the United States Naval Institute*, v. 25, 533-84, 799-849. 1900.

Sturtevant, William C. "First Visual Images of Native America." In: *First Images of America*, Fredi Chiappelli, ed., v. 1, pp. 417-54. Berkeley: University of California Press. 1976.

Sveistrup, Poul P. "The Economy of Greenland." *Meddelelser om Grønland*, v. 182, no. 1. 1967.

Swadesh, Morris. "Unaaliq and Proto-Eskimo." *International Journal of American Linguistics*, v. 17, 66-70. 1951.

Swaine, Charles. *An Account of a Voyage for the Discovery of a North-West Passage*. 2 v. London: Jolliffe, Corbett, and Clarke. 1748-9.

Swinton, George. *Eskimo Sculpture*. Toronto: McClelland and Stewart. 1965.

———. *Sculpture of the Eskimo*. Greenwich, Conn.: New York Graphic Society. 1972.

Szathmary, Emöke J. E. "Human Biology of the Arctic." In: *Arctic*, v. 5, *Handbook of North American Indians*, David Damas, ed., pp. 64-71. Washington D.C.: Smithsonian Institution. 1984.

Taylor, J. Garth. "Demography and Adaptations of Eighteenth-Century Eskimo Groups in Northern Labrador and Ungava." In: *Prehistoric Maritime Adaptations of the Circumpolar Zone*, William Fitzhugh, ed., pp. 269-78. The Hague: Mouton. 1975.

Taylor, William E. "The Arnapik and Tyara Sites." *Memoirs of the Society for American Archaeology*, no. 22. 1968.

Tester, Frank J., and Peter Kulchyski. *Tammarniit (Mistakes)*. Vancouver: University of British Columbia Press. 1994.

Thalbitzer, William. "A Phonetical Study of the Eskimo Language." *Meddelelser om Grønland*, v. 31. 1904.

———, ed. "The Ammassalik Eskimo." *Meddelelser om Grønland*, v. 39, pt. 1, 1914; v. 40, pt. 2, 1941.

———. "A Note on the Derivation of the Word 'Eskimo' (Inuit)." *American Anthropologist*, n.s., v. 52, 564. 1950.

Tunes, Nicholas. *See:* Poincy, Louis de.

Turner, Lucien M. "On the Indians and Eskimos of the Ungava District, Labrador." *Proceedings and Transactions of the Royal Society of Canada*, v. 5, 99-119. 1888.

———. "Ethnology of the Ungava District, Hudson Bay Territory." *Eleventh Annual Report of the Bureau of Ethnology*, 159-350. 1894.

Usher, Peter J. "The Canadian Western Arctic." *Anthropologica*, n.s., v. 13, nos. 1-2, 169-83. 1971.

———. "The Use of Snowmobiles for Trapping on Banks Island." *Arctic*, v. 25, 172-81. 1972.

Valentine, Victor F., and Frank G. Vallee. *Eskimo of the Canadian Arctic*. Toronto: McClelland and Stewart. 1968.

VanStone, James W. "Commercial Whaling in the Arctic Ocean." *Pacific Northwest Quarterly*, v. 49, 1-10. 1958.

———. *Point Hope*. Seattle: University of Washington Press. 1962.

———. *Eskimos of the Nushagak River*. Seattle: University of Washington Press. 1967.

———. "Tikchik Village." *Fieldiana Anthropology*, v. 56, no. 3. 1968.

———. "Masks of the Point Hope Eskimo."*Anthropos*, v. 63-4, 828-40. 1968-9.

———. "Akulivikchuk." *Fieldiana Anthropology*, v. 60. 1970a.

———. "An Introduction to Baron F. P. von Wrangell's Observations on the Eskimos and Indians of Alaska." *Arctic Anthropology*, v. 6, no. 2, 1-4. 1970b.

———. "Nushagak." *Fieldiana Anthropology*, v. 62. 1972a.

———. "The First Peary Collection of Polar Eskimo Material Culture." *Fieldiana Anthropology*, v. 63, no. 2. 1972b.

———. "V. S. Khromchenko's Coastal Explorations in Southwestern Alaska, 1822." *Fieldiana Anthropology*, v. 64. 1973.

———, ed. *Russian exploration in southwest Alaska*. Fairbanks: University of Alaska Press. 1988.

Vaughan, Richard. *Northwest Greenland*. Orono, Maine: The University of Maine Press. 1991.

Wein, Eleanor E., Milton M. R. Freeman, and Jeanette C. Makus. "Use of and Preference for Traditional Foods among the Belcher Island Inuit." *Arctic*, v. 49, no. 3, 256-64. 1996.

Wentzel, Willard-Ferdinand. "Notice of the Attempts to Reach the Sea by Mackenzie's River, Since the Expedition of Sir Alexander Mackenzie." *Memoirs of the Wernerian Natural History Society*, v. 4, pt. 1, 19-23. 1822.

Wenzel, George. *Animal Rights, Human Rights Ecology, Economy and Ideology in the Canadian Arctic*. London: Belhaven Press. 1991.

Weyer, Edward M. *The Eskimos*. New Haven: Yale University Press. 1932.

Wilber, Charles G. "Physiological Regulations and the Origin of Human Types." *Human Biology*, v. 29, 329-36. 1957.

Woodbury, Anthony C. "Eskimo and Aleut Languages." In: *Arctic*, v. 5. *Handbook of North American Indians*. David Damas, volume ed., pp. 49-71. Washington D.C.: Smithsonian Institution. 1984.

Wrangell, Ferdinand P. von. "The Inhabitants of the Northwest Coast of America." *Arctic Anthropology*, v. 6, no. 2, 5-20. 1970.

Zagoskin, Lavrentiy A. "Lieutenant Zagoskin's Travels in Russian America, 1842-1844." Henry N. Michael, ed. *Arctic Institute of North America, Anthropology of the North: Translations from Russian Sources*, no. 7. 1967.

Zimmerly, David W. "Cain's Land Revisited." *Newfoundland Social and Economic Studies*, no. 16. 1975.

Index of Personal Names

General Index